LEADING
THE CHURCH'S
SONG

LEADING THE CHURCH'S SONG

Augsburg Fortress

Minneapolis

LEADING THE CHURCH'S SONG

The art on the cover, commissioned for this book, is by Nicholas Markell.

Book design by Circus Design.

Project Coordinators: Scott Weidler, Norma Aamodt-Nelson
Editors: Robert Buckley Farlee, Eric Vollen
Music Engravers: David Matsen, Ryan French

Library of Congress Cataloging-in-Publication Data
Leading the church's song / Robert Buckley Farlee, general editor ; [contributors, Mark Bangert, et al.]
    p.   cm
    Includes bibliographical references and index.
    ISBN 0-8066-3591-6 (pbk. : alk. paper)
    1. Church music—Instruction and study.
I. Farlee, Robert Buckley. II. Bangert, Mark Paul.
MT88.l4   1998
782.25'145—dc21

                                       98-33961
                                          CIP
                                          MN

Manufactured in the U.S.A   AF 3-402
03   02   01   00   99   98   1   2   3   4   5   6   7   8   9   10

With grateful appreciation to

Aid Association for Lutherans

for its generous support of this project.

CONTENTS

This book reflects the complexity of music in the church at the moment. Various authors describe different approaches to the music of the church's song, from the array of musical styles and perspectives in play among us. The point, as the book's title indicates, is to help leaders lead and the church sing the song it has been given. The intention here is cause for rejoicing.

As soon as you look behind the intention to the various details, your rejoicing may be dampened. It may even turn to despair. If you are like most human beings in and out of the church, you are likely to find such an array confusing and bewildering. Before you turn away in frustration, step back far enough from the individual leaves in order to see the trees and your place among them. Here are a few suggestions for doing so.

• First, leaders of the church's music and members of their communities of faith ought to know as much as possible about as many liturgical and musical styles as possible, but they still have to reckon with the implications of the first commandment. God is God, not they or the communities they serve. That means the leader and the community are finite creatures in one time and place. None of us can be everything or know everything or be proficient at everything. You and your people will know some styles better than others and be able to sing those styles more easily than others. That's the way the world is made, as my son used to tell me when he was quite small, expressing more wisdom than he probably knew. This does not mean that there is only one way you can sing, but lusting for more than is humanly possible—trying to be God—is not good. Said another way, neither you nor your community can sing everything.

• Second, you and your community can sing far more than any of you individually could sing alone or imagine to be possible. A community of Christians who sing around word, font, and table is not a trained choir, but it is like a choir in that the whole is greater than the sum of its parts. The parts contribute in various ways with surprising gifts which together enable the song to take more shapes and contours than you can anticipate. We are not God, but we are gifted by God with talents that are not to be buried. This is as true where two or three are gathered together, as where there are twenty or thirty, two or three hundred, or two or three thousand. Do not underestimate what is possible. Do not sell yourself or your people short.

• Third, we are called to steward the resources we have been given. That means discovering and knowing our own idioms well. They cannot be neglected without serious damage to ourselves and to the body of Christ beyond us. To neglect them is to lose our memory, to lose our memory is to lose our being, and to lose our being is to lose the part of Christ's body that lives for the life of the world in our corner of it. But our own idioms, if they are healthy, need the ballast of other ones. By themselves they become ingrown and idolatrous. The key here is to work out gradually and explore the wealth with which God has graced this creation and its many creatures.

• Fourth, there is no quick fix in this book or anywhere else. As in all worthwhile pursuits, we learn to lead by leading and to sing by singing, just as the runner learns to run by running. A community learns to sing together by the discipline of singing together in the bonds of the more general discipline of love that binds us to one another and to the service of the neighbor and the whole creation. This learning curve does not happen overnight by the intrusion of a prerecorded sonic environment that gives the impression a community is singing when in fact it is silent or at best singing along. The Christian church sings naturally, to be sure, in response to the grace of God. But once the song has been sensed, it takes shape by hard work, just like all other worthwhile human endeavors. John Wesley was blunt about this when he admonished the people to sing even if they found it a burden at first. They would eventually find it a blessing, he said. This admonition stands against a culture of immediate gratification, but the church's message is deeper than quickly disappearing superficialities.

• Fifth, this book can serve you in all sorts of helpful ways, but it increases rather than decreases your responsibilities. The more possibilities there are, the more you have to make distinctions. The song of the church is for the long haul, not the short run. Not everything is worth its time and effort. Not everything is congregational. There are standards of musical craft and fittingness for worship which we flaunt at our peril. Since we are finite and cannot sing everything, appropriate choices have to be made in loving respect for the people of God who sing. Leaders have to make choices as thoughtfully and lovingly as possible.

• Sixth, the goal is not complexity. The goal is a song which sings around word, font, and table. A simple unison line sung by a congregation is far superior to complex confusion and a silent congregation. Complexity has its place (usually in its essence quite simple). Choirs and instruments are part of such a place because they can embody more complexity than a congregation. They should sound alone at times, and they can lead and enliven the congregation's song in splendid ways. But the ideal is not some imaginary complex intrusion. The ideal is the sound you and your people make which will vary in complexity depending upon the resources that are available.

• Seventh, in our atomized world of isolated group after isolated group, it is easy to see an array of resources as a menu to be dished up for various segments of the society—for young, old, rich, poor, men, women, certain ethnic backgrounds, this taste, that taste, this class, that class, urban, rural, and so forth. A discriminatory

presumption often accompanies such a perspective and assumes that a given slice of the population is only capable of, deserving of, responds to, or likes a narrowly defined kind of music. The analysis itself is inaccurate, as poor people who like art music, rich people who like folk music, and the inquisitive spirit of the human race amply demonstrate. The sinful divisions of the church nonetheless reflect our atomization and then tempt the church itself to embrace inaccurate and discriminatory bifurcation as a positive good.

As it said already in the first century of its existence, the church at its essence knows another reality, that we are one in Christ and sing with one voice. The reality is broken in this world, to be sure, but the church remembers that the foretaste of the feast to come is already present among us. We deny our nature as one body of Christ when we allow the world's divisions to keep us from singing together. How to sing together in our age is no easy matter. But the situation we face and a book such as this heighten the necessity and increase the church musician's ingenuity and responsibility. In the church and its song there is no distinction between high and low, rich or poor, male or female, old or young, slave or free, suburban or rural, one ethnicity or another. Nor is anybody a statistic in one of these segments on a spreadsheet, no matter how helpful such charts may be. We are all human beings rescued in Christ, all freed to sing together, and all worthy of the best and most fitting music.

Rejoice then in the freedom you have been given, the song you have to sing, and the multiple ways you can embody it. Savor the array with which we are graced and to which this book gives you access. If details become too heavy, back off for perspective and recall your place in God's good creation. Then sing as the Spirit bids and remember to delight in the song of One whose yoke is easy and whose burden is light.

CONTRIBUTORS

Leading the Church's Song has developed out of a passion for revitalizing the singing of the Christian assembly, including the varied and rapidly expanding repertoire of the present day as well as the riches of the church's many traditions. The vast diversity of this material called for a diversity of authorship, in order to bring together voices that can speak with assurance about their own areas of experience and knowledge. Through writing, oral presentation, and interview, the following contributors have brought to the contents of this volume gifts of discernment, helpful information, and practical advice. The chapters to which they have contributed are noted next to their names.

In addition to the contributors listed below, a number of other individuals who have played a significant part in the preparation of this book are here acknowledged: Corean Bakke, Dori Erwin Collins, John Ferguson, Patricia Kazarow, Naomi Rowley, and Paul Manz, for review and helpful suggestions based on the original manuscripts; and Carol Carver, Robert Hobby, and Matt Wolka, for preparation of the tune index. Contributors to the accompanying compact disc of musical examples are noted on page 162.

May this book and recording find a place among the many and varied instruments employed by those who lead the church's song.

Scott Weidler
Associate Director for Worship and Music
Division for Congregational Ministries
Evangelical Lutheran Church in America

Norma Aamodt-Nelson
Acquisitions Editor, Instrumental Music
Augsburg Fortress, Publishers

Project Coordinators

Mark Bangert (Chapter 9)
John H. Tietjen Professor of Worship and Church Music at the Lutheran School of Theology at Chicago, artistic director of the Bach Cantata Series and choir director at the Lutheran Church of St. Luke. Bangert has studied at Ruhija Church Music School in Bukoba, Tanzania, and at the Asian Institute for Liturgy and Music.

Marie Rubis Bauer (Chapter 4)
Director of liturgical music at the St. Lawrence Catholic Center, Lawrence, Kansas.

Michael Bauer (Chapter 4)
Associate professor of organ, church music, and choral conducting at the University of Kansas and organist/educator at Crossroads Reformed Church in Overland Park, Kansas.

Lorraine Brugh (Chapter 10)
Assistant professor of music and university organist at Valparaiso University, Indiana. The subject of Brugh's doctoral dissertation was contextualization in worship.

Mellonee Burnim (Chapter 6)
Associate professor in the Departments of Afro-American Studies and Folklore/Ethnomusicology at Indiana University-Bloomington and minister of music at Bethel African Methodist Episcopal Church in Bloomington, Indiana.

Gerhard Cartford (Chapter 8)
Editor of *Libro de Liturgia y Cántico*. Cartford is a retired Lutheran church musician and professor of worship and music who worked for over twelve years in Latin America in the area of worship renewal among South American Lutheran communities.

Robert Buckley Farlee (Editor; Afterword)
Director of music and pastor at Christ Church Lutheran in Minneapolis. In addition to his parish duties, Farlee is active as a composer, writer, editor, and workshop leader.

Robert Gallagher (Chapter 3)
Minister of music at Wayne United Methodist Church in Wayne, Pennsylvania. Gallagher is a member of the organ faculty at the Benjamin T. Rome School of Music of the Catholic University of America in Washington, D. C.

Mark Glaeser (Chapter 7)
Minister of music at Christ Lutheran Church in Charlotte, North Carolina. Glaeser coordinates a twenty-choir/ensemble music program that ranges from traditional to contemporary.

José Antonio Machado (Chapter 8)
Pastor and musician at Todos Los Santos Misión Luterana in Minneapolis, Minnesota.

Angel Mattos (Chapter 8)
Project director representing the ELCA for *Libro de Liturgia y Cántico* and choral director for First Baptist Church in Carolina, Puerto Rico, at the Free School of Music in San Juan, and the All-State Puerto Rico Choir.

Mark Mummert (Chapter 2)
Cantor at Lutheran Church of the Good Shepherd, Lancaster, Pennsylvania, and seminary musician at the Lutheran Theological Seminary in Philadelphia.

William Dexheimer Pharris (Chapter 8)
ELCA pastor, musician, and chaplain at Fairview-University Medical Center in Minneapolis. Pharris resided in El Salvador from 1986 to 1989.

James Notebaart (Chapter 1)
Priest and director of the Office of Indian Ministry in the Outreach Division for the Archdiocese of St. Paul and Minneapolis.

Charles Ore (Chapter 4)
Professor and chair of the Music Department at Concordia College, Nebraska, and cantor at Pacific Hills Lutheran Church in Omaha, Nebraska.

Mark Sedio (Chapters 1, 2, 4, 8)
Lead writer for this volume, Sedio is cantor at Mount Olive Lutheran Church in Minneapolis and serves on the music staff at Luther Seminary in St. Paul.

Robin Knowles Wallace (Chapter 5)
Assistant professor of worship and music at the Methodist Theological School in Delaware, Ohio.

Richard Webb (Chapter 7)
Associate director of evangelism in the Division for Congregational Ministries, Evangelical Lutheran Church in America, specializing in ministry to postmodern generations with a focus on worship and evangelism.

Richard R. Webster (Chapters 2, 4)
Organist and choirmaster at St. Luke's Episcopal Church in Evanston, Illinois, where he directs the Choir of Men and Boys, the Girls Choir and Schola, and the St. Luke's Singers. In addition, he serves on the faculty of the Organ and Church Music Department at Northwestern University in Evanston.

Paul Westermeyer (Foreword)
Professor of church music at Luther Seminary in St. Paul, where he is cantor for the seminary community and administers a masters of sacred music program with St. Olaf College, Northfield, Minnesota.

WORSHIP BOOK ABBREVIATIONS

AME   *The A.M.E.C. Bicentennial Hymnal.* Nashville: The African Methodist Episcopal Church, 1984.

H82   *Hymnal 1982* (Episcopal). New York: The Church Pension Fund, 1985.

LBW   *Lutheran Book of Worship.* Minneapolis: Augsburg Publishing House; Philadelphia: Board of Publications, Lutheran Church in America, 1978.

LLC   *Libro de Liturgia y Cántico.* Minneapolis: Augsburg Fortress, 1998.

LMGM   *Lead Me, Guide Me: The African American Catholic Hymnal.* Chicago: GIA Publications, 1987.

LW   *Lutheran Worship.* St. Louis: Concordia Publishing House, 1982.

NCH   *The New Century Hymnal.* Cleveland: The Pilgrim Press, 1995.

NNBH   *New National Baptist Hymnal.* Nashville: National Baptist Publishing Board, 1995.

PH   *The Presbyterian Hymnal* (PC-USA). Louisville: Westminster/John Knox Press, 1990.

SB   *Sound the Bamboo.* Manila, Philippines: Christian Conference of Asia and the Asian Institute for Liturgy and Music, 1990.

SZ   *Songs of Zion.* Nashville: Abingdon Press, 1981.

TLH   *The Lutheran Hymnal.* St. Louis: Concordia Publishing House, 1941.

UMH   *The United Methodist Hymnal.* Nashville: The United Methodist Publishing House, 1989.

VU   *Voices United: The Hymn and Worship Book of the United Church of Canada.* Etobicoke, Ontario: The United Church Publishing House, 1996.

WOV   *With One Voice.* Minneapolis: Augsburg Fortress, 1995.

W3   *Worship: A Hymnal and Service Book for Roman Catholics.* 3d ed. Chicago: GIA Publications, 1986.

CHAPTER 1

Since Christ is Lord of heaven and earth,

how can I keep from singing?

Robert Lowry

INTRODUCTION

Grant Park, Chicago, 1979. The newly elected Polish pope makes his first visit to the "second largest Polish city in the world, after Warsaw." A crowd pushing one million has been gathered for hours. Finally the pontiff arrives; the mass begins. At several points the congregation, almost as large as the population of some countries, breaks into song—a million people singing together. Faces stream with tears. Eyes bear witness to the power and the Spirit. A million people recite the creed in unison. An enormous community of faith. A congregation.

August, 1995. A crowd gathers in the park near the Liberty Bell in downtown Philadelphia. Through the sea of baggy denim clothing, candles and flowers, a large portrait draped in black is visible. The crowd is singing, obviously in mourning. The most popular member of the Grateful Dead is, well, dead. The presiders, three long-haired women in patchwork finery, lead the chant: "Amazing grace, how sweet the sound." The stanza ends. There is silence. A split-second scanning of memory banks proves futile. The result: stanzas two and three, four through eight are the same as the first. Those involved in this event feel the need to cry out in song, to join their voices with one another in a ritual of melody, a blending of community, an act of corporate support. And here, mourning one who devoted his life to providing new songs, the gathered congregation senses that what belongs here is an old hymn—if only they knew more than one stanza!

Sunday morning. The sanctuary is full. It's time to reflect on the Word in song. The musicians have creatively introduced the designated piece. The refrain is appealing, yet not many in the pews are singing. A soloist presents the verses which are clear and intelligible. Again, the refrain. The singing is better, but you can't help feeling that something is missing. Strangely, singing out makes you feel more alone. You understand that you are there, part of a worshiping community. Yet the idea of a community joined together in a song of praise seems evasive. The idea of a community joined together by a song of praise is virtually impossible if those present, for whatever reason, are not adding their voices to the assembly.

What connects these three incidents? The song of the assembled people—when it works and when it doesn't. The gathering around the pope's visit demonstrates the promise of communal song, that potential that has drawn us into the calling of leading it. The incident at the memorial for the Dead's Jerry Garcia illustrates that even in a culture that doesn't outwardly value singing together, people realize on a deep level that such song is powerful, maybe even essential. The church illustration strikes home for us, in our real world. We know how much the church's song can add to our life together in faith—but how do we reach the plane of effective song?

Congregational Song: A Lesson in Community

Throughout history, the arts, and especially music, have played a vital role in the rituals of humankind. There is evidence of this in every culture, in every religious community. Most often, though not always, worship is a community event. Music, through its intimate connection with human emotion, on one hand helps heighten individual responses, and on the other nurtures community in the deepest sense. Music, by nature, usually requires some sort of community. It does not and cannot exist in a vacuum. Certain elements are necessary for music to take place. Like theater and dance it is an art "active in time." A *composer* creates a piece that is passed on to another either by rote teaching (oral

tradition) or in writing. The next necessary element is that of *performer*. The person being taught the piece—the *listener*—fills out this trinity of musical prerequisites. Variants on this theme are countless. Composer and performer may be the same person. The roles of performer and listener are often themselves made up of communities. An orchestra, for example, is a community of performers. So are a trio ensemble, a rock band. Two children singing "Row, row, row your boat" as a round make up a community of performers—and, simultaneously, of listeners. Composer, performer, listener: community.

Music unites—it is an important aspect of communal worship, of *being* congregation. Singing together is the quickest way to unite a gathering of individuals, no matter how large or small, into one corporate worshiping body, the body of Christ. Something happens when we sing.

Countless factors influence the way we sing—one of which, unfortunately, is that we *don't* sing. Here, at the turn of the third millennium, perhaps for the first time in history, the practice of group singing, at least in the United States, has become all but extinct. When was the last time, other than in church, you joined your voice with others in song? The only remnants of group song (and of ritual song) we own today are the "Birthday Song" and "The Star Spangled Banner." How strange it is that, for most people, the corporate singing of our national anthem has become associated solely with the opening rites of various sporting events. Even this is becoming more and more a solo piece in its orientation! Thankfully, some do still

Important to keep in mind is that anthropologically—and theologically—speaking, the idea of listening being the end of music is a novelty. Music is, at its heart, a form of communication; those who heard a piece would be expected to learn it, to repeat it to others.

gather for seasonal Christmas caroling but even this is not in any way widespread.

The waning practice of group singing also has diminished our repertoire. Ask a child to sing any of our folk tunes, nursery rhymes excluded. What *are* our folk tunes? Not many seem to know. Because of budget cuts most music programs in schools, especially in public schools, have suffered greatly. If music is a part of the curriculum, the focus is most often on instrumental rather than vocal training. For most children, commercial jingles seem to have taken root as the "folk" idiom, a sad commentary both on our culture and our priorities.

So where is the music of the people today? Has music in the popular idiom supplanted folk music as the music of the people? Many Americans are generally literate in the popular music of their respective eras, maybe even of the eras that preceded or followed their own. For the most part, however, music on the popular scene is solo oriented, having nothing to do with communal song. Some pieces do resemble music that could actually be sung by groups—"Don't Sit Under the Apple Tree," "Unchained Melody," the music of Joan Baez and Woody Guthrie, even the Beach Boys' "California Girls." But the popular music of the past half century, employing bended and strophically varied rhythms, unpredictable phrase elongation and vocal note coloring, simply is not conducive to group use. This type of music, while artistic, compelling, and often a real treat to listen to, is just that: *it is meant for listening*. Quality is not an issue here. The fact is, simply, that this is music meant for solo or small group *performance*—not for group vocal involvement. The way it is constructed—rhythmic changes

between verses, stylistic vocal embellishments, and complex text construction— makes it too unpredictable for group song. The popular music of today is solo music.

Are there pieces possessing characteristics from the solo popular idiom which the members of the congregation might be able to sing if they become familiar with them through repeated use and education? This is possible and indeed commendable providing the congregation actually can sing them as group song. This means that the song produced by the assembly itself must remain primary.

The Primacy of the People's Song

Congregational singing of any sort requires leadership—people don't just begin to sing spontaneously—but this leadership should *never* overshadow the song of the people. The vocalist who "leads" the congregation by means of an over-amplified microphone connected to a powerful sound system, the organist who employs harsh detachments in articulation and overpowering registrations to beat the congregation into submission, and the pastor who bellows from the side of the chancel are all guilty of replacing rather than nurturing the song of the people. Songs in a solo style that are attempted as group song often require such dominating leadership, which is why they don't, as a rule, work well. If, in the music of worship, the voice of the congregation is not *primary*, then simple, profound silence would be preferable. Leaders need to consider ways they can help congregations find their collective voice, not fill in for them, taking

> As musicians of the church, we are facilitators who help those gathered for worship use their gifts, their offerings of heart and voice to the glory of God.

5

1

their place. The key here is *facilitation*—helping it happen, not making it happen. This should be the starting point for any decisions regarding leadership in congregational song.

Now, to use a good catechism phrase, "What does this mean?" For us as leaders of the church's song, it means:

● Choosing music that is congregationally based, which has the characteristics necessary for ease in group singing.

● Selecting tunes that sing well, that are sufficiently predictable as well as interesting, that are both memorable and worthy of memory, that bring the text to life, that embrace textual accents in a natural way.

● Selecting texts that sing well, texts with chains of vowel patterns that flow, that follow predictable rhythmic structures from one stanza to the next, that do not overreach in their rhyming schemes.

● Nurturing the development of the congregation's collective voice so that, on occasion, they may sing unaccompanied—a great way to allow them to really hear themselves.

● Cultivating an awareness for placing those musical entities in the service so they are meaningful and contribute to the flow of worship rather than attracting attention to themselves.

● Reflecting musically on texts to help the congregation digest the words, concepts and images, as they are being sung.

● Introducing the hymn, song, or liturgical piece in such a way that there is no question in the mind of the participant as to what his or her part is to be, and in such a way that no one can help but participate.

● Taking time to analyze both tune and text, ascertaining where the difficulties in singing may lie, and determining how the congregation might best encounter them.

● Researching the origins of both text and tune, learning what spawned their creation, to better communicate what is essential.

● Learning the musical languages of other cultures to enhance the congregation's awareness of its place in the worldwide church.

● Varying the accompanying instrumentation, highlighting ethnic styles, supplying supportive yet colorful harmonic structures, and—for organists—not always using the same registration.

● Making friends with the element of surprise.

One of the characteristics of congregational hymns, songs, and responses is that they are often based on repetition. Repetition of stanzas or refrains can facilitate the process of familiarization, thereby increasing the congregation's comfort zone. In singing each successive stanza, the singer becomes more comfortable with the natural twists of melody and rhythm. The text is able to unfold. A good marriage of text and tune allows this to happen with both a degree of expectancy *and* surprise. A good music leader acts both as supporter and guide.

> The strophic structure of most congregational hymns, songs, and responses is full of potential. Such structure offers the musician ample possibilities for "play."

> Serving as a musical facilitator of congregational song is a lot like dating or courting. It always includes a little give and take, both on the part of the musician and on the part of the congregation. There is also a little teasing, a good dose of surprise, and a lot of caring.

Helping the Congregation Find Its Voice

The musician, in facilitating the song of the people, must take into account a multitude of factors. Who will make up the assembly? This obvious question deserves careful attention. The size of the congregation, for example, has bearing on decisions regarding instrumental accompaniment, organ registration, and the choice of the music itself. What is their age range? What are they used to singing in church? The purpose of the gathering also needs to be taken into account. What part does music play in the flow of the service? How might the musician facilitate not only mood but also drama and flow? How musically literate is the congregation? A miscalculation here can lead to frustration for everyone.

Anyone who has served as a substitute organist or, for that matter, who plays more than one service in the same parish, understands that no two congregations sing exactly alike. While there is likely some degree of predictability from week to week and from service to service, the musician constantly needs to be aware of the current disposition of the assembly. Are they singing well today? How can I best encourage their participation? What can I do to make the congregation "gel" as a worshiping unit? While the structure of the service combined with elements such as expectancy and anticipation on the part of those gathered foster at least a fundamental base, the question still must be addressed: What can I do to help expand and uplift?

Leaders of congregational song who tend to be most effective understand the importance of working *together*—of leading through the building of relationship, of working from within as a part of the congregation, of keeping one eye toward beauty of tone and color as well as one eye toward meeting the people where they are on this particular day. Anticipate musical problems before they arise and learn to deal with them as they come up. Know the congregation you serve. Familiarize yourself with their existing repertoire, their cultural heritage, their likes and dislikes. Then build on this base: set a vision for incorporating areas of growth—new literature, hymns from unfamiliar traditions. At the same time, remain respectful of the songs they love. You may not have much use for "Great is thy faithfulness"—or Luther's "May God bestow on us his grace"—but before you think about easing it into disuse, consider the person for whom that hymn is incomparably moving.

The one who facilitates the church's song also needs to consider the environment in which the community worships. This includes instruments available in the space, acoustics, visual lines, seating design, amplification system, lighting, tone of intimacy or grandeur, as well as the positioning of the choir and other worship leaders. Consult

> The acoustical character of a space governs the way a given instrument sounds in a room as well as the way the congregation responds to that instrument and how it is played. In rooms with little or no reverberation, members of the congregation may feel they are singing alone, even though surrounded by other worshipers. In rooms with abundant resonance or reverberation, members of the congregation can get "caught up" in the sound of their own singing, resulting in a constant slowing of tempo.

1

with others who plan and lead worship to determine how such factors can be used together to enhance not just the song, but the entire worship.

Exactly *what* the congregation will sing raises another issue. We start with what we have: what hymnals are in the pews? What hymns and songs do the people already know? Finding something that would work particularly well in a given setting at a specific service is the first step; next, how do we go about getting it before the eyes of the congregation? Do we put everything in the service folder, whether it is in the hymnal or not? Would visual projection work in our sanctuary? Should both notes and text be reproduced, or text alone? *Are we breaking copyright laws?* These are major questions. The final one is very important.

In a time when convergence of denominational traditions (musically, liturgically, theologically) is on the rise, musicians need to explore and familiarize themselves with the music and performance practice of their church neighbors. The church musician needs to be familiar not only with the German chorale, the tunes from the Genevan Psalter, and the hymns of the English and Welsh traditions, but also with a plethora of other genres: white spirituals, Black gospel, revival hymnody, African call/response form, Asian scales, and so on. Books, articles, recordings, telephone calls to friends, seminars—the learning never ceases.

This book is intended to be one resource among many in that learning process. Beginning with considerations applicable to any form of communal song, we then move through a more detailed—though by no means exhaustive—exploration of many genres of song available to the worshiping community today. It is not intended to prescribe how the assembly and the leader must do things. It is, rather, an invitation: "Give this form of song a try." "Would this technique help your congregation?"

Conclusion

Augustine said, "The one who sings prays twice." As the church, we possess an enormous and wonderful treasure chest of hymns, songs, chants, psalms, and canticles. In singing them, by participating and adding our own voices to the song, we make them our own. We join the song of all creation, of Hannah, of Miriam and Moses, of Zechariah, of Simeon, of Anna, of Mary, of our Christ.

And something happens to us when we sing. On a communal level we become more conscious of how we fit into the group, of our role in the larger gathering. On a spiritual level, tune, text, and the sound of our singing can transport us to places we never thought possible. Catechetically, we internalize that which we sing. Propelled by the wings of melody, rhythm, and perhaps harmony, the message and images of the text pass through our lips finding ways into our memories as well as our hearts. The kernel of

The breaking of copyright laws is stealing and is, unfortunately, more prevalent than it should be. Publishers and licensing agencies have worked to make it easier to obtain legal permission to reprint music and text. Both musicians and clergy need to become familiar with copyright permissions and licensing procedures. A simple first step is to call the publisher of the resource from which you would like to reprint something. They will be glad to help you.

faith is nurtured. It has often been said that the way in which we pray *(lex orandi)* has great bearing on that which we believe *(lex credendi)*. It is probably just as valid to say that what we *sing* also shapes our faith—*lex cantandi lex credendi.* We who lead that song are by nature servants of God's people and serving them well requires work. The task calls us to continuous study of things churchly: scripture, historical models and the function of liturgy, the cycles of the church year. It requires of us constant study and practice to keep musical skills (instrumental, vocal, choral, conducting) at sufficiently high levels. And it challenges us frequently to risk something we have never done before.

Our calling is also pastoral. We function in and serve a community. In some ways we are means by which the Holy Spirit creates community, for that which we do serves to gather, unite, and bind individuals together. This is indeed a high and holy calling.

INTRODUCTION TO GLOBAL MUSIC   Crossing into another's culture reminds us that we are all neighbors, and that our church is truly a global church. It is not unusual to find a hymn from Tanzania, Brazil, or Taiwan in a North American worship service today. What does it take, though, truly to sing another's song? How much do I need to understand about the performance practice of the original culture before I attempt it in my local context? What can I know of the cultural and theological background from which a song comes? When is it time to step into the waters and try to make music from another culture?

The chapters in this book that deal specifically with global music step into the waters of various cultures and describe how they might be applied in a North American context. The cultures represented here are not exhaustive; for example, no attention is given to music from the Middle East, nor to American Indian traditions. This is not because there is not a dynamic tradition of church music in those places. It merely reflects that music from those cultures is still making its way into our worship books and hymnals. We still have much to learn from many places, at home and around the globe. These chapters are a humble beginning to encourage our efforts to meet the neighbor in the church's music.

When learning another culture's music, we are not attempting to replicate a hymn's original context. In each local context any hymn takes on its own life through its contextual presentation. That is as it should be. In order for any new hymn to become meaningful, it must become an expression of the community which sings it. By learning what we can about another cultural context, however, and by drawing connections between that context and our own, we can find entry points into a culture different from our own. The global music chapters point us to signs we can look for when we first approach a Latino, African, or Asian tune or text. The authors show us what to look for, and what we might want to know in order to sing it. These are some of the clues which provide the willing musician with some equipment for trying new cultural music.

In sharing one another's music, it is more than music that we share. Music of various cultures brings us a glimpse of each other's experience of God. As any culture connects its experience of the holy to its music, a unique context for God's presence is created—we experience together the way God weaves a varied, diverse tapestry of revelation among us. The church's song gives us this place to experience this sharing. Step in; the water's fine.

2

Everything should be made as simple as possible,

but not more so.

Albert Einstein

The music of Christian song is, as we shall see, a grand and richly varied world. Each locale within that world has its own vocabulary and syntax: we sing and lead each in different ways which will be treated under "Performance Practice" in each chapter. Yet all these styles of song are united in important ways. They help people to speak the faith. They are true to themselves and to the Word. And because their language is that of music, they possess basic elements that don't change from one style to another. It is those common aspects of leading congregational song that are addressed in this chapter.

Tactus

L ife is rhythm: the beat of the heart; the rising and the setting of the sun; the turn of the seasons; the church year. Life is rhythm and all God's creatures have it. It is rhythm that gives music its life.

Of all technical rhythmic considerations, none is more important to leaders of the congregation's song than that of tactus, more commonly called the "beat." Tactus (pronounced TAHK-toos) is the pulse that propels melody and harmony in time. Depending on the style of music, the tactus may be experienced very differently, from the subtle pulse of chant to the beat of a drum, but it always governs the movement of a piece.

The key element regarding tactus is dependability. A dependable and steady beat sets the structure that allows the congregation

the freedom to participate. A dependable tactus fosters trust between singer (on both individual and group levels) and leader. The musician gains the congregation's trust by setting and maintaining the tactus appropriate to the particular stylistic and cultural considerations of a piece. A congregation that trusts its musician sings.

Tactus is the life of congregational song. From the book of Genesis to the present, life is breath. The congregation is made up of people who need to breathe. When the leader (especially a keyboard player) hasn't taken this into consideration, the person in the pew is often left feeling either rushed or dragged. Breathing is a natural process, and singing is (or should be) a natural process as well. Songs should virtually float out of people with their breath. Those leading the song need to learn how to breathe with the congregation in much the same way a good choral conductor

2

breathes on his or her preparatory beat. For those who lead from instruments, this does not mean singing along with the congregation, which actually impedes the leader's listening and responding role. Rather, it highlights the necessity that the musician understand each piece's phrasing and know the places where a subtle "give" in the tactus might facilitate corporate breath.

Tempo

Tempo is another rhythmic factor to consider in leading the congregation's song. It is the responsibility of the leader not only to set a steady and dependable beat, but also to determine at what speed the beat will move.

Few factors are more deadly to congregational singing than a leader who makes only limited use of the spectrum of tempo possibilities. Hymns, songs, liturgical responses, psalm settings, the musical portions in which the congregation participates through singing—all are bound to texts. The music to which a text is set is intended to reflect the character of that text. Some texts are more inward and contemplative in nature; others are merry and joyful. Just how much can this all be reflected in the congregation's participation in the text, that is to say in their actual singing? A fair amount. Next to awareness of

the function of a steady tactus, setting the tempo should be one of the music leader's foremost concerns. Reflection on text is the starting point.

- What is the text saying? An analysis of the content of the text's message, imagery, character, position, and use within the context of the service is always in order.
- How does the text make you feel? How does the text sing?
- Are there any words or phrases which do not roll easily off the tongue? (The word *baptism*, for example, is always hard to sing.)
- How would you sing a given text and tune? Try it. Try to capture the character of the text in your own rendition. Think about the speed at which you're singing. Think about the way you're singing. Are you using *legato* (connected) or more bouncy, detached phrases? See how you can make the text come alive just by means of the tune.

INTERNALIZING THE PULSE   The ability of a musician to produce a reliable, steady pulse in a hymn is essential if anyone is to sing along. Unfortunately, we don't always know if we are prone to erratic pulse in playing. The solution? Tape a service and listen to the hymns. If your hymn playing suffers from unsteadiness, the tape recording will tell you. If so, make a habit of practicing the hymns with the metronome, not so that you will play them rigidly and unmusically, but so that you can play them steadily and with the reliable pulse that every hymn needs. It is critical to understand that a hymn usually is not over when you reach the bottom of the page. Although a slight stretch may be needed, the internalized tactus must remain present even when moving from the end of one stanza to the beginning of the next. (This transition is addressed in Chapter 4.)

Next, look at the character of the melody. Is the marriage of text and tune a good one? Does the tune capture the text's message? (Sometimes it is appropriate to substitute a different, more suitable or more familiar tune that has the same meter and stresses.) Considering the tune alone, what tempo might work best? Adding the words and imagining your congregation and setting (size, acoustics, instrumentation, familiarity), what tempo would best serve the situation as a whole? Imagine the congregation singing the piece without any accompaniment. Would this tempo work?

One function of an introduction, whether instrumental or vocal, is to help the congregation determine the tempo at which they are going to sing. In presenting the introduction, the leader must already have the corporate voice of the congregation in mind. The first two measures the congregation actually sings are the most vital. They have heard the introduction; now they actually open their mouths, the vocal cords begin to vibrate, and the song of the people begins, either tentatively or with assurance. The tempo of those first measures must be solid and unwavering. Trust in the tempo is determined by the introduction and those first measures.

The tempo is set during the introduction. Whatever the content and form of the introduction, the tactus must be clear and unwavering during the introduction so that the congregation begins the hymn at the speed the leader has determined. The player who introduces a hymn at lightning speed, only to play stanza one at a decidedly slower pace, has defeated both hymn and congregation. The organist who spins out a beautiful, sub-dued, improvisatory reverie as an introduction, only to throw on big sounds and play the hymn faster at the outset of the first stanza also has missed the mark.

Leaders of song are interpreters of song, and interpretation calls for research. In their sermon preparation most preachers try to determine the message of the scripture on which they will be preaching. To do so they use a process called exegesis in which they may translate the section from original Greek or Hebrew, making note of key words or word plays. They then study what passages precede as well as follow the portion in order to put it into context regarding the larger picture. The preacher then asks the question, "What was the original speaker (or writer) trying to convey to the original hearers or readers?" Another immediately follows: "Who were those listeners, readers, and what was their situation?" This is called determining the scripture passage's *Sitz im Leben* or "life setting." It is only after such preliminary work that a preacher sets about determining what the message of the text is for us today and how, if at all, our setting differs.

Musicians in the church who are entrusted with the people's song can benefit by doing the same type of study and preparation. This can be helpful especially in determining things like tempo. We can begin by asking questions concerning a tune's *Sitz im Leben*.
- Who is the composer of the tune?
- When was it written?
- Was it written specifically for this text?
- How does this tune relate to other music written by this composer?
- Is there anywhere I can go to hear other music by this composer?

- What type of musical instrument or ensemble may have accompanied the tune at the time of its first appearance?
- How does the melody move—mostly in a stepwise fashion (which tends, for the most part, to be easier to sing) or by leaps?
- Is it memorable? (That is, will it be easy for the congregation to remember its contours after the introduction and maybe one stanza?)
- Was it conceived as a vocal piece (for one singer), a choral piece (a part song for many singers)?
- Was it most likely sung in harmony or unison?
- Does the melody relate to any other type of music popular at the time (e.g., dance tunes, ballads)?
- Are there any repeated motives that deserve attention?

Delving into such research might even change your opinion about how a piece might be done, regarding tempo or otherwise.

The position of the piece within the context of the service also may play a role in determining the tempo at which it will be sung. Does it serve as a reflection on something that has just happened liturgically? What was the spirit of that specific action? Worship is alive and fluid, never static. In the course of a service the congregation experiences and participates in many different functions, each with its own specific mood or flavor. These might include praise, prayer, reflection, or proclamation. Tempos should reflect these accordingly. Because it is the function of the introduction to set the spirit, the place of a piece in the service will undoubtedly have some influence on the way it is introduced.

Another consideration regarding tempo is the harmonic movement of a piece. Compositions that have predictable harmonic structures are often easier to sing, even when the harmony is relegated only to instrumental accompaniment, the voices singing in unison. More complex harmonic structure will have some bearing on tempo, as will the congregation's familiarity with the piece.

THE SINGING VOICE OF THE ASSEMBLY When we read a volume such as this, we might at first consider the leadership of congregational song to be the function of instruments. But if we review the history of Christian music, we note that much more often than not, Christian ritual music existed—even flourished—as unaccompanied communal song. Christians inherit the musical tradition of the synagogue in which the gathering is led by the solo voice of the *hazzan*, the cantor. Early Christians battled over the inclusion of instruments in the liturgy at all, much less to accompany singing. As congregations influenced by the reforms of Martin Luther sought to wrestle corporate singing back from the domination of the choir, they appropriated the prevailing communal folk song style of the day—a rugged, rhythmic, and unaccompanied *lied*. The organ was used first as an accompanying instrument as late as the last half of the sixteenth century. Prior to that, the organ introduced the hymn and interpreted selected stanzas of the hymn in alternation with the unison and unaccompanied congregation. Even the term we use regularly for unaccompanied singing—a cappella—derives from the method of singing "as in the chapel."

When Christians gather we become the very body of Christ. Our assembly constitutes church—ecclesia—and our communal expression becomes the very breath of the living God. Communal singing is seen then to be the living voice of Christ in our midst. At its most natural state, unencumbered by instruments and harmonies, the unison sound of corporate song contains a unique power. However, our recent fascinations with harmonies and vocal perfection have had a tendency to displace this power and fool us into thinking that we need accompaniment for assembly song to exist. Perfect recordings made through a series of takes and edits condition our ears to surreal sounds with which we simply can't compete, so we shame ourselves into silence. The national anthem is piped into the ballpark, the television replaces song in the home, and boom boxes fill our lives with endless, mindless tunes that leave us mute. In order to reclaim the voice of the church we are invited to rediscover the core musical expression of the assembly: unaccompanied communal song.

Good unaccompanied assembly singing depends on several factors. First, it must be led by a voice or voices that lead with grace. Just as in any good instrumental accompaniment, leadership in this case will first need to establish a tempo, tactus, and determine the tonality. To begin a strophic metrical hymn that will be sung a cappella, the cantor or choir might sing one selected phrase that will indicate the regular pulse of the hymn that the assembly will count on to remain regular and establish the key center. Once the assembly enters, modifications may happen naturally to conform to the space, acoustic, and community. Rather than fight such modifications, the leadership ought to lead with grace, bending where necessary and leading as needed.

Second, all congregational singing, accompanied or not, depends on good acoustics. Rooms with carpet, cushions, porous walls, and "acoustical" tiles dampen corporate sound. Placement of vocal leadership will also enhance the assembly singing. A cantor or choral voice that envelops the sound from behind or around the congregation seems to work best for this purpose. At times, however, visual as well as audible leadership may be required which may draw the leader to the front. Avoid the tendency to amplify the leadership meant for unaccompanied singing. Such electronic means drives the sound "at" people rather than "with" people and draws connections to pop culture's performance methods which simply don't encourage participation.

Assemblies who are unaccustomed to singing without accompaniment will need help to find their "solo" voice. Begin with the simple dialogues of the liturgy such as the preface dialogue to the eucharistic prayer. Psalm tones work quite well, perhaps even best, without any accompaniment. A stanza of a hymn might be selected on occasion for unaccompanied singing. Ostinato (repeated) chants such as the ones from the community at Taizé are also fine places to begin. In all of these, expectations of singing in harmony should not be imposed, but allowed to occur freely. There is exquisite beauty in a full assembly singing in unison.

Finally, good assembly singing, accompanied or not, depends on trust. The community must trust that the leadership will not "leave them comfortless" but will support and lead as needed. And in such days of media perfection a word of consolation to any congregation engaged in unaccompanied singing that welcomes their imperfections and vocal flaws will be necessary. Praise the effort of the community, charge the choral leadership with the stewardship of all communal song, and work diligently to lead in a way that fosters trust, support, grace, and love.

2

although individually not strong readers, may rise to surprising challenges. Get to know the people in the pew. Gain an idea of what to expect and make appropriate decisions.

The leader must be aware of the general musical ability of those making up the gathering.

• Are these people here gathered used to singing at all?
• What is the level of musical literacy?
• How can I, as one called here to facilitate them in this endeavor, help them find their voice?

Musical literacy does not necessarily equal ability to sing just anything at any given tempo. A group that has done much singing together,

In view of all the variables, there is no "ideal" tempo for any given congregational piece. Factors to consider include:

• the number of worshipers
• the acoustics of the worship space
• the musical leadership—ensemble, solo instrument, voice
• the time and nature of the gathering.

The tempo of a joyous hymn of praise sung by a group of ten worshipers in a chapel with little reverberation and no instrumental accompaniment may be very different from

---

CHORALE PRELUDES AS INTRODUCTIONS A simple, straightforward hymn introduction will give the congregation necessary information on key, tempo, and style of a hymn. But an honored tradition especially in the Germanic churches is the chorale prelude—generally a longer, more elaborate form of hymn introduction. The genre includes everything from the small-scale masterpieces of Bach's *Orgelbüchlein* to a tonally challenging contemporary piece. What is the place of such works within today's worship?

The answer to that will depend in large part on the history and character of each congregation. St. Bartholomew's may value chorale preludes, even insist on them, as helpful frameworks particularly for principal hymns in the service. The assembly is quite willing to allow the extra time required so that they may consider the commentary provided by the composer. However, across town at Lord of Life Church the regular use of chorale preludes within the service would

feel like an imposition, the organist grabbing the spotlight. The congregation wants to have the hymn tune identified simply and then begin singing.

Often in church music this matter requires sensitivity. If chorale preludes within the service are undesirable they may still add much as pre- or post-service music. If they are used to introduce hymns, the organist needs to balance artistic considerations with the liturgical character of that part of the worship. What sort of piece would work well here? Does this prelude work with this text? Are the keys the same? If not, how will I deal with that? Perhaps the most important consideration is whether the tune is clearly presented in the prelude so that at its conclusion the hymn can simply begin. If not, the organist should play the last phrase of the hymn to help the assembly. Similarly, if the tempo of the hymn is not obvious from the prelude, the organist needs either to play a phrase of the hymn for the congregation's reference, or at least deliberately play the first few notes of the hymn.

the same hymn sung by hundreds in a large, reverberant cathedral, supported by organ and brass. Even so, the spectrum of tempo possibilities can (and should) be narrowed as much as possible. It's most likely that the

example 2-1

Now, my tongue, the mys - tery tell - ing

shed for this world's ran - som - ing.

group in the chapel will be able to progress at a much brisker tempo than the cathedral congregation. The reverberant acoustics of a large space would advise against swiftly moving group song. An index with suggested tempo ranges for some common hymns is provided in the back of this book.

Is there a difference between the sense of tempo employed for hymnody and that for liturgy? One would hope not, yet that is always a danger in congregations that regularly use particular liturgical settings. Familiarity with these texts and tunes sometimes gives way to "liturgical time" in which the leader and congregation make mad dashes through the responses and canticles, all sung at the same pace. The liturgy is not something simply to rush through for the sake of accomplishing it. As in hymnody the text is the governing factor. Does the singing of the Sanctus conjure up Isaiah's great vision of God's majesty (Isa. 6) or are these simply

---

FLEXIBILITY Once the pulse is established, is it inviolable? Of course not. In the case of most hymns the most obvious "give" in the tactus is the relaxation that occurs naturally at the end of the final stanza. A judicious *rallentando* is nearly always in order at this point. Sometimes it should be grand, other times modest. This slowing down gives the hymn a sense of finality and completion. Most of us do this instinctively. To prove it try accompanying a hymn all the way through with no tempo relaxation whatsoever at the last stanza's final cadence. It just does not work and leaves the singers feeling as if they have hit a concrete wall. (Note: Plainsong hymns are an exception to this practice.)

A few hymns call for tempo fluctuations within a stanza, specifically where rhythmic intricacy and/or angular melodic lines require a bit more time and effort for the assembly to execute. For instance, in the case of the tune GRAFTON ("Now, my tongue, the mystery telling"—H82 331), what may seem a reasonable tempo at the beginning suddenly becomes unworkable in the penultimate bar on the third and fourth beats. (See example 2-1.)

The inverted triad outlined by the tune's three ascending, slurred eighth notes is followed immediately by the drop of a fifth along with a new word (or syllable) to sing. This presents a challenge even for experienced singers. The sensible solution is to slightly relax the tempo for those two beats only, resuming normal speed for the last bar of the hymn.

words and tune to tear through in order to get to the Words of Institution? Is the Kyrie sung at the same speed as the Gloria? They differ greatly in both function and content. Does the opening dialogue of the Great Thanksgiving ("The Lord be with you. And also with you.") actually embrace the characteristics and rhythm of a spoken dialogue? Is the natural rhythm (and mode—spoken or sung) of the minister's part consistent with the congregational response?

Accent and Articulation

If tactus and tempo together provide the heartbeat of music, it is articulation that brings the spark and rhythm of life to the rest of the body. Articulation is the key to movement, to helping a piece, either individual or corporate, instrumental or vocal, take on life and color. Basically, articulation is the connective tissue between notes in a melody or chords in a harmonic progression. It is the contextual relationship of one note to

another. Movement from one note to another may be accomplished in a smooth, even fashion without any break between the notes *(legato)*. It may be *marcato*, accented and stressed. It may be *staccato*, detached, with each note separated from the next by quick releases. Some notes may be more accented than others. Some may achieve greater stress (or weight) by being "leaned into." In general the overall articulation of a specific phrase may appear fairly uniform. The actual movement from note to note, however, may be comprised of a rich mixture of subtle nuances (some notes more detached, louder, softer, etc.). Again, but in another way, the text, rich in word accents, vowel colors, and natural flexes, serves as the best guide.

Vocal Leadership

Those who lead the congregation vocally (song leader or choir) most likely do so by example. Through vocal leadership a congregation can learn what it means to sing sensitively with an eye to the text. This type of leadership is usually simultaneous, occurring while the congregation is actually singing. As cited in the discussion concerning the setting of tempo, the first measures are vitally important. The solo leader or choir set the stage, giving the congregation

PERFORMANCE ANXIETY A common challenge in setting the tempo is performance anxiety. All musicians deal with nervousness now and then. When nerves take over, the result can be a hymn that is too fast, hard driven, and unsingable. Before you start the hymn take a few seconds to be still, quiet, and prayerful. Focus on God rather than on the altercation you may have had with a disgruntled choir member before the service. Let go of any anger and honor your calling. Then take a deep breath and begin.

NURTURING ARTICULATION   It is in the area of articulation that the leader of the congregation's song can be most nurturing. The leader, having read the text and thereby having become more familiar with its mood and flow, can set the scene for the congregation's participation. The leader must understand in advance the climaxes of each musical sung phrase, of the melody and text as a whole. The leader understands how to magnify these elements to make use of them, thereby sharpening the congregation's sense of text and tune and, in fact, heightening their participation. This is the way the notes and text on the page become a *living* entity.

cues as to the spirit, tempo, dynamics, and flow of the piece.

Vocal leadership has nothing to do with singing out "over" the congregation or with overpowering them. Vocal leadership should be conceived as coming from within the group. It's like the elementary school teacher who speaks in a whisper in the midst of a noisy classroom so the children have to quiet down in order to listen. It's learning to be community. It involves learning to listen, both on the part of the leader and on the part of those in the congregation.

Instrumental Leadership

For those who lead from instruments (keyboard or ensemble) the task is somewhat different. They face a challenge: how can this type of leader, without the luxury of words or explanation but simply by the way in which they play, communicate to the congregation the sense of the piece as a whole, particularly its spirit and flow? How can they

actually take what the congregation is producing (singing) and simultaneously, by means of articulation, heighten their awareness of the magic that is happening in that production, the mystical union of text and tune, of composer and performer, of creator and creature, of art?

Articulation at the keyboard is a helpful tool indeed. Outside of its coloring properties, the way in which a keyboard player articulates a phrase can do much to assist the congregation in the way they are singing. It is by means of articulation that the person at the keyboard can provide real leadership in very subtle ways. Sometimes it becomes necessary for the leader to highlight a specific element or area of the music, such as tempo, ritards, or dynamic climaxes. On instruments which are dynamically touch sensitive (piano and some synthesizers) this can be accomplished by means of employing accents, of playing some notes harder (hence louder) than others or by placing more space between the notes. On keyboard instruments that are not

---

DANCING WITH VOICES Leader-ship through articulation is showing the congregation how to dance with their voices. The steps may vary—some higher, some lower, some faster, some slower—but they all constitute vocal movement.

HYMN HELPS Where does the conscientious hymn leader go to learn the history, the *Sitz im Leben*, of hymns? Hymnal companions or commentaries are excellent sources. Most major hymnals have had companions published for them. These will often provide essays on various types and eras of hymnody as well as specific notes on each hymn tune and text. In most cases, they are available from the same publisher that issued the hymnal itself. A list of major hymnal companions is included in the bibliography at the end of this book.

Another helpful font of information (as well as a place to order hymnals and companions) is The Hymn

Society in the United States and Canada. The Hymn Society publishes a journal, *The Hymn*, and holds annual conferences—both of which address a wide spectrum of hymn-related issues. For more information, phone 800-The Hymn, E-mail hyperlink mail to: <hymnsoc@bu.edu>, or write to:

The Hymn Society
Boston University School of Theology
745 Commonwealth Ave.
Boston, MA 02215-1401

Note: The E-mail and postal mail addresses are correct at the time of publication, but are subject to change at a later date.

dynamically touch sensitive (organ, harpsi-chord, some synthesizers), expression comes through an entirely different approach. Since on these instruments the way in which a note is struck (attacked), firmly or lightly, has no effect on the way it will sound, the secret of articulation here lies in how the notes are released. This has bearing on the way the following note will sound. Playing a melody at the organ and making it come to life involves varying degrees of separation with great attention to the notes' endings. Just how much space, if any, is placed between the notes gives a phrase character as well as clarity. (This is covered in more detail in Chapter 4.)

Keyboard players can learn much about articulation from bowing techniques on stringed instruments and tonguing techniques on woodwind instruments. An oboist or flutist achieves flavorful phrasing by tonguing (creating a "stop" by executing

---

YOUR BEST ALLY—THE CHOIR Church choirs exist to lead God's people in worship. Every church choir director should be clear on this, and take every opportunity to remind their choirs that this is their primary calling and most important business. No matter how polished an anthem may be, if the hymns and liturgical music in a service do not have the choir's full attention and commitment, then the music hasn't fulfilled its mission.

Before any service the music leader should decide how each hymn is to be rendered. Choices about which stanzas will be sung in unison, harmony, with descants and so forth, should be made by the director and communicated to the instrumentalists and choir. Then, a portion of every Sunday morning choir warm-up should include adequate rehearsal on the hymns so that the choir can lead the congregation competently. Hymn rehearsals should cover phrasing, punctuation, treatment of tactus between stanzas, and anything else that will contribute to the assembly's ability to sing a hymn well. Remind the choir of any unaccompanied stanzas or phrases and that its leadership role then becomes doubly important.

Too many choir directors neglect or ignore the hymns assuming that they will take care of themselves or that they are not worth the same care and effort as the choral pieces. They may even think that the thoughtful rehearsal of hymns with the choir would be lost in the midst of congregational singing. This is a serious mistake. Corporate worship demands and deserves only our best efforts. Nothing in a service should ever be considered "throw away" or unimportant, particularly the hymns. The choir is in a unique position to support the instrumentalists in bringing the hymns to life.

Insisting on a conscientious approach to the hymns also brings fringe benefits. The musical concepts that every director wants to impart to the choir—phrasing, intonation, word painting, rhythmic vitality, dynamic control, blend, and subtlety—are available in the pages of a hymnal. Hymns provide wonderful teaching tools for building the skills of choir members. This is particularly true with children or singers of limited experience.

The choir that is well rehearsed on the hymns enables a congregation to soar to new levels in their singing. Everyone is enriched, and God is praised.

the syllable *doo*) on important notes while slurring (no tonguing) others that are less important. Bowing provides a safeguard concerning phrasing on stringed instruments. The way in which the hair of the bow grips the string, the sound it makes when changing directions, and the different quality between up and down bow aurally resemble the process of breathing. If a hymn is played with the same degree of separation between each note the result can be monotonous. Again, music needs to breathe. Players, especially players who do not make use of their own breath (keyboard and string

players), need to be aware of this. Articulation is breath.

"I don't know what you did today to help us sing like that, but thanks!" is the highest compliment any music leader in a congregational setting can receive. The way in which we support and lead congregational singing through sensitive articulation can be our greatest gift to that community. Subtle nuances in articulation are valuable tools by which we can help propel the congregation to new levels of musicality, of textual awareness, of community. Then, we can get out of the way and let them "do their thing!"

WHAT YOU HAVE   Work with what you have. Just as in Jesus' parable of the talents, we have been given certain gifts. What we do with them is up to us. We may or may not have wonderful musical resources at our disposal. For every grand and glorious organ there are a dozen that are less than adequate. For every trained professional choir there are thousands of modest ones with fewer than a half dozen voices. Yet within every limitation lurks opportunity. The challenge is to get the most out of what we have. Stretch yourself. Demand high standards from your choir. Challenge your congregation. Take them all as far as you think they can go without breaking them.

Some of the most wonderful hymn singing comes from small congregations in out-of-the-way places with only humble organs to lead them. Even with a dismal instrument there are ways to bring out a hymn's full potential. Perhaps there are at least a few stops that blend well together. If the pedal sounds are pale, consider more frequent "manuals only" hymn stanzas. Consider working with a good high school instrumentalist and write a simple obbligato for the last stanza. Encourage your choir to take its rightful leadership role in the hymn singing. Train your congregation to sing unaccompanied on a stanza or part of a stanza now and then. It can be thrilling when a congregation can hold its own without the aid of accompaniment. They will love it and their singing will improve dramatically over time.

Accompaniment

The type of instrumental accompaniment the leader employs to support congregational singing affects the way the congregation sings and influences their participation. The foremost question always should be, "Will this accompaniment serve to help and support the congregation in their corporate song?" Of course, the words *help* and *support* are relative. The leader should always begin with the idea of unaccompanied singing as the model for all congregational song. When a congregation is asked to sing without the aid of instrumental forces, the individuals making up the congregation listen to themselves and to others. It is here that the congregation can best become aware of and find its true voice. Something happens when a group of people joins their voices in song, especially in unison song. Voices, each with their own character and timbre, come together. Barriers drop. The individual gives

2

way to the corporate. The singing takes on a life of its own. The group "gels." This is the goal of the leader of the people's song.

The leader's role is never to overpower or lead by means of force, dynamically or otherwise. The operative terms here, again, are *support* and *guidance*. Certain things we do (dynamic or timbral variations, for example) can serve to heighten the emotional connection experienced by those in the congregation. But experiences enhanced by emotion always depend on some mode of participation. It is the leader's task simply to take what the group is doing and help them do it better.

In choosing the type of accompaniment best suited to a certain group singing a specific piece, several factors need to be taken into account:
- the size of the group, the spatial setting, and the acoustical environment
- an inventory of the instruments that are or could be used
- some exegesis of the piece, determining its *Sitz im Leben*, including original instrumentation
- deciding what kind of accompaniment would best bring out the character of the tune, of the text
- the possibility and advisability of recasting the accompaniment for a fresh take on the hymn—a sixteenth-century chorale, for instance, sung in unison with a jazz-style

UNISON SINGING   Because it is completely bound to the Word, the singing of the congregation in its worship service, especially the singing of the house church, is essentially singing in unison. Here words and music combine in a unique way. The freely soaring tone of unison singing finds its sole and essential inner support in the words that are sung. It does not need, therefore, the musical support of other parts. The Bohemian Brethren sang: "With one voice let us sing today, in unison and from the bottom of our heart." "So that together you may with one voice glorify the God and Father of our Lord Jesus Christ" (Rom. 15:6). The essence of all congregational singing on this earth is the purity of unison singing—untouched by the unrelated motives of musical excess—the clarity unclouded by the dark desire to lend musicality an autonomy of its own apart from the words; it is the simplicity and unpretentiousness, the humanness and warmth, of this style of singing. Of course, this truth is only gradually and by patient practice disclosed to our oversophisticated ears. Whether or not a community achieves proper unison singing is a question of its spiritual discernment. This is singing from the heart, singing to the Lord, singing the Word; this is singing in unity.[1]

Dietrich Bonhoeffer

accompaniment of a flute and string bass might simultaneously jar, enlighten, and uplift.

Then, we face accompaniment questions centered on the topic of harmony.
- What is the character of the tune—long, floating lines? Rhythmically energetic phrases?
- Is it better sung in unison or is sung harmony a necessary element?
- Is the printed harmony singable or is it intended for keyboard?
- Might the group want to sing in harmony?
- Might singing in harmony intimidate some and hinder the song?
- What kind of accompaniments might be

HARMONY

The melody of congregational song is prime. Harmony acts as its nurturing cradle, facilitating leaps, rhythm, and flow.

possible if the group sings in harmony or in unison?

• Could I do something in my accompaniment—playing the harmony up an octave, for example—that might help the group's endeavor to sing in harmony?

• Might the congregation even be able to "go it alone," sing without any instrumental accompaniment?

In recent years some hymn tunes have suffered because the harmonies with which they were published do nothing to support congregational singing. In fact, these harmonizations sometimes get in the way of congregational singing. Supportive harmony provides a sense of predictability and of movement. In a strophic (multi-stanza) piece that is sufficiently familiar, alternative harmonies can refresh, surprise, and enlighten successive stanzas. This is, in fact, a basic principle for more orally-conceived genres like African and gospel. Strong, supportive harmonizations must be the norm, providing the groundwork. Leaders from the keyboard especially need to be aware of this. Those who lead from instruments that are capable of producing harmonic accompaniments other than the keyboard (guitar, autoharp, accordion) also need to be aware of this, although it is less of an issue because these instruments, by design, are grounded in primary and root chordal structures. Although chordal inversions and more complex structures certainly are possible, when leading group singing these instruments tend to utilize root position. When leading group song, for example, the guitar is often strummed. Even if it is picked, the chordal structure, based on fret harmony, remains fairly solid.

Most hymns, psalms, spiritual songs, and liturgical settings are published with keyboard accompaniments. Some harmonizations are more supportive to the singer than are others. Again, those harmonizations that are predictable in their harmonic movement and exhibit a firm grounding in the rules of music theory offer the greatest support. In instances where printed harmony actually hinders the song of the group the musician should not hesitate to reharmonize or search out more supportive, exciting harmonizations. The keyboard leader should never feel bound by the book (even a denominational hymnal) if the harmony printed in it doesn't offer adequate support. The leader should feel free to find a harmonic setting that does give support, or create one's own.

Acoustic Versus Electric

As previously stated, congregational song is, by nature, participatory—a group of individuals singing together. Since the dawn of civilization communities, especially those drawn together for the purpose of ritual, have joined their voices in some type of chant or song. Sometimes chanting served communication in settings too expansive for spoken word. Chanting—speaking on pitch—is more easily projected and heard. Children know this instinctively when they make themselves heard by voicing a descending minor third (often set early on to the word *Mommy!*). Is it any wonder Gregorian chant developed the way it did? Unison chant helped propel the sound of both voice and text in the cavernous, reverberant architecture of great medieval cathedrals and churches.

The advent of electronic amplification and technology revolutionized communication. With relatively little effort an amplified singer or speaker could be heard even in extremely large spaces. Electronics have played a major part in the evolution of music in general. The wind chests of pipe organs are filled and sustained by means of electrified motors. The tones of some instruments are generated totally by electronic means. Electronic organs, electric guitars, synthesizers all offer new sounds with which we can experiment. By means of sequencers and MIDI, the church musician's palette of colors has broadened enormously. New sounds blend with old, old songs take on new sonorities. Even a congregation that doesn't own congas or a marimba nor have in its membership anyone available to play the guitar or string bass can experience these sounds by means of electronics. A hymn from Japan might be accompanied by organ and synthesized koto; a South American refrain could be orchestrated for piano, guitars, trumpet, and synthesized marimba; computer-sequenced loops of multi-layered African drum patterns might underlie a Tanzanian hymn; we are bound only by our own creativity.

Great care must be taken, however, lest electronic synthesis or amplification in any form interfere with or worse, supplant the voice of the people. Synthesizers can be useful tools, or they can become toys that divert the leaders and the people from their fundamental song. Sequenced music, whether percussion or organ, is lifelike but not alive. Such technology has its place in church, but calls for careful discernment from those who facilitate the people's song. We will see in the chapter on African music how electronic instrumentation can, in some instances, be antithetical to the people's song.

Similarly, in both corporate speech and musical vocal leadership, amplification has the power to make the role of the people superfluous. Have you ever been in a service in which a congregational reading or prayer is "led" using a microphone? In situations like this, members of the congregation often do not participate with the enthusiasm they may have had they been left to their own capabilities. Rather than participating, they find themselves listening: the leader's voice has become primary, usurping the role of the people. This does nothing to nurture the community to respond on its own, with its own voice. One solution might be to make use of a small group of unamplified singers, even two or three, to serve as a nucleus around which the voices of those in the larger assembly can gather. The small group can model group singing or verbal response acting as "leaders" for the larger group.

Conclusion

Tactus, tempo, articulation, vocal and instrumental leadership, unison and harmony singing, the role of electronic amplification—these are the sorts of issues that need to be addressed for any type of church song. Clearly, some questions will be more urgent for some styles than for others. (Amplified Gregorian chant, for instance, is scarcely imaginable) But even when the answer seems obvious it can be beneficial to ask the question. For example, "At what tempo should I play this hymn?" A fresh look at it, a slower or faster tempo, might be just the thing to give it new life. This sort of continual reexamination takes energy, but in approaching church song of all forms, we would do well to heed the advice of the apostle Paul: "Do not lag in zeal, be ardent in spirit, serve the Lord" (Rom. 12:11).

1. Dietrich Bonhoeffer, *Dietrich Bonhoeffer Works.* Vol. 5, *Life Together: Prayerbook of the Bible.* Minneapolis: Fortress Press, 1996.

3

Chant is a form of spirituality,

a way of reaching up to God

and of leading souls to God.

Dom Joseph Gajard, trans. R. Cecile Gabain

CHANT

Gregorian chant, as Ismael Fernandez de la Cuellar has said, is "ancient, but not antiquated." It lies behind much of today's western church music, but deserves its own place in the foreground as well. In its monophony it appears simple, yet it is very rich and is subject to a complex history of interpretations. Nevertheless, with attention to a few important principles chant is well within the reach of choirs and, yes, of congregations. In a time when we are always looking for the new, exotic sound for worship we should not overlook this voice from the western church's own past.

Chant takes us back to a fundamental aspect of worship: people reaching out to God and to each other with our singing voices. The mysterious and profound beauty of its pure melody, at once distant and detached but also intense and personal, has for centuries drawn people closer to their divine creator. The melody style of chant can range from a simple recitation of a prayer on a single note to a long melodic line sung on a single syllable.

The repertory of these sacred melodies is so vast and so varied that only the very smallest fraction of it is readily available in performance editions. Most chant belongs to an oral tradition that came to be written down simply to remind the musicians of melodies that they had already committed to memory. Eventually, the availability of notated versions resulted in a decline of the oral tradition. Most chants found in modern hymnals are derived from the so-called Gregorian repertory, the body of chant (also called plainsong or plainchant) which is best known to western culture, and that which will be treated in this chapter.[1] Although the term *Gregorian* refers to the pope and church father Gregory I (c. 540–604), much of the chant which bears his name was probably composed long after his time—in fact some of the best loved chants were composed as late as the seventeenth century. And as new liturgical celebrations were added to the Roman calendar, new chants were arranged, or centonized ("patched together," from the Latin *cento*, patchwork) to accompany new texts. Even today many gifted composers are writing new music based on the flowing movement and the modality (or at least diatonicism) of chant.[2]

The history of chant development is treated in a host of music dictionaries, encyclopedias, anthologies, and textbooks. An initial source

example 3-1

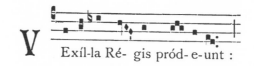

V Exíl-la Ré- gis pród- e-unt :

of information would be a college level music history text. For more detail, one should study a text or anthology focusing specifically on medieval music. A comprehensive treatment of the subject may be found in David Hiley's *Western Plainchant* (see bibliography).

An understanding of modern chant notation is also helpful, and most texts will contain a short treatment of notation, both ancient and modern. The following example indicates the three ways that this music is generally notated in modern chant books and hymnals. (See examples 3-1, 3-2, and 3-3.)

example 3-2

example 3-3

example 3-4

OTHER FORMS OF CHANT   Most people, upon hearing the term "chant," will tend to think of Gregorian chant or plainchant. However, other important historic forms of chant are used in the church throughout the world. The most widespread of these are Byzantine chant and its national forms, and Anglican chant.

Byzantine chant is the historic church music of the Eastern Orthodox churches. It has been adapted into the forms found in the Armenian, Syrian, Georgian, Russian, and Slavonic Orthodox churches. As with Gregorian chant the earliest manuscripts point to a much older oral tradition. Byzantine chant shares with its Latin cousin the use of eight ecclesiastical modes in which psalmody and hymnody are set. While many Byzantine hymns are based on scripture, non-scriptural hymns are common and have contributed to the liturgy of the West as well as the East. One example is the *troparion* "Phos hilaron" (known by translations such as

"O gladsome light" and "Joyous light of glory") used in evening services. Other important forms of Byzantine hymns are the *kontakion* (a long, metrical sermon sung during the morning office), the *kanon* that developed in the late seventh century, and the *sticheron*, a short, monostrophic hymn with a variety of uses in the liturgy.

Anglican chant is notable for its characteristic use of four-part harmony. Originally developed in the Anglican church as a harmonization of Gregorian chant with the melody in the tenor, after the middle of the seventeenth century the connection with Latin chant was largely lost. Used primarily to set psalm and canticle texts, the typical Anglican chant is a binary form, each part beginning with an unmeasured reciting tone and closing with a measured cadence. It is, of course, a much newer tradition than Byzantine and Gregorian chant; nevertheless, Anglican chant has been influential, particularly in the English-speaking church.

For more than thirteen centuries Gregorian chant has undergone a series of renewals and reforms. This constant process of change has affected the way chant has been copied, edited, printed, and sung. Aside from the various interpretive practices in use today, there have been many older practices, each in its own day claiming authenticity, dating back to the Middle Ages. As often happens, these quests for authenticity are more a reflection of the times of the individual reformers than of the era from which the original chant comes. In the Baroque period, for instance, chant came to be accompanied by a wind instrument or by the organ; ornaments were added and modal cadences were "tonalized" by the addition of accidentals. Sixteenth- and seventeenth-century reform-ers of chant, such as the editors of the *Medicean Gradual* (1614), removed "extrane-ous" notes in the belief that the ancient melodies had been corrupted over the cen-turies. Although subsequent research has proven this approach to have been erroneous, a reasonably authentic vocal/organ perfor-mance of a work such as Frescobaldi's *Fiori musicali* of 1635, in which organ would alter-nate with chant, might include the use of the abbreviated melodies as they appeared in the *Medicean Gradual*. In other words, chant has not stayed the same over the ages. And the more perspective we can gain on this genre, the more we will be led to richer and better informed performances of chant with our congregations.

CHANT TERMINOLOGY   As befits one of the oldest branches of music, the study and practice of chant have developed certain terms to describe chant's notation and interpretation. Among the more common words are:

arsis   (French *élan*; adjectival form, *arsic*) Especially in the Solesmes method, a rising or leaning into the beginning of a group of notes or a phrase.

episema   A short horizontal line above or below a note in some chant books. According to Solesmes theory, this calls for a slight lengthening on that note. A vertical *episema* indicates the ictus when it would not otherwise be clear.

ictus   The beginning of a group of notes; not an accent, and may or may not fall on an accented syllable.

neume   The sign used to notate Gregorian chant in manuscripts and older chant books. A single neume may indicate from one to four or more notes.

thesis   (French *repos*; adjectival form, *thetic*) The opposite of *arsis*: a falling or backing off from the end of a group of notes or a phrase.

Performance Practice

Throughout the twentieth century the many important musicological discover-ies in the area of chant have led to both controversy and confusion among chant per-formers. Conflicting guidelines for interpreta-tion found in current treatises can be intimi-dating and overwhelming. For a church musi-cian the difficulty often lies in finding guide-lines that can be applied systematically to a wide range of chant melodies. Several ways of singing chant, some featuring distinct regional attributes, can now be heard on recordings of masterful chant choirs from England, France, Germany, Austria, Hungary, and North America. Unfortunately, few com-prehensive performance editions are available which would explain the particular approach implemented by each individual director on these recordings.

important thing. In DIVINUM MYSTERIUM ("Of the Father's love begotten"—LBW 42), for example, one would count the first two phrases as follows. (See example 3-5; track 1.)

In this example the groupings seem perfectly logical: the accents of the text and the flow of the music are never in conflict. A thorough study of the entire hymn would reveal that the English text has been carefully worked out to fit the ancient melody. Although not all chant hymns demonstrate

example 3-5

1 2 1 2 1 2 1 2 1 2 1 2 1 2 1 2 3 1 2

VALUING THE NOTES A common mistake in reading unstemmed notes is to overvalue the longer note. Remember that the black note receives *one* count and the open note *two*, not four (it is not to be sung as a whole note in this context). Show your singers a page of the keyboard accompaniment so that they can see its parallel "stemmed" notation most often in eighth and quarter notes. (See example 3-6; track 4.) The "feathered whole note" (see the first note in 3-6) indicates a reciting tone to which any number of syllables may be sung.

---

example 3-6

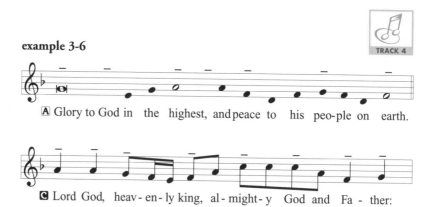

[A] Glory to God in the highest, and peace to his peo-ple on earth.

[C] Lord God, heav-en-ly king, al-might-y God and Fa-ther:

The current methods of interpretation can be divided into two schools of thought: mensuralism and equalism. The mensuralists believe in an exact metrical relationship between long and short notes (proportional rhythm) based on rhythmic signs found in several important medieval manuscripts.[3] Most equalists heed the medieval rhythmic signs, but they do not believe in adherence to any type of strict meter.[4] Among followers of each of these two categories, there are, of course, divisions. *The Hymnal 1982* offers alternative versions, one mensuralist, the other equalist, for several hymns. Two interpretations from that hymnal of VEXILLA REGIS, one equalist, the other mensuralist, demonstrate the contrast. (See examples 3-2 and 3-4.)

The beautiful and gentle wave of movement in chant is not entirely arbitrary. Chant does have rhythm, that is, "ordered movement." On the basis of this concept, most chants or chantlike music found in modern hymnals can be grouped into two- or three-note units. This division into binary and ternary groups, by defining the rhythm/movement, allows for greater precision in performance. Keep in mind that the first note of a unit, commonly called the *ictus*, is not necessarily accented or stressed. (Let's not call it "beat one," if only for that reason.) It is simply a touchpoint, a place in time. Many singers like to either circle or bracket ternary groups, while others prefer a slur for twos and a bracket for threes. Consistency is the most

example 3-7

3 1 2 3 1 2 3 1 2 3 1
Come, Ho - ly Ghost, our souls in - spire,

example 3-8

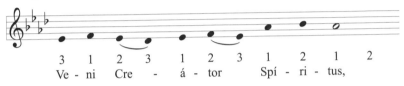

3 1 2 3 1 2 3 1 2 1 2
Ve - ni Cre - á - tor Spí - ri - tus,

example 3-9

3 1 2 3 1 2 3 1 2 3 1 2
Come, Ho - ly Ghost, our souls in - spire,

this ideal alignment, there are solutions to any potential conflicts between accent patterns of the text and the flow of the melody. Despite the differences among the following versions of VENI CREATOR, a workable pattern of twos and threes can be established for each. (See examples 3-7, 3-8, and 3-9; tracks 2 and 3.)

Many settings of the liturgy, even those composed in recent years, are also based on patterns of twos and threes. For instance, look at the beginning of Richard Hillert's setting of "Glory to God in the highest" (LBW Setting 1). Notice how in both the intonation and the congregation's part, triple and duple patterns are established. Using a mensuralist approach in which the ictus are equally spaced, it is easy to make a rhythmic correlation between the two parts. (See example 3-6; track 4.)

Conducting Chant

As you lead a choir in chant, your conducting gestures must be intentional and consistent, and they must be unmistakable to those

THE SOLESMES STYLE In the early- to mid-twentieth century the preeminent school for the study of Gregorian chant was at the Abbey of Saint-Pierre de Solesmes (usually simply called Solesmes, pronounced so-LEM), southwest of Le Mans, France. Under the direction of Dom André Mocquereau (1849–1930) and practiced for more than fifty years by their choirmaster, Dom Joseph Gajard (1885–1972), a system of performance was developed that, despite scholarly controversy, is still capable of producing consistently beautiful results. This system, explained in the "Rules for Interpretation" at the beginning of the chant book *Liber Usualis*, once found almost universal applica-

tion: it has great practical value, especially for choirs rehearsing with different directors but planning to combine for a chant performance. One of the most important principles of the old Solesmes style is that the ictus does not always fall on an accented syllable. In fact it often coincides with the last syllable of a two-syllable Latin word (e.g., *Deus, sanctus, lauda, dies*). In regard to Dom Mocquereau's approach, chant scholar Richard Crocker relates, "I have had the experience of singing chant with a complete stranger, as if from the other end of the world, and enjoying on the first try perfect ensemble as well as authentic Solesmes style."

who sing. Decide how you will group your twos and threes, then conduct in such a way that the singers know where "one" (the ictus) is. One clear and comprehensible conducting pattern is the sideways figure eight advocated by the "old" school of Solesmes.[5] It is divided into two gestures, arsic and thetic. Briefly, this pattern works as follows:

- Arsic movements (inward part of the figure eight) are reserved for accented syllables—not necessarily the ictus—especially in a rising melodic pattern. They are also used as preparation for a chant which begins on "2," where "1" is a rest. The hymn CONDITOR ALME SIDERUM ("Creator of the stars of night" or "O Lord of light, who made the stars"—H82 60), for instance, begins on "2." Simply add an eighth rest before the first note—this rest is the ictus, that is, the touchpoint. Then conduct the rest as "1" and have the choir begin on "2." This allows you to set the tempo for the chant.
- Thetic movements (outward wavelike gestures) occur on unaccented syllables and falling melodic patterns.

Many directors conduct chant convincingly with a repeated circular movement. Nonetheless, the figure eight has two advantages:

- it is comprised of two gestures rather than one, providing greater flexibility
- the first note of a group (that is, the ictus) can be more clearly identified by the singers because of the sideways motion of the gesture.

The editors of the *Liber Usualis* marked binary and ternary groups for all of the chants, and some of these editorial decisions are a matter of dispute. Many chant directors prefer a more intuitive approach, marking their own groups according to the accent of the Latin (or English) text. The pitfall of attempting to follow verbal accent in Latin can be seen in many hymns in which verbal accents shift position from stanza to stanza. In such cases, a reliance entirely on verbal accent would require a change in conducting patterns for each stanza. Other chant methods, especially the mensuralist interpretations, are best suited for small groups of singers led by directors who are willing to devote time to transcribing chants from sources that contain the early medieval rhythmic signs.[6]

The following are some practical hints that may help the leader of chant in working with choirs or congregation.

- Prepare! The introduction of any unfamiliar music to your congregation should begin with careful preparation by the musical leadership. Whether you are the director or the accompanist, it is imperative to study the chant

---

LIBER USUALIS   The *Liber Usualis* is a comprehensive twentieth-century edition of chants for the Mass and the Office. Although intended for very practical use in the Roman Catholic church, it was the result of intense scholarly effort. In the *Liber Usualis* the printed transcription of a given melody generally represents a fusion of more than one medieval chant source. Out of print until recently, a reprint of the 1953 printing (1952 copyright) with introduction and rubrics in English is now available through St. Bonaventure Publications in Great Falls, Montana.

and to sing the entire chant as part of your preparation. Then work with the rest of your leadership team—the choir and/or cantor. Often the choir/cantor will serve as a barometer of the entire congregation, thereby giving you a better idea of the problems that might arise when you try something new. And if you have instilled confidence in your choir/cantor, the congregation will follow their lead.

● Begin your warm-up by humming the "Amen" found at the end of the hymn (it's simple and short). Change to "oo," then "ah." Be creative. Have the choir sing that short "Amen" formula in parallel fourths or fifths. Tune up those whole and half steps.

● Sing the whole chant without the text, perhaps on the syllable "noo." This is the best time to shape the melody. A gentle accompaniment is not harmful. It can, in fact, help support the pitch. Encourage people to sing gently and to blend. Their leadership in worship should be based on clarity and beauty, not volume.

● Try different tempos, but do not rush. Some choirs now tend to sing chant hymns at brisk tempos which are "listenable" but not "singable" by the average congregation. If your chant rhythm is arranged in groups of notes, you are probably not in danger of singing too slowly.

● Add the text, remembering the shape and sound of the music you have already created on vowels alone. You may be surprised at how well the music launches the text, rather than the other way around.

In the end, no matter how many different systems of interpretation are available or which one you choose, it is important to lead a beautiful and inspiring performance that embodies one key element—prayerfulness.

Keyboard Accompaniment

Most people are aware that Gregorian chant was originally performed by unaccompanied voices, and that is still the best way to capture its beauty. However, especially when using chant as congregational song, circumstances will often call for supporting accompaniment, most often from organ or other keyboard. This is particularly true of modern compositions built upon chant style, such as David Hurd's *New Plainsong Mass* (W3 264–69) or hymn tunes like Richard Dirksen's INNISFREE FARM ("Christ, mighty Savior"—H82 34).

Generally speaking, accompaniment for chant is best kept as unobtrusive as possible. With congregational chant you may at first need to solo out the melody; as soon as feasible, though, move into the background, accompanying almost imperceptibly. Listen, for example, to how the accompaniment to UBI CARITAS ("Where true love and charity are found"—W3 598) supports the melody, but doesn't dominate it. (See example 3-10; track 5.)

example 3-10

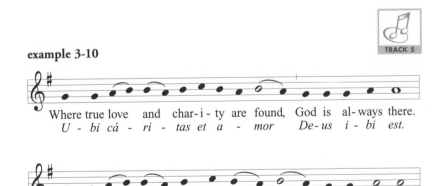

Where true love and char-i-ty are found, God is al-ways there.
U - bi cá - ri - tas et a - mor De-us i - bi est.

Since the love of Christ has brought us all to-geth-er,

3

Just as the performance of a 4/4 hymn is often improved by thinking in two pulses to the measure rather than four, the movement of chant benefits by thinking in groups of notes rather than in single notes. In most cases the placement of chords will coincide with your groupings or vice versa. If you disagree with the groupings implied by a particular published accompaniment it is possible to shift certain chords to a rhythmic position that is one pulse earlier or later than notated in order to avoid conflict with your binary and ternary groups.

Also note that despite the fact that accompanying chords will most often change with the ictus, there are drawbacks to accompanying chant always in this manner. For one thing, the changing chord tends to accent the ictus (which, as we have seen, is undesirable). In addition, changing the chord every two or three notes can establish a rather restless harmonic rhythm. Consider at times changing the underlying chord only once or twice in a phrase and then not always on the ictus.

Be judicious and informed about the use of harmony. Be discreet in the use of functional harmony, especially dominant and diminished seventh chords. More to a medieval style would be an accompaniment that employs parallel fourths and fifths or parallel 6/3 chords *(fauxbourdon)*.

Basic principles of hymn leadership apply.
- Introduce the chant as you expect it to be sung.
- Vary the texture by adding or reducing the number of voices in the accompaniment.
- Pay attention to the touch or articulation, being sensitive both to the acoustic and to the text and structure of the piece.

Finally, remember that in chant accompaniment "less is more"—it is better to err on the side of simplicity. Chant singing can be memorable without turning it into a grand production.

Conclusion

To many people, chant can be rather daunting—enjoyable to listen to, perhaps, but not suited for congregational song. (The exception, of course, is "Oh, come, oh, come, Emmanuel.") There are times, though, when it can add just the right tone of reflection, a reference to things timeless. It is also particularly well suited to carrying the text without overshadowing it. The music leader who includes it now and then will probably be surprised at how positively the congregation responds.

---

1. Old Roman chant, which is represented by manuscripts dating between the eleventh and thirteenth centuries, was probably sung in Rome between the eighth and thirteenth centuries. Mozarabic chant was sung in Spain, Ambrosian in Milan, Beneventan in southern Italy, Gallican in France before the imposition of Roman practice by Pepin and Charlemagne, and Byzantine in Constantinople. These were widely varying repertories, whereas Sarum chant, which was used in Salisbury, was more of a dialect of what we now call Gregorian chant.

2. Gregorian chant employs the medieval system of modes; that is, scales organized around what we now know as the white keys of a piano but beginning on various notes. A major or minor scale is considered diatonic if no sharps or flats have been added beyond the original key signature.

3. See, G. Murray, *Gregorian Chant according to the Manuscripts* (London: L. J. Cary, 1963) and J. M. A. Vollaerts, *Rhythmic Proportions in Early Medieval Ecclesiastical Chant*, 2d ed. (Leiden, Netherlands: E. J. Brill, 1960). Also, John Rayburn, *Gregorian Chant: A History of the Controversy Concerning its Rhythm* (New York: 1964; reprint, New York: Greenwood Press, 1981) contains a bibliography of this subject.

4. See, Dom Joseph Gajard, *The Solesmes Method* (Collegeville, MN: The Liturgical Press, 1960). The rationale for the Solesmes chant editions is dealt with more fully in Dom André Mocquereau, *Le Nombre Musical Grégorian: A Study of Gregorian Musical Rhythm* vol. 1, parts 1 and 2, trans. Aileen Tone. (Solesmes: Editions de l'Abbaye Saint-Pierre de Solesmes, 1989). There is also a "school" of Eugène Cardine, author of *Gregorian Semiology* (Solesmes: Editions de l'Abbaye Saint-Pierre de Solesmes, 1982) and *Beginning Studies in Gregorian Chant*, trans. ed. William Tortolano (Chicago: G.I.A. Publications, 1988). Although Cardine's research has led to new developments in the understanding of the meaning of the earliest chant notation, the path from his important theoretical insights to a practical method of performance has not yet been made smooth.

5. See, Theodore Marier and Justine Ward, *Gregorian Chant Practicum* (Washington: The Catholic University of America Press, 1990). This "Manual for Adult Beginners" is a thorough primer on chant interpretation according to Dom Mocquereau and Dom Gajard. More detailed instruction on this approach to Gregorian chant can be found in Dom Joseph Gajard's book *The Solesmes Method*. Recordings of the monks of Solesmes singing according to these principles are widely available, although the most recent recordings document a slight shift in their approach to rhythm.

6. Our modern ears are accustomed to chant interpretations that would have been inconceivable to nineteenth-century ears. What a pity it would be, though, to ignore the work of so many musicians who edited and arranged chant melodies at that slower, more solemn pace. Take, for example, Eugène Gigout's *Chants du Gradual & du Vespéral*, which contains four-part harmonizations of over 150 chant melodies. In that collection, Gigout assigned a chord to each slowly moving chant note. As old-fashioned as this approach seems to us now, it represents a valid attempt by Gigout to adapt chant melodies to his own time. How will they look back on us in a hundred years?

CHAPTER 4

Shout for joy loud and long,

God be praised with a song!

To the Lord we belong:

Children of our maker,

God the great life giver.

David Mowbray

Engulfed by a plethora of "new" forms of congregational song, we can at least take the classic hymn for granted, can't we? Yes, but only if we're willing to risk stagnant, rote singing. Hymnody, which draws from roots in northern Europe, remains the core of North American Protestant song and deserves a fresh look now and then, however familiar it is. Tactus, articulation, the space between stanzas, variety in settings, and organ registration—all of these are potential sources of renewed vigor in this important part of the church's song.

If asked to name four hymns, the average North American might come up with "Oh, come, all ye faithful," "Praise God, from whom all blessings flow," "Holy, holy, holy," and "Praise to the Lord, the Almighty." Although the repertoire of congregational song is greatly varied, these examples represent the most common experience of many Christians. Most hymns that are well known to North Americans come from the northern European tradition. True, some may have been written in the last decade in the United States or Canada, or they may originate in some other part of the globe, but their musical language—and thus how we leaders interpret them—is grounded in northern Europe.

The examples discussed in this chapter fall into the sometimes overlapping categories of metrical, rhythmic, and folk hymnody. Some definitions are in order. A metrical hymn (such as most English and later German hymns) is one that has a regular meter and a recurring pulse. Such hymns may exist in

four-part harmony, as a unison line with organ or other instrumental accompaniment, or sung by voices alone.

A rhythmic hymn (such as earlier German chorales and Genevan Psalter tunes) is also characterized by a steady pulse (tactus), but does not necessarily have a consistent number of beats in a measure, if there are measures at all. This steady tactus usually underlies a rugged, often syncopated, melody. These hymns were generally sung in unison with or without organ accompaniment. Many metrical (also called isometric) hymns evolved from early rhythmic forms.

Folk hymnody requires a somewhat more extensive introduction. In regard to meter, a folk hymn might have the characteristics of either the metrical hymn or the rhythmic hymn. What sets the folk hymn apart is its origin outside the culture's art traditions. In addition, the distinguishing characteristics of this repertoire are:

4

- its evolution, or re-creation by a community over time
- its eventual acceptance into the oral tradition of the community
- the community's use of this music to define its own boundaries in relation to the surrounding culture.

In addition, many folk hymns are the product of rural areas and come to us from the distant past, the composition of unknown authors. In a sense, virtually all styles and genres of hymn writing have, at one time or another, become folk literature for one or more communities. These hymns have spoken to their communities and, in turn, the character of the hymns cherished by a community accurately reflects the spirit and character of the people within that community.

A few other observations might be made regarding European folk hymnody in particular. First, the tunes tend to fall in one of several forms:

- AABA (FOREST GREEN)
- ABCD, through-composed (SLANE)
- ABBA, a variant of French *virelai* form (KING'S LYNN)
- AABB, a variant of French *ballade* form (GREENSLEEVES).

Second, in their current form, most of these tunes are written in major keys. Modal, pentatonic, or minor tunes are the exception.

Third, as mentioned, these hymns have evolved and may continue to do so. One reason for this evolutionary process is that folk hymns are a product of oral tradition. They either originate there or they are first notated and then gradually enter the oral repertoire of a community. As they become part of oral tradition, folk hymns are slowly altered to fit the requirements of the present-day community in which they are sung. These alterations ordinarily occur within individual motives or phrases of a tune. Change is slow and incremental. The presence of folk hymns in hymnals does not stop the process of change. In the production of hymnals many editorial decisions are made that alter folk tunes either in the direction of earlier versions of the tune or toward an amalgamation of features from several versions. Thus, oral and written traditions interact in an ongoing evolutionary process that forms the basis for the assembly's song at any given moment along the way.

Another reason for the gradual alteration of folk hymns is their geographical movement. One of the fundamental characteristics of folk hymnody is migration. Folk hymns are on a journey. They wander from one cultural and geographic setting to another, finding new homes in diverse communities far removed from the original traditions that created and nurtured them. Along the way, new cultural expectations affect the performance of these hymns. Modal intervals might be altered to fit a tonal system. In particular, flatted sevenths from the mixolydian mode are often exchanged for raised leading tones. Folk hymns that were originally sung as solo melodies are set in four-part harmony for the purpose of choral singing. This practice began in Germany during the nineteenth century and later moved to England and North America.

Finally, most of the folk tunes in current use are coupled with comparatively newer texts. In part, this results from the nature of these tunes themselves. Folk hymns are often *contrafacta*—tunes with secular associations that subsequently have been paired with sacred texts. In addition, the striking melodic patterns of folk hymns help the singer remember the text. Since the tunes themselves are memorable they tend to inspire poets to produce new texts, which are in turn readily adopted by the assembly.

Mainstream Hymnody

The vast genre discussed in this chapter encompasses the mainstream of northern European and American Christian hymnody from the Reformation to the present, drawn from many subcultures. Much of the practical material discussed here can be applied to the leadership of other hymnic styles.

The question might be asked, Why is this mainstream hymnody? What has made this form of congregational song so well accepted? With the Reformation's encouragement of active congregational participation in worship there arose an urgent need for music that the average worshiper could manage. The German chorale and the Genevan Psalter tune, with their straightforward lines and appealing, earthy rhythms, soon took hold. In England this new congregational music took the form of the metrical psalm tune. At the same time, influenced by this more formally composed

hymnody, communities were nurturing their own folk hymns that, in time, would be brought into wider use. Within a short time hymnody had taken root within the hearts and musical minds of worshiping Christians, forming the backbone of congregational music as many know it. Every century since the sixteenth has had its metrical hymns; they are still being composed today.

Why is this form of congregational song so firmly entrenched in the fabric of Christian worship? The reasons are as simple as its elements:

- it repeats itself (stanzas, as well as phrases)
- it has a recurring pulse
- its movement is predictable
- it is easily remembered
- a large gathering is able to sing it together as a unified voice.

Thomas Day, in *Why Catholics Can't Sing*, characterizes the hymn in terms that, at first glance, seem to have pejorative connotations: "The classic Christian hymn is big and broad and essentially simple in its construction; it can hold a group of people in its large motions." He continues to describe the music of the Protestant church as "quite mediocre—honest and plain stuff, but nothing to write home about. For approximately five hundred years this mediocrity has been the secret of success for the music in most Protestant churches." He labels this "homely music," and continues that "behind the 'mediocrity' in the music there is a reverberating profundity."[1] This is really an accurate and beautiful description of the metrical hymn.

4

use more often for metrical hymnody. Since the organ is the standard support for this type of hymnody, though, we will focus on it. Those using other instrumentation may find many of the suggestions applicable.

Performance Practice

In many ways the Northern European hymn was made for the organ and the organ for it. When we think of "O God, our help in ages past," we probably imagine it sung by an organ-led congregation. This is not to say, of course, that other instruments cannot be used—in the keyboard realm, piano and synthesizer are possible—and unaccompanied song is an option we should

Tactus

How do we begin to play a hymn effectively? The notes, of course, must be learned. It is far better to play something simple—even a hymn—for prelude or postlude than to put all one's effort into artful works for the "before and after" while floundering through the hymns and detracting from the worship itself.

HOW FAST? Much has been said on the subject of appropriate tempos for hymn singing. The arguments for *faster* or *slower* are heated. National and denominational customs emerge and fade. What is popular today may be passé in the next generation. Generally, the terms "fast" and "slow" are unhelpful and misleading. More descriptive and accurate terms include "less fast," "not too slow," or "moderate." How do we establish a reasonable and intelligent tempo range for any hymn, remembering that the goal is the full and authentic participation of everyone present?

Factors calling for a "less slow" hymn tempo include: dry acoustics, small or medium size rooms, smaller organs, small gatherings in small *or* large rooms, a lethargic assembly. In a gross oversimplification, it is possible to say that hymns from Germanic traditions are generally sung "less slow."

Naturally, the opposite conditions would suggest tempos that are "not fast." The longer a room's reverberation, the more time it takes for musical phrases to unfold, particularly when a large crowd is involved.

Hymns simply cannot be taken quickly in a room with five-second reverberation. In another gross oversimplification it is possible to say that hymns from the English tradition are generally sung "less fast."

Any metronome indications suggested for hymns, including the suggestions on pages 150–57 of this book, are helpful provided they are viewed as negotiable, as demonstrated with CWM RHONDDA on the following page. In some cases, these tempo markings force one to rethink old assumptions about certain hymns.

When playing most northern European hymns, it is a common misinterpretation to treat the quarter note as the primary pulse. More often than not the tactus is discovered in the half note. Reimagine the music with a half note pulse and see what a difference it makes. Hymns take on a new level of energy, becoming more lively, more forward-moving, even easier to sing. They are also more dangerous if the accompanist is not prepared for this speed.

Certain hymn tunes, such as TRURO ("Christ is alive! Let Christians sing"—LBW 363), present a special challenge in finding the right speed. A sprightly tempo that works for the first phrase, in which the half note pulse is strong, clear, and predominant, seems hurried when faced with the quarter notes in the second phrase. By the last phrase, with its large leaps and quarter note energy, the original tempo is positively frantic. How can these opposing needs be reconciled? Consider the hymn as a whole, taking into account the contrasting requirements of the first and last phrases, and then strike a compromise. The right tempo will accommodate both.

Let's take CWM RHONDDA as a test case for hymn tempos. It is a familiar tune to most churchgoers, appearing with at least two classic texts in many hymnals ("God of grace and God of glory" and "Guide me, O thou great Jehovah/Redeemer").

Case A. CWM RHONDDA is scheduled for a summer Sunday service with a small congregation (20–30) in a modest-sized church with dry acoustics, a low ceiling, and four-rank unified organ. In this instance, a speed of ♩=60 would not be unreasonably fast. A radically slower tempo would be a mistake. Why? The few singers present would be overtaxed physically and musically and would not be able to sustain their energy beyond the first two stanzas or so. The third and fourth stanzas then become a chore and endurance test rather than a joyful, life-giving event. The last thing a hymn leader wants is a congregation thinking, "Can we just get this hymn over with, please?"

Case B. The same hymn is slated for the dedication service of a new church—a cavernous building with ample reverberation and a large, commanding organ. A crowd of a thousand is expected for the service on this grand occasion. Practicality necessitates a more relaxed pace of perhaps ♩=84 (♩=42). This broader pulse allows phrases to unfold naturally and musically with crescendo and diminuendo emerging effortlessly as the congregation unites in song. It also leaves plenty of room for everyone to breathe between phrases. A significantly faster tempo would soon deteriorate into a jumble, or worse, a contest between organist and congregation to see whose notion of speed will prevail. Singers in the back of the church (if the organ and choir are in the front) will inevitably fall behind and likely give up, as did the singers in Case A, but for very different reasons.

Whatever the selected tempo, stick with it. The congregation needs to be able to rely on a steady tactus. When you come to the end of a stanza (except for the final one), *don't slow down*. Make the final note longer, add some breathing room (see "The Space Between Stanzas" on pages 48–49), but maintain the pulse.

Finally, a rallentando lends a sense of dignity and finality at the very end of the hymn. The same principles that determine the hymn's tempo also govern the amount of slowing down that is appropriate in the final cadence. As in previous stanzas, the final chord should be of determinate length. It is best to hold this chord the same number of beats as in earlier stanzas. Because the rallentando has just altered the tempo, however, the final chord will last somewhat longer in real time. In any event, a chord of indefinite length is not helpful anywhere in the hymn, including the last chord. If held too long, the congregation inevitably runs out of breath long before the organist lets go. With consistency of leadership, the congregation can be conditioned to sing together with the leader; they just need to know what to expect.

Most current hymnals have dispensed with the "Amen" at the end of hymns. Whatever the theological arguments, a sung "Amen" at the end of a hymn invariably drags things out, weakens the final cadence, and dampens whatever mood was achieved during the hymn.

example 4-1

example 4-2

Once the notes are learned, then focus on the pulse, the tactus, of the hymn. A strong, clear, and steady rhythm is critical to lead an assembly in song. It needs to be consistent, and the congregation has to be able to hear it. Generations of organists were taught a thoroughly legato style of organ playing, destroying the rhythmic vitality of many hymns.

German chorales (c. 1517–1650) and hymns from the Genevan Psalter (after 1536) were written at a period in history when bar lines and time signatures were largely nonexistent. The natural pulse of the music, the tactus, was felt rather than discovered through music notation. In fact, modern notation is often misleading. For example, hymns that appear to be in 4/4 time usually have a half-note tactus; hymns that appear in 3/4 often have a dotted-half tactus. Two examples with stress marks indicating where the tactus would fall are shown. (See examples 4-1 and 4-2.)

This broader feel of the tactus has a profound effect on how the hymn is played and sung, propelling the melody along. The English tune KINGSFOLD ("My soul proclaims your greatness"—WOV 730), for example, though it appears to be in 4/4, has a half-note tactus; the Welsh tune THE ASH GROVE ("Sent forth by God's blessing"—LBW 221), with its triple meter, has one pulse per bar. (See examples 4-3 and 4-4; tracks 6 and 7.)

The same technique works for more conventionally composed hymns. The popular

example 4-3

TRACK 6

example 4-4

TRACK 7

example 4-5

TRACK 8

EASTER HYMN ("Jesus Christ is risen today"—LBW 151), for example, can march along with a quarter-note tactus; spread it out to a half-note tactus, though, and it soars. (See example 4-5; track 8.)

Lutheran Book of Worship and *Hymnal 1982* are modern worship books that have followed the early practice: no time signatures appear in those books. Bar lines are omitted from early hymnody as well. The tactus must be discovered naturally by playing the melody and rhythm and sensing where the strong and weak beats of the music occur. More often than not, that tactus is a half note.

Consider the tune ES IST DAS HEIL ("Salvation unto us has come") as it appeared in 4/4 time in *The Lutheran Hymnal* (1941). When played with each quarter note getting a strong pulse, the result is laborious. (See example 4-6; track 9.) In 1978, it appeared in *Lutheran Book of Worship* as shown in example 4-7.

Without understanding the concept of tactus, one could still feel this is a laborious 4/4. However, when applying a "strong" accent to the larger beat, allowing the in-between pulse to feel "weak," a rhythmic, dance-like quality results. (See tracks 10 and 11.)

The rhythms of some early hymns can be quite energetic as is the case with ES IST DAS HEIL. Others, especially from the Genevan Psalter and folk traditions, are quite rhythmic

example 4-6

TRACK 9

example 4-7

TRACK 10   TRACK 11

LEGATO HYMN PLAYING   Legato technique, since it is *applied to* the music and not *derived from* the music, tends to iron out the gentle rhythmic groupings and much of the syncopation. There is nothing to indicate that early music was conceived or played using late nineteenth- and early twentieth-century legato style. While there are no recordings of sixteenth- and seventeenth-century musicians playing their own music, it is possible to ascertain from historic documents that each major period had its own unique style of keyboard articulation. One wouldn't normally play WOODWORTH ("Just as I am, without one plea") in a marcato style; neither, then, will the informed organist want to play a rhythmic chorale in a Romantic style. Simply put, a single keyboard style cannot serve to accompany all of the songs, hymns, and spiritual songs of every time and place. For hymnody dating from the seventeenth century and before, mastering the *leggiero* (baroque "one finger" legato) style from the Baroque period can restore rhythmic life. The sidebar on articulation in this chapter has some helps for mastering that style. More information related to early keyboard technique can be found in *Organ Technique: An Historical Approach* by Sandra Soderlund (Hinshaw Music, 1980); *J. S. Bach's Keyboard Technique: An Historical Introduction* by Quentin Faulkner (Concordia, 1984); and *Organ Technique: Modern and Early* by George Ritchie and George Stauffer (Prentice Hall, 1992).

example 4-8

French carol; arr. Marie Rubis Bauer © 1998 Augsburg Fortress

but in a more gentle dance-like way. The addition of some light percussion (triangles, tambourine, hand drum, finger cymbals) can help communicate this style, as in the case of NOËL NOUVELET ("Now the green blade rises"—LBW 148). (See example 4-8; track 12.)

Both rhythmic chorales and Genevan Psalter hymns originally were sung in unison without accompaniment. We should encourage our congregations to sing them in this way today, at least occasionally. When accompanying them on the organ, be certain that the registration is gentle and does not dominate the voices. At the same time, keep the tactus clear and strong. This can be a bit more challenging with non-metered tunes than it is with a regular number of beats in a measure and clearly delineated bar lines. One possibility for FREU DICH SEHR (PSALM 42—"Comfort, comfort now my people"—LBW 29) is to think of a steady half-note pulse. With this established, some of the "stronger" notes—such as the second "*com*fort"—actually fall on a weak beat. This sets up a feeling of syncopation and helps to propel the melody.

Alternatively, the same melody can be thought of more along the lines of chant: a combination of twos and threes. In this case the second "*com*fort" falls on a strong beat, and the melody's interest lies in the alternation of triple and duple meter. (See example 4-9; track 13.)

example 4-9

1 2 3 1 2 3 1 2 1 2 1 2 1 2 3 1 2 3 1 2 1 2 1 2

Similarly, the concept of tactus can be applied in a number of ways to the original rhythmic version of EIN FESTE BURG ("A mighty fortress is our God"—LBW 228). One idea would be to conduct a simple "down-up" pattern with a half note every downbeat. Then sing the melody on the syllables "down" and "up." This will provide a sense of the lively syncopation inherent in the tune. (See example 4-10; track 14.) Or, alternately, number the melody with twos and threes as in chant (beginning on the upbeat 2) to sense the alternating pattern of duple and triple meter. (See example 4-11.)

It is important to remember that there is no one absolutely correct way to articulate a particular hymn in every case. An organist must learn all the possibilities, then listen carefully to your instrument, space, situation, and assembly, applying all the techniques as you go. (See track 15.) In every instance attention to tactus and articulation will give more life to a hymn

Articulation

The careful handling of repeated notes is essential to keeping the tactus strong and evident in effective hymn playing. Think of the hymn tune HANOVER ("Oh, worship the King"—H82 388). The tactus is the dotted-half note (one pulse per bar). By giving weight to the strong beats (beat one in 3/4 time), the organist solidifies the tempo immediately. He or she accomplishes this by treating the first note/chord (on the "Oh") as an upbeat, playing it in a detached manner. This gives that particular note a sense of lift as well as adding weight (agogic accent) to the following downbeat.

The soprano line (if that's the melody, as in most cases) should articulate every repeated note with a slightly larger articulation before the strong beats. Repeated notes in the bass line might be tied together from strong to weak beat but articulated when leading into a strong beat. The bass line can help reinforce the tactus. Repeated notes in the inner voices (alto and tenor) can either be tied together or detached to reinforce the tactus, depending on the circumstances. Consider the following possibilities. (See example 4-12; tracks 16 and 17.)

example 4-10

example 4-11

example 4-12

Notice that the soprano line articulates every repeated note. In the third system, the bass line ties two notes together between beats one and two, and the inner voices are all connected. This particular combination might work well in a room with dry acoustics. (See track 18.)

When a stronger tactus is needed (a livelier acoustic or more lethargic assembly) the articulation should be adapted. One possibility is shown in example 4-13; track 19.

In this example, in addition to the articulations marked above, repeated notes in the inner voices as well as arrivals to the tactus in

the bass line are now articulated. Occasionally, in 3/4 time, a 2+1 articulation can be very strong. That means consistent articulations before the tactus (beat 1) but also separating the upbeat (beat 3). (See track 20.)

Again, these are only possibilities that will need to be adapted to fit individual circumstances. When you think of all the possible subtleties within articulation, the levels of gradation between these examples are many. As a

example 4-13

TRACK 19

ACCENT AND ARTICULATION ON THE ORGAN   On instruments such as a piano, where a particular note can be struck more loudly than others, the tactus can be heard by applying this method of accent to the appropriate beats. On instruments such as an organ, where striking a particular note harder than others does not result in an accent, the same effect is achieved by careful use of articulation, the slight separation before and subtle elongation of the stressed pulse (agogic accent). Articulation is one of the principal components in determining how the listener will perceive tactus, phrasing, and texture.

On the organ, try playing a simple C-major scale completely legato using the fingering 1, 2, 3, 1, 2, 3, 4, 5. Next, try to achieve the same legato, but playing the entire scale with the same finger 1, 1, 1, 1, 1, 1, 1, 1. Using that technique again, try to slightly lengthen

every other note, **1**, 1, **1**, 1, **1**, 1, **1**, 1, thinking "down-up-down-up" as you do this. (Note, however, that the finger shouldn't "pop" up even after the shorter notes, but be drawn inward toward the palm.) After practicing this skill, a crisp duple rhythm will be heard. Experiment with the "size" of the articulation preceding the lengthened beat to create stronger or more gentle accents. Shift the larger articulation and elongated notes to create a triple rhythm **1**, 1, 1, **1**, 1, 1, **1**, 1. It takes a lot of patient practice to master this technique.

This is the kind of legato that is very effective in hymn playing on the organ. Of course you won't be playing hymns with one finger. However, once you have a sense for how the notes flow together using this type of legato, you will more easily achieve a clear sounding of the tactus, which in turn will result in confident, rhythmic congregational singing.

new concept to an organist this kind of thinking can seem overwhelming: suddenly, a simple hymn becomes quite complex. However, once mastered, careful control of every articulation can help a hymn come alive and will result in better assembly singing. (See track 21.)

example 4-14

written:

example 4-15

played:

It is critical not to become stuck in a rut, playing a hymn tune the same way every time, no matter what. An organist must be prepared to alter her or his plans as the singing progresses. The assembly may not need as much rhythmic help at a particular service and you may need to lessen the articulation planned for inner voices. You may expect a rousing opening hymn only to discover that the gloomy weather has done its worst, and more articulation is needed than you had thought.

Once a song, hymn, or liturgical piece is begun the tactus must be maintained. Nothing is more detrimental to congregational singing than the delay of a strong beat at the beginning of a phrase. The key to allowing for congregational breathing lies not in the way a phrase is begun but rather in the way the phrase that precedes it is concluded. This means that, rather than actually adding "breathing time" at the beginning of a phrase, time for a breath can be "robbed" from the final note of the preceding phrase. Again using HANOVER as an example, moving from the first phrase to the second, it is written as example 4-14 but played as example 4-15. Depending on the acoustic, the rest could be lengthened to a quarter, again stealing from the preceding note.

It is important for the organist to remember that releases of notes, as well as attacks, are part of the rhythm. Be certain to lift the chord precisely on the pulse that you intend. The assembly will hear that lift as part of the beat. If, in the example above, a stronger tactus is needed, a quarter rest would be better because the lift would be on a quarter-note beat. Musicians who understand this also know that in great

4

pieces of congregational literature this structure is built-in—it's what makes the piece easy to sing. A phrase that ends with a whole note in common meter most often requires a quarter-note breath on the final beat. This does nothing to disturb the downbeat of the next phrase or the tactus of the piece in general. In some circumstances, slight tactical elongation on certain beats at the end of a phrase may be necessary to facilitate breathing. These should be done in a natural sounding manner with as little "give" to the tactus as is possible. The best way to decide how to breathe in the context of a specific phrase is simply to do it—either try it yourself or ask a group, however small, to undertake the feat. Choir warm-ups, staff devotions, gatherings at the coffee maker in the church kitchen are great places for solving these (and other) problems.

Musical Phrasing

Another factor in adding or deleting articulation is phrasing, both musical and textual. Three schools of thought in the phrasing of hymns are:

- follow the musical phrase with both singers and organ breaking at the end of the musical line, no matter what the text

---

THE SPACE BETWEEN STANZAS   How do you handle the transition from the end of one hymn stanza to the beginning of the next? Some organists use the "parking" technique: they hold the final chord of the stanza interminably while searching the stop jambs for some new combinations. When the chord is finally released, the new stanza begins abruptly without the tiniest pause to recover, breathe, and prepare for what comes next. On the other hand, there are organists who subscribe to the "rolling stone gathers no moss" tactic: they charge from one stanza to the next absolutely in time, leaving the singers gasping for breath and just as discouraged as in the first method.

Organs don't need to breathe, but singers do. A good organist understands that a sense of breathing is fundamental to making music whether in the organ works of Bach and Reger or the accompaniment of hymns. All organists should be required to sing in the choir and the congregation from time to time in order to better understand that singing is a physical pursuit requiring breathing, and that breathing takes time and effort.

Learn to breathe with the congregation. Some organists sing along as they play. This is helpful in regard to breathing with the congregation but not for listening to them. If the organist is singing, it is more difficult to discern the collective voice of the assembly, particularly in dead acoustics where *everyone* feels as if they are singing alone. The organist can help the assembly breathe and sing together by giving attention to the transition from one stanza to the next.

Moving from one stanza to another is a matter of timing. The factors are the amount of time the last chord is held and the space between that chord and the downbeat of the first chord of the next stanza. As with any issue regarding tactus, predictability is the key!

In the case of HANOVER ("Oh, worship the King") the following formula works nicely:

• Hold the final chord exactly three beats *in tempo*. Do not slow down or place a fermata over it. Rallentando is appropriate only at the very end of the hymn.

example 4-16

written:

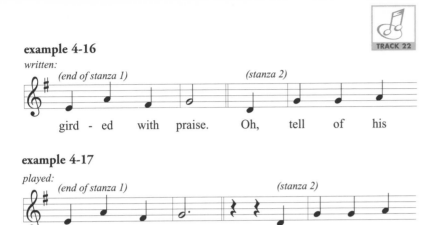

(end of stanza 1)   *(stanza 2)*

gird - ed with praise.   Oh, tell of his

example 4-17

played:

(end of stanza 1)   *(stanza 2)*

gird - ed with praise.   Oh, tell of his

• Release the chord and count out two empty beats *in tempo* before beginning the new stanza, also *in tempo* (See examples 4-16 and 4-17; track 22.)

In other words, the last note equals three beats, the space between stanzas equals two beats. This brings the congregation back in on a third beat. In shorthand, the organist and choir can write "3+2" over the last note in their hymnals. The plan should then be followed religiously. The congregation will quickly catch on. They will sense how long to hold the last note and, more importantly, how much time they have to breathe before the new stanza begins.

The 3+2 plan works for most, but not all, triple meter tunes that begin on the upbeat (e.g., WAREHAM, ST. PATRICK'S BREASTPLATE, ST. CLEMENT, ST. DENIO, THE FIRST NOWELL, ROCK-INGHAM). Triple meter tunes that start on the downbeat are more problematic (e.g., ABBOT'S LEIGH, KING'S WESTON, ST. AGNES, MARYTON, HYFRYDOL). On such hymns, a 3+3 treatment will require a tempo that is either quite broad or one that is a brisk, one-beat-per-bar feeling. Other factors pointing toward 3+3 are a generous acoustic and a large congregation. With a moderate speed, drier room, and smaller crowd one can make a case for 3+2. Losing a beat will at first seem awkward, but if this method is consistently used in this meter, the singers will catch on. In the case of 3+1, congregations feel pushed and hurried. There is not enough time to breathe.

The same general guidelines—adding beats to the final note in a stanza, then "breathing" for a determinate number of counts—apply for hymns in duple meter. Test out JUDAS MACCABAEUS ("Thine is the glory"—LBW 145). Assuming that the tactus is a half note (the only practical choice, no matter what the tempo), what are the possibilities? 2+1? 1+1? 2+2? Each has its advantages and drawbacks. Try ST. MAGNUS ("The head that once was crowned"—LBW 173), a duple meter tune with a quarter note tactus that starts with a pickup note. Possible solutions include 2+1, 2+2, and 3+2. Tunes such as LAUDES DOMINI ("When morning gilds the skies"—LBW 546) present similar problems.

Remember, these are general suggestions; hymn playing is an art, not a science. If you are uncertain about the best approach for a given meter, try out different solutions with your choir. You will know from their response (musical and verbal) what works best. If the connection feels artificial or forced, abandon it in favor of something more natural. With a consistent approach and firm leadership from both organist and choir the congregation will soon know what to expect. Once they have a sense of what you are doing, they will go along automatically.

4

- adhere to the phrasing of the text, breaking at punctuation, regardless of the musical line
- strike a compromise.

The purpose of singing any text in worship is to illuminate, heighten, and enliven the words. Music is the means to this end and should therefore give increased clarity and resonance to a text. The music should never obscure the words. A hymn tune exists to serve its text.

In HANOVER ("Oh, worship the King") consider the line "Oh, gratefully sing his power and his love." Read these words aloud. Because there is no comma following "sing" a pause is unnecessary, even intrusive. A break in the musical line here only weakens the impact and integrity of the text. How much better for the organist to carry through the musical line while the choir makes a crescendo to emphasize the idea. By adding a passing C or C♯ quarter note in the pedal on the second beat the organist reinforces the idea that a breath at this point is not desirable. In carrying the musical phrase *through* these eight words their meaning and clarity are enhanced. (See example 4-18.)

Now examine the corresponding place in stanza 2 "Whose robe is the light, whose canopy space." When read aloud, a break at the comma makes perfect sense. Handled properly, it also makes musical sense to lift the phrase here by inserting either an eighth or quarter rest, depending on the tempo.

When preparing to lead a hymn, carefully consider every punctuation mark in light of the musical phrase in which it occurs. When would a break in the musical line be helpful, even thrilling? When would such a break weaken or destroy text, music, or both?

Playing the Text

Articulation can help express the text, but it is only the beginning. It is always important for the leader to have a general understanding of the text and its architecture. Is the text iambic (unstressed-stressed: "O sons and daughters of the King"), trochaic (stressed-unstressed: "Let all mortal flesh keep silence"), dactylic (stressed-unstressed-unstressed: "Sent forth by God's blessing"), or some other pattern? Are there any mood changes in the hymn as a whole? Does the text involve dialogue? Is there an emotional climax in any single stanza? Is the text doctrinal, devotional, didactic? Is it a hymn of praise or a prayer? Who is being addressed in the text? Then ask, Which of these facets do I want to emphasize for the congregation in this time and place? How might I do that?

example 4-18

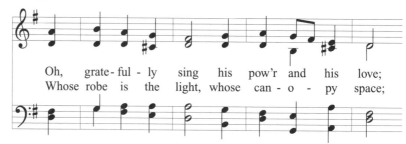

Oh, grate-ful-ly sing his pow'r and his love;
Whose robe is the light, whose can-o-py space;

There are many ways to enhance the meaning of the text through creative hymn playing. One simple idea is to revert to unison accompaniment, playing the melody in octaves in the manual and the pedal, when accompanying texts that articulate messages of unity or oneness. The hymn "Sent forth by God's blessing" is one such example. The middle of the second stanza reads:

Unite us as one in this life that we share.
Then may all the living
With praise and thanksgiving
Give honor to Christ and his name that we bear.[2]

When accompanying this hymn, it would be appropriate to play the phrase "unite us as one in this life that we share" in unison, followed by four-part playing during the subsequent phrases. In a similar manner, whole stanzas can be played and sung in unison,

building on the melodic power embodied in these tunes. Returning to parts for later stanzas lends new energy to the singing.

Where texts employ a dialogue or a refrain, consider some form of alternation between soloists and/or choir and the assembly as a means of heightening the dramatic character of the hymn. For instance, in the hymn "The angel Gabriel from heaven came" (WOV 632), the first three stanzas of the hymn could be divided between a narrator, the angel Gabriel, and Mary. The assembly itself would sing the fourth stanza, summing up the message of the hymn.

Registrations

Successful hymn playing requires variety of all kinds, including color—and part of the fun of being an organist is playing with the

---

HONORING NOTE VALUES Some hymn accompanists are prone to robbing notes of their full value, particularly longer or dotted notes. The dot in a dotted quarter note should be given its full value rather than glossed over or ignored. A dotted half note in common time should be held out for three full beats. In such matters organists and singers behave very differently and with potentially calamitous consequences for the hymns. When people sing in groups, they commonly fall behind the beat, dragging because they often indulge the long notes. A dotted rhythm will invariably slow down when sung. (Think of *by the* dawn's early light" in "The Star Spangled Banner.") In contrast, organists tend to move off a longer note too soon, cheating it of its full value. Dotted rhythms are crushed. Consider the beautiful siciliano-like character of KREMSER ("We gather together"—UMH 131). Organists

often hurry these elegant dotted rhythms allowing them no time to unfold naturally. By the last line of even such a well-known and beloved hymn the congregation and organist are often quite out of sync.

Another example is LOBE DEN HERREN ("Praise to the Lord, the Almighty"—LBW 543). The tendency of many organists to rush the dotted figures leaves the congregation behind by the second measure. Often the glorious climax of this hymn (third phrase, second measure—also the tune's highest note) is ruined by organists who simply move onto the next note too soon. How much better it would be to count out the dotted half note for three full beats, even slightly stretching the third beat for the sake of musicality. In doing so we allow the congregation to savor the glory of that moment and increase the odds of getting organist and singers *together* before proceeding in tandem to the final cadence.

colors, or timbres, of the instrument. Consider this an invitation to vary the registrations frequently. What "frequently" means, of course, depends on the hymn, the player, the instrument, and perhaps the congregation. Many organists will change registrations every stanza and often within each stanza. Others prefer more consistency within a hymn, although not to the point of boredom. A question to ask would be "How can I best carry this text for this congregation at this time?" That may mean getting out of the way or it may mean doing some tone painting, if that is within your abilities.

The possibilities for hymn registrations are unlimited. Some of the basic sounds (depending, of course, on the instrument available) include: principal chorus (principal or diapason 8', 4', [2⅔'], 2') with or without mixtures, chorus reeds (those which add color rather than dominate), 16' manual sounds for thickness and grandeur, pedal reeds and 32' for emphasis, and solo colors such as reeds, gapped registrations such as 8' and 2', and mutations. (Some classic solo combinations using mutations are 8', 4', 1⅓' and the cornet of 8', 4', 2⅔', 2', and 1⅗'.) There are many others and the organist is limited only by his or her imagination.

One of the frequently overlooked tools for thrilling hymn playing is the swell box. Forget the old rule about keeping your right

foot off the swell pedal. Go ahead and use it for occasional effect during the hymns. Consider the line from "Oh, worship the King," "It streams from the hills, it descends to the plain." Begin with full Swell coupled to Great foundations and the box completely closed. Gradually open the shades over the course of the four-bar phrase. The sheer musical effect is stunning, as is the lift it will give the singing. A well-placed diminuendo using the Swell box is equally effective.

One might think that the same principles would hold true for the volume pedal on an

ALTERNATION Many German hymns were written as teaching tools, and other hymns from the northern European tradition were paraphrases of scripture. In these and other cases it wasn't uncommon for hymns to have from ten to twenty stanzas—or more. Singing that many stanzas in a row can challenge anyone's endurance, so a dialogical technique called "alternation practice" was developed. Today, even though most of those long hymns have been shortened, this practice is still useful and appreciated by congregations.

Using this technique one simply divides stanzas between different forces—even if the hymn has only three stanzas. Some options are obvious:

1. cantor		1. all
2. congregation	Or	2. higher
3. choir		3. lower
4. congregation		4. all

But don't let your creativity stop there. Look at your worship space; it will probably suggest some logical divisions between sides or areas. It is also possible on occasion to employ a purely instrumental stanza. If this is new to your congregation, you might include a note in your service folder inviting people to meditate on the words of the stanza at that time. (Of course, the setting should be expressive of those words.)

electronic organ. However, because the timbre doesn't change as it does (however subtly) with an opening Swell box, the effects are not totally comparable. Use the volume pedal, but be very judicious with it, lest one call to mind the worst stereotypes of funeral home organists.

Accompanying Folk Hymns

European folk hymns are a diverse body of music that calls for an equally diverse approach to accompaniment. In the process of making decisions regarding the accompaniment, one important element to consider is instrumentation—or lack of it. With the help of a good cantor or choir, one of the most effective ways to sing folk hymns is unaccompanied. It is almost certainly the most historically accurate approach to much of this literature.

Alice Parker has championed unaccompanied singing in connection with American folk hymnody.[3] Many of her ideas are equally effective with European repertoire. First, remember that visual cues are important in unaccompanied performance. Without the presence of an accompanying instrument the assembly relies on sight more than it would otherwise. Yet, the assembly as a singing body does not require a conductor in the same manner as a choir. It is capable of sustaining its own song with the occasional use of subtle hand gestures to unify the beginning and ends of stanzas.

Tempo is also a critical consideration in an *a cappella* performance. Help the assembly find a natural, communal tempo that provides ample space for the text and supports the melodic properties of the tune. In general, unaccompanied performance works better with tunes that are stately or lyrical such as IN BABILONE ("Son of God, eternal Savior"—LBW 364). When singing an unaccompanied folk hymn it might be wise to scatter individual choir members throughout the assembly as a means of assisting the singing.

Of all the accompanying instruments used with folk repertoire, the organ remains the most popular. Many standard approaches to hymn playing on the organ work well for folk

---

SOLOING OUT Every organist should develop the ability to solo out the tune. Aside from lending variety to your hymn treatments it is a means of highlighting the melody, particularly helpful on new or less familiar hymns. It is also an opportunity to exploit the solo colors of the instrument. Bolder reeds, whether penetrating or noble, are highly suitable for this, as are mixture sounds. A cornet or diapason color works well for quieter hymns.

The technique of soloing out may seem clumsy at first but quickly improves with practice. Begin by learning to read and play the alto and tenor voices together in the left hand on more subdued stops, omitting right hand and pedal for purposes of practice. Though it takes getting used to, your skill will improve so that you can do this at sight. The bass line remains in the pedal on a sound that is balanced with the left hand. The next step is to combine the left hand, and pedal (alto, tenor, and bass voices). Then practice soprano and bass voices together (right hand, on solo stop[s], and pedal). Finally, combine right hand, left hand and pedal. The tune will soar out over the supporting voices. A solo treatment of the tune need not last for an entire stanza. It can come and go, phrase by phrase, as the text dictates. Always read the text first and use your imagination.

hymns. In addition to the organ, a number of other instruments possess unique properties that enable them to function effectively with folk repertoire. The piano is particularly important in this regard. The combination of its inherent lyricism and percussive qualities makes it a wonderful option for accompanying folk music. Try playing folk hymns like BUNESSAN ("Praise and thanksgiving"—LBW 409) that have slow harmonic rhythm on the piano. A simple arpeggiated figure could work well. (See example 4-19; track 23.)

If you are able, improvise (or work out ahead of time) simple accompaniments based on the harmonies provided in the hymnal. These accompaniments do not necessarily need to be tied directly to the tune at all times. You can cue the congregation by playing a few notes of the tune at the start of important phrases or after rests, but spend the remainder of the hymn working out creative counter-melodies (either improvised or octave transpositions of inner voices) and playing harmonies both above and below the singing range of the assembly. (See example 4-20; track 24.)

Handbells are another option to consider when making choices regarding instrumentation. They may be used to accompany canons by ringing randomly the five pitches of a pentatonic scale, by playing harmonies of the hymn, a rhythmic ostinato, or a free harmonization.

When additional instruments are available, consider using an ensemble to lead the hymn. One effective technique with folk hymns is to form a quasi-continuo group by employing a bowed or plucked cello to play along with the organ or harpsichord. Advise

example 4-19

Music: Gaelic; arr. Mark Sedio © 1998 Augsburg Fortress

your cellist to play the bass line lightly rather than in romantic style. Adding obbligato instruments to this texture creates a charming chamber ensemble which can either lead the assembly in song or play occasional solo stanzas in alternation with the assembly through the course of a hymn. Obbligato instruments might either play the melody line or descants that are based on the alto and tenor lines of the harmony.

In more intimate settings, instruments that strum, arpeggiate, or improvise counterpoint, including harpsichords, lutes, and guitars, can be effective either in a solo capacity or in combination with wind or string instruments. While harpsichord is most commonly associated with music from the renaissance and baroque periods, it is also appropriate to accompany much nineteenth- and twentieth-century folk music in this fashion.

European folk culture has often treated instrumental music as an independent genre. Nonetheless, traditional folk instruments can contribute to the performance of vocal folk literature. Among the most important and accessible folk instruments are the fiddle, the flute, various percussion instruments, the bagpipe, the hammered dulcimer, and the hurdy-gurdy.

example 4-20

Music: Gaelic; arr. Mark Sedio © 1998 Augsburg Fortress

Types of Folk Hymns

European folk hymns can be organized into several general categories based on the melodic and rhythmic characteristics of the tune. The following discussion will consider the implications for performance arising from these categories.

Dance Hymns. Tunes of dance origin or character probably constitute the largest single category in folk hymnody. Indeed, dance and movement itself are often connected with the origins of folk song. The word *ballad* comes from *ballare* which means "to dance," and is related to "ballet."[4]

example 4-21

The most prominent characteristic of dance tunes is their rhythmic vitality. Meters range from simple duple (2/4) to compound triple (9/8), although the bulk of these tunes are in triple meter of some sort. Texts generally speak of animation, activity, travel, rejoicing, or singing ("Good Christian friends, rejoice," "Let all things now living," "Come rejoicing, praises voicing," "My soul proclaims your greatness"). Given the positive nature of these texts, as one might expect, dance hymns are usually written in major keys.

Since rhythm and tempo are such important features of dance hymns, these elements strongly impact the performance of this literature in the context of the assembly. The first step in deciding how to sing and play dance hymns is to arrive at an appropriate tactus or pulse for the music. Note that feeling hymn tunes in one beat per measure does not necessarily imply a fast pulse, but does allow for a natural ebb and flow necessary for anyone who dances this music. Playing these hymns in a manner that provides a strong, constant tactus, coupled with a buoyant, open touch throughout, will enable members of the assembly to "sing lighter on their feet."

When playing these tunes on the organ, it is best not to over-register. Transparent combinations, for instance 8' flute, 4' principal, 2' principal, with or without a light mixture, work very well. Solo out lines with a clear, bright trumpet that is not too heavy in char-

acter. Marcato pedaling, either on strong beats or harmonic changes, may further stress the dance-like character of these tunes. This idea may be extended to include chords played by the left hand. With good choral leadership it is even possible to abandon the tune altogether, playing marcato chords in vital, enlivening rhythmic patterns, which are intended to energize the assembly's singing. Along these same lines, consider playing a drone or percussive ostinato figure in the left hand and pedal while the right hand plays the melody.

Hymns of Lament. These hymns often couple tunes possessing a strong character of longing with reflective texts. KAS DZIEDAJA ("By the Babylonian rivers"—WOV 656) is an example. They usually lean toward step-wise motion and are often in minor keys. Yiddish and other Jewish tunes like TIF IN VELDELE ("Light one candle to watch for Messiah"—WOV 630), based on plaintive eastern European scales, are excellent examples of lament.

example 4-22

INTRODUCING THE HYMN   The minimum requirements for a hymn introduction are to inform the assembly of the tune and to set the key and tempo. Through the kind of articulation applied it can also identify the spirit of the hymn—whether joyous or contemplative, for instance. Unless a hymn is new, unfamiliar, difficult, or all of the above, it is unnecessary (though not wrong) to play the entire hymn as an introduction. Some would say that playing all the way through a well-known hymn serves only to disengage a congregation; others would counter that it aids their preparation. Whatever the length, the introduction should draw in the congregation, making even the most reluctant churchgoer want to stand and sing.

• Play the introduction with the same tempo and rhythmic feel you will be using when the assembly sings.

• In general, keep the tactus going between intro and first stanza, just as you would between stanzas (see "The Space between Stanzas" on pages 48–49).

• If it's a familiar hymn, you might play just enough to make the melody, pitch, and rhythm clear. For HANOVER this could be the first and last lines, the third and last lines, or the first and second lines (which would end on the dominant). (See example 4-21.)

Introductions to familiar hymns are an excellent place to begin composing or improvising. In devising hymn introductions, write them out, particularly if you are uncomfortable with improvisation. Putting them on manuscript paper will improve your compositional skills, force you to think about voice leading and harmonic progressions, and provide you with a written record of your hymn treatments. To stimulate your creativity, take time to study some of the excellent published collections of hymn introductions and harmonizations. Writing your own hymn settings, whether simple or elaborate, will bring you satisfaction and growth. (See example 4-22.)

4

Perhaps the single characteristic of this genre of hymnody that stands out the most is the poignant lyricism of the melodies. This suggests the use of particular instruments to accompany these hymns. Oboe and violin are two especially good choices for descants or simply to double the melody. For hymn introductions, experiment with allowing either of these instruments to play the melody through unaccompanied. Encourage the instrumentalist to play as lyrically as possible within the confines of a singable tempo. A sparse effect will result, which matches the character of hymns in this category. If a solo instrument plays on the introduction, bring it back to play the melody and then a descant on later stanzas. Phrases

VARIETY When an organist becomes confident in basic hymn playing with clean articulation and a clear tactus, variety in hymn playing can be achieved through the use of passing tones, neighboring notes, and other decorations, primarily in the supporting voices. Such devices help the singing—by propelling a line forward, by suggesting a crescendo, by setting up a rallentando, and the like. They should never get in the way, however. A walking bass line can give a hymn wonderful new energy on the last stanza. If such a pedal line is clumsy or ill-conceived, though, it will call undue attention to itself and hinder the flow of the hymn.

Singing a hymn is a pilgrimage complete with preparation and anticipation, the first step, the journey itself, the final stretch, and the arrival. The organist serves as tour guide—coaxing, encouraging, inspiring, giving directions, and pointing toward the goal. The last stanza, being the final stretch, calls for something different. People want to move with renewed vigor for the end is in sight. A reharmonization, descant, or decorated version may be just what is needed, and will serve to bring the assembly in a strong unison.

Reharmonizations. There are hundreds of published collections of hymn harmonizations on the market, most intended for unison singing. Playing through

some of them may spur you to create your own. The most helpful harmonizations are those in which the new harmonies are logical, tasteful, and supportive of the tune. The more intricate ones tend to get in the way rather than lift the singing to new heights. You will soon see which ones are helpful and which are not. Any reharmonization should be well rehearsed by the organist prior to the service. The element of surprise should be a pleasant one for all who are gathered to sing, but a harmonization ought not be a surprise for the organist.

While looking for varied hymn accompaniments, also keep in mind that the harmonization printed in the hymnal usually should not be abandoned. Many people enjoy singing hymns in harmony and will appreciate it (and sing more enthusiastically) if you frequently use the printed harmony on a quieter registration. Try to do this when appropriate unless the published harmonization is ghastly or unsuited for four-part singing.

Transposing the Last Stanza. Some organists improvise or compose a brief interlude before the final stanza during which time a modulation sometimes occurs, usually up a half step. Judicious use of this practice is critical. As is true with all good ideas, when used too often it weakens the hymn and destroys its integrity.

of the descant and of the hymn tune might overlap, as opposed to starting and ending at the same time.

Once again, in hymns of lament, unaccompanied singing is always an option. Lovely tunes known by the assembly, such as LONDONDERRY AIR ("O Christ the same," but well known as the tune for "O Danny boy"), are good candidates for *a cappella* performance. When the assembly is singing a unison, unaccompanied stanza, having either a soloist or the choir sing a descant that emerges organically from the unison line can provide a memorable moment.

Organ registrations for these tunes should be warm. As the text changes during the course of a hymn the registration should follow suit. The Latvian tune KAS DZIEDAJA elegantly parallels the text "By the Babylonian rivers." Try this: in the pedal, play a 16' flute descending the D-minor scale in a dotted half note rhythm while the left hand sustains a four-note cluster (maybe E-F-G-A) and the right hand (or solo instrument) plays the melody. This could provide a dark ambience and the image of weeping as a backdrop for the lament.

Pastorales and Lullabies. Another prominent style in the genre of folk hymns is the pastorale or lullaby. Though not identical in affect, lullabies such as W ZLOBIE LEZY ("Infant holy, infant lowly") and pastorales such as ST. COLUMBA ("The King of love my shepherd is") share a characteristic gentleness and calm. Texts about Christmas, the gentle nature of the good shepherd, and general blessings are common. These folk hymns are often in triple or compound meter.

Gentle organ registrations (perhaps 8' and 4'), depending on your congregation, are appropriate for these hymns. Consider introducing them using a single voice, such as an 8' or 4' flute (resembling the speaking range of a soprano recorder) or solo oboe stop. You may wish to employ a cello doubling the bass line. Try registering the pedal at 8' pitch or with a light 16'.

In addition to the organ, the flute is a particularly appropriate instrument to use for hymn introductions or descants. For hymns that work in canon such as ST. COLUMBA, consider using the flute as the second voice in the canon.

Ballad. These are narrative folk songs, and the repertoire of folk hymnody includes several fine examples, THE FIRST NOWELL and DEO GRACIAS ("Oh, love, how deep") among them. While these hymns are beloved, their nature as stories or folklore mean that they are lengthy, presenting a special challenge to the leader of the assembly's song.

To capitalize on the narrative nature of these hymns, try dividing the stanzas so that each is taken by a different part of the assembly. If there is a refrain, allow the entire assembly to sing it. When leading the assembly in these ballads, the organ accompaniment should support the drama of the text. Reserve full organ for those occasions when the entire assembly is singing together.

Hymns of Procession or Proclamation. While folk hymns of this type often have texts similar to those of the dance genre of folk hymnody—rejoicing, moving forward with purpose—they are more often in duple meter and more conducive to performance in a stately, walking tempo. The strong tactus apparent in HAF TRONES LAMPA FÄRDIG ("Rejoice, rejoice, believers"—LBW 25) and the similarly powerful, angular melody of KING'S LYNN ("O God of earth and altar"—H82 591) suggest the need for sturdy, rhythmic leadership. A marcato touch and strong plenum registrations, perhaps incorporating solo and chorus reeds, provide the powerful image of grandeur associated with these tunes.

Several Welsh hymns, richly melodic and solidly harmonized, fall into this category. Welsh hymnody is most often sung in four parts, historically unaccompanied—a tradition spanning several hundred years. Many of the original harmonies of Welsh folk songs are versions of a part-singing tradition that was passed on orally, written down only after generations of practice. When a good four-part harmonization exists in the hymnal, use it and stick with it, employing reharmonization as the variation rather than the norm. While improvised and varied hymn accompaniments may enhance

hymns, their overuse may also distract the assembly from singing its own song. Especially in the case of folk song, simplicity is desirable. It is important to recall the roots of this genre and remember that these are the songs of the people.

Conclusion

This survey of techniques for bringing metrical and traditional hymns to life has been only cursory. Many techniques that lie at the heart of effective hymn playing defy written description. They can only be learned by doing them with a congregation. We also learn from hearing other organists and song leaders. It is easy for church musicians to become isolated and absorbed in our corner of the vineyard. We should make opportunities to break out of our routines and participate in the worship of neighboring churches or go to church music conferences where we are sure to hear a variety of hymn playing. How crucial it is to our musical growth to attend a live concert of chamber or symphonic music, or a solo recital. Our musical horizons can never be too broad. Such enrichment is sure to enhance our hymn playing. God's people gathered at worship depend on us. They deserve our finest efforts.

---

1. See, Thomas Day, *Why Catholics Can't Sing* (New York: Crossroad Publishing Co., 1992).

2. Omer Westendorf from *Lutheran Book of Worship* #221.

3. See especially, Alice Parker, *Melodious Accord: Good Singing in Church* (Chicago: Liturgy Training Publications, 1991).

4. See also, Philip V. Bohlman, *The Study of Folk Music in the Modern World* (Bloomington: Indiana University Press, 1988), p. 8.

CHAPTER 5

L et each singer perform in church properly,

enchoired, and in the manner that it ought to be done,

and grand effects will be the unavoidable result,

if the music itself be good.

from The Columbian Harmony

Drawing on what they had inherited from northern European traditions of hymnody, North Americans of the eighteenth and nineteenth centuries proceeded to mold new categories of hymns. Shape note, fuging tune, revival song, gospel hymn—these forms and more have enriched the church's song. By paying attention to the original uses and styles of these songs we can hear them speak in their own clear tones and enjoy their refreshingly simple message.

North American indigenous hymnody includes a wonderful variety of music which can add energy and joy to our praise in worship. Often, as in secular classical music, our indigenous composers have been slighted in preference to European composers. But most recent hymnals from 1978 on include tunes from the singing school and shape note hymnals. Music of the Sunday school movement and revivals will be found primarily in United Methodist, Baptist, and other evangelical hymnals such as *The Worshiping Church.*

The earliest tune written in the United States and still in common use is CORONATION by Oliver Holden (1792), usually matched with the text "All hail the power of Jesus' name." Other early American tunes include LEWIS-TOWN ("O Son of God, in Galilee")[1] by William Billings (1794) and TWENTY-FOURTH ("Where charity and love prevail"), attributed to Lucius Chapin around 1813.

The spread of music throughout the early colonies into the frontier was accomplished primarily by singing schools led by teachers who often published their own songbooks, primarily using religious texts. As the 1800s began, Little and Smith's *The Easy Instructor* introduced the use of shape notes to facilitate music reading. Shape notes and the related songbooks became very popular, particularly in the South, and day-long "sings" are still held today in many locations. These tunes are often pentatonic and set with parallel fifths and octaves. Many well-loved tunes come from this era: BEACH SPRING ("Lord, whose love in humble service"), FOUNDATION ("How firm a foundation"), HOLY MANNA ("God, who stretched the spangled heavens"), LAND OF REST ("Jerusalem, my happy home"), NEW BRITAIN ("Amazing grace"), and WONDROUS LOVE ("What wondrous love is this").

Over the last several decades North American composers, particularly in the church, have rediscovered the strength in shape note tune, and many recent hymn writers have written texts in those meters. These tunes have often been called "North American folk tunes" or "white southern spirituals" as they captured the flavor of life particularly in the Appalachian Mountains, combining indigenous American elements with music from the British Isles. This part of our heritage is being renewed as we discover that these tunes have wonderful possibilities for enabling congregational singing.

Lowell Mason (1792–1872), the most famous of early North American educators, was very influential in church music as well, particularly in the urban North. Mason set European tunes for North American congregations and encouraged classical settings of American tunes. Two frequently used tunes showing Mason's influence are OLIVET ("My faith looks up to thee") and TOPLADY ("Rock of ages"). In worship these hymns will be treated like European metric hymns (see Chapter 4). Another tune found and arranged by Mason, AZMON ("Oh, for a thousand tongues to sing"), was also popular in its shape note setting in singing schools, camp meetings, and revivals.

The camp meeting and prolonged camp meetings (like Chautauqua, Ocean Grove, and Lakeside) included particular forms of music. Tunes from this era, such as THE LAMB ("O the Lamb") and BREAD OF LIFE ("Break thou the bread of life"), may be found in United Methodist, Baptist, and other evangelical hymnals.

SHAPE NOTE SINGING   Shape notes (also known as character notes) were a method of notation invented by William Little and William Smith, first published in their book *The Easy Instructor* in 1801. Concerned that many North Americans could not read music, they set hymns in "fa–sol–la"-based (or solmization) symbols. In this way singers could tell from the shape of the note which scale degree it represented. At the same time these shape notes were placed conventionally on a five-line staff so that music readers could interpret the notes as usual, and non-music readers could tell if the pitches went up or down.

The exact shapes evolved over some years as different books used different systems. Some used four shapes, others seven, and there was variety in which shapes were attached to which pitches. However, the most influential and widely used shape note books used the pattern set out by Smith and Little. The two most common patterns are shown. (See example 5-1.)

As can be seen in the four-shape pattern, what we would call "do–re–mi" and "fa–sol–la" have the same set of three shapes; what we would call "ti," the leading tone, has a diamond shape. In both systems the shapes represent scale degrees, not pitches.

A great number of shape note hymnals were published in the nineteenth and twentieth centuries. Among the most widely used and reprinted were Ananias Davisson's *Kentucky Harmony* (1817), William Walker's *Southern Harmony* (1835), and Benjamin White and E. J. King's *Sacred Harp* (1844). All of these books combined original tunes and those which had been compiled and arranged by the editors.

example 5-1

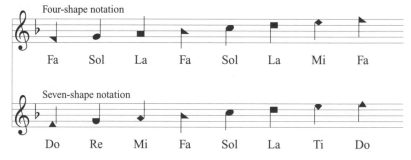

Revivals grew out of the camp meetings and flourished in the United States on the frontier and in urban and rural areas, crossing racial and economic boundaries. Revivals (and their extended forms, camp meetings) depended in part on songs and choruses to bring sinners to salvation. Choruses were prevalent as they were easily taught and remembered, singable by young and old, literate and illiterate, long-time believers and new converts alike. For many of the same reasons, praise choruses are important in many churches today, particularly those focused on seeking new believers. Revival tunes still in use include MARCHING TO ZION ("Come, we that love the Lord"), HANSON PLACE ("Shall we gather at the river") and HOW CAN I KEEP FROM SINGING ("My life flows on in endless song").

The Sunday school movement which began in the United States in 1824 produced a number of songbooks and composers including William Bradbury, Robert Lowry, and William G. Fischer. The familiar children's hymns "Away in a manger" (AWAY IN A MANGER and CRADLE SONG) and "Jesus loves me" come from this movement, as do HANKEY ("I love to tell the story"), HE LEADETH ME, and SWEET HOUR. Like Lowell Mason, many of the composers of Sunday school tunes were classically trained musicians, often active in the musical life of larger U.S. cities.

The first use of the word *gospel* in connection with congregational song was in an 1874 collection by Philip Bliss, a musician who was influenced by Dwight L. Moody to become a singing evangelist. Bliss wrote the tunes VILLE DU HAVRE ("It is well with my soul") and WORDS OF LIFE ("Sing them over again to me"). The texts of Fanny Crosby inspired many gospel song composers, who wrote, among others, the tunes ASSURANCE ("Blessed assurance"), RESCUE ("Rescue the perishing"), and TO GOD BE THE GLORY.

Songs from camp meetings, revivals, and the Sunday school movement have often

GOSPEL SONGS   Gospel hymns or songs are an authentically North American contribution to world hymnody. The streams flowing into this genre are many. Folk hymnody played an important role, as did collections of songs written for camp meetings, singing school tune books, and songs composed for the Sunday school movement. Sunday school collections alone accounted for a vast number of hymns in the mid-nineteenth century, helping to develop a taste for this lighter form of hymnody. Later, Ira D. Sankey (who worked as song leader with evangelist Dwight Moody) further popularized the gospel style both in the United States and in England.

Among the distinguishing characteristics of gospel songs are their high emotional content. These were songs designed to stir people toward making a commitment to Christ; they weren't much interested in the finer points of theology. Simple tunes are employed, often including a refrain. The underlying harmonic structure matches this simplicity with chord changes sometimes restricted to one per bar.

Despite these seeming limitations, gospel hymnody has had a profound impact both on individuals and on North American church and culture. As Robert M. Stevenson has commented in *Patterns of Protestant Church Music*, "its very obviousness has been its strength."

been looked down upon as having "inferior" or sentimental texts and repetitive music. Thus, this repertoire has been largely ignored in many mainline denominational hymnals. Many of these texts and tunes are wedded rather than being independent of each other as in the shape note repertoire. The descendants of this music may be seen in "contemporary Christian" music's use of refrains and in the work of the Gaithers and African American gospel artists and composers. Perhaps as time goes on and styles change, we will look again at these songs for their teaching qualities and memorability, as well as the energy and excitement they can generate.

Performance Practice

Tempo

Rhythm is vital in performing music from this genre. In the singing school and shape note traditions the downbeat is very strong. If you have a chance, attend a "Sacred Harp Sing"[2] where you can watch the traditional song leader's direction, given with upper arm at the side, wrist straight and basically stable, forearm moving in a straight line up and down, flexed only at the elbow, while the upper arm remains basically still. Once the tempo is set, it doesn't vary except perhaps for a slight ritardando and lengthening of the final chord. The strength of these tunes needs to be evidenced in their tempos without sacrificing their energetic

nature; so don't drag, but move the tempo confidently.

For camp meeting, revival, and Sunday school songs, the tempo is derived both from the text and from its function in the worship service. JESUS LOVES ME takes a confident, energetic tempo, while a reflection

example 5-2

TRACK 25

TRACK 26

REFRAIN OR CHORUS? A refrain is a recurring section of music and text. Refrains appeared in the early Christian church as psalm responses or antiphons; now they also have a place in hymns and songs. An example is the refrain "Yes, Jesus loves me" from the song "Jesus loves me, this I know."

A chorus is a short song, generally with only one stanza (for example, Taizé choruses like "Jesus, remember me"). Some choruses were originally the refrain to a hymn but now are sung independently (for example, "Lord, listen to your children praying," originally from a longer hymn by Ken Medema). Conversely, some choruses have later become attached to hymns as refrains (for example, "We're marching to Zion," a refrain added by Robert Lowry to Isaac Watts's text "Come, we that love the Lord").

on the saving death of Jesus Christ, such as THE LAMB, has a much slower tempo so that each note has its own sounding as does each word. As many of these songs depend on a combination of quarter and eighth notes, the intelligibility of the text when sung with the eighth notes is an important factor in determining tempo. In those hymns where the harmony changes are slow (once per measure, or every two measures) those accompanying on organ may find it more effective to articulate in order to reinforce the primary beats, rather than using ordi-

nary articulation (lifting between every repeated note) which in this case will produce a "choppy" accompaniment. (See example 5-2; tracks 25 and 26.)

Melody

Melody is the most important element in the hymn tunes that come from the shape note tradition. The melody in these hymns is traditionally sung by both men and women, with basses singing a lower part and some high voices (both men and women) taking a descant-like part. Thus, these hymns were most often originally written in three parts, with the melody in the middle. The melody has similar characteristics to folk melodies: very strophic, lyrical, perhaps ornamented with passing notes and grace notes when sung as a solo, but generally "straight on" for congregational singing. These melodies may be introduced by a solo stop on the organ (diapason, trumpet, oboe) with a simple I–IV–V accompaniment in open fifths, by unison octaves on the piano, or by violin (in the style called "fiddle playing"). (See example 5-3.) Melodies from the shape note tradition include BEACH SPRING, CHARLESTOWN, COMPLAINER, DETROIT, FOUNDATION, HOLY MANNA, KEDRON, LAND OF REST, MIDDLE-BURY, MORNING SONG, NETTLETON, NEW BRITAIN, PLEADING SAVIOR, RESIGNATION, RESTORATION, STAR IN THE EAST, TENDER THOUGHT, and WONDROUS LOVE. During the singing of these tunes the melody should remain prominent.

Early North American tunes, such as CORONATION, LEWIS-TOWN, and TWENTY-FOURTH, are often related to "fuging tunes" with imitative sections between various voices. The melodies may be appropriately

---

FUGING TUNES Though the name of the fuging tune implies a relationship to the fugue, the only connection is an imitative, contrapuntal style. Developed in England in the early eighteenth century, the fuging tune became very popular in North America and indeed remains so in some communities.

An ABB form characterizes fuging tune hymnody. The A section is homophonic and usually has a strong tonic cadence. The B section is the "fuging," imitative section. No principles determine which voices enter when; however, each has the same text and a similar melodic pattern. After the B section is repeated, the hymn may end with a brief homophonic closing.

William Billings (1746–1800) is the best known composer of fuging tunes. Others who wrote in this style include Supply Belcher (1752–1836), Lewis Edson (1748–1820), Daniel Read (1757–1836), and Timothy Swan (1758–1842).

---

example 5-3

phrase "bring forth the royal diadem," perhaps using trumpet or oboe stops here, going to full registration for "and crown him Lord of all." (See track 27.)

introduced by trumpet or oboe, as well as reed stops on the organ or bright diapasons 8' and 4'. During the singing of these tunes the various voices retain equal prominence.

Hymn tunes from the later 1800s, from the revival and Sunday school movements, depend more on harmonies. Therefore, if the melody is unfamiliar, the introduction might include the melody soloed out on the organ or with an instrument, ending with full harmony on the last phrase. In addition to trumpet and oboe these melodies can be introduced appropriately with flute, clarinet, trombone, French horn, viola, or cello. Tunes of this sort include ASSURANCE, CONVERSE, FAITHFULNESS, HANKEY, HANSON PLACE, MARCHING TO ZION, PILOT, SHOWALTER, THE OLD RUGGED CROSS, THE SOLID ROCK, THOMPSON, WEBB (MORNING LIGHT), and WOODWORTH. During the singing of these tunes the melody will be equal with the harmony parts.

Accompaniment

The early North American tunes call for organ registration of bright 8', 4', and 2' diapason stops or piano accompaniment with equal volume in each part. For celebratory occasions a brass ensemble or string quartet would be appropriate for this European-influenced music. In the tune CORONATION, organ accompaniment could highlight the duet between the soprano and bass voices on the

example 5-4

The tunes of the shape note tradition have been set in many different styles by arrangers past and recent. It is very appropriate for the congregation to sing these tunes unaccompanied in unison, alternating with the choir singing a stanza in the traditional three-part setting. Three-part settings reflecting the tradition may be found in *Hymnal 1982*: FOUNDATION—636 (accompaniment edition only, incorporating two-part canon), HOLY MANNA—580, and STAR IN THE EAST—118. *Supplement to The United Methodist Hymnal* includes BOYLSTON (a Mason tune in a setting adapted from *The Sacred Harp*), DETROIT, and RESTORATION. In addition, reprints of the original oblong shape note hymnals are available through The Hymn Society and other sources.

Beware of settings of these tunes that seem "busy" or are primarily chordal. The signature of these harmonies should reflect the original use of open fifths with parallel fifths and octaves. Alice Parker's wonderful book *Creative Hymn-Singing* includes performance suggestions (all unaccompanied) for

DAVIS, FOUNDATION, LAND OF REST, and STAR IN THE EAST which use two-part canons, ostinatos, pedal points, and unison melodies. Canons may be used for many of these tunes; KEDRON is shown as an example. (See example 5-4.)

Even if your congregation sings these shape note tunes in unison, the accompaniment should reflect the above ideas. On the organ

---

ORGAN AND PIANO DUETS Unfamiliar to many mainline churches, organ and piano duets are frequently employed in evangelical settings and can add a new sound to worship. One can consider combining organ and piano on the refrains: as the organ sustains the written harmonies, the piano fills in the chordal structure with arpeggios, accented bass notes on the primary beats, or echoes on the refrains. (See example 5-5.)

On the stanzas, alternate piano and organ, supporting the congregation or soloists but varying to avoid tedium in the accompaniment.

---

use 8' and 4' principals, occasionally using an 8' or 4' string stop to flavor the accompaniment. String trio or solo violin, viola, oboe or English horn are appropriate for use. In a quiet worship setting a dulcimer would be appropriate for introduction and perhaps an introductory solo stanza (it would be lost under congregational singing). Occasionally acoustic guitar or autoharp might also be used, perhaps on an introduction with violin, viola, or oboe, and then to accompany a small group of singers; don't depend on guitar or autoharp chords throughout the entire hymn, however, as that detracts from the open-fifth flavor of these tunes.

Orff instruments and handbells can also be used with shape note tunes. Orff settings by Shirley McRae and Betty Ann Ramseth may be found in *Supplement to The United Methodist Hymnal* for HOLY MANNA, PROMISED LAND, and MORNING SONG. In many instances the ostinato patterns for Orff accompaniments can be directly transferred to handbells with only the occasional need to lower the bass xylophone or metallophone part one octave to provide ease of playing.

The popular Shaker hymn tune SIMPLE GIFTS ("I danced in the morning"—PH 302), like the shape note tunes, draws its strength from melody. Its accompaniment is usually chordal and should have a dance-like rhythm without being heavy-handed. Piano would be preferred with a wide variety of instruments possible to solo out the melody—violin, flute, clarinet, oboe, recorder, or trumpet. Guitar accompaniment is also appropriate.

example 5-5

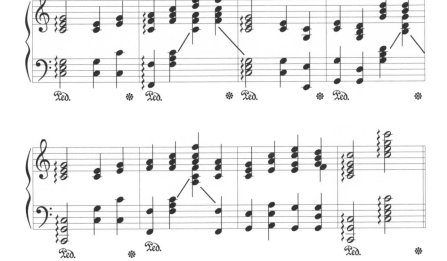

example 5-6

Hymns from the revival and Sunday school tradition fall into several accompaniment groupings: duet songs, solo/congregation, and suggested four-part songs. All these hymns lend themselves to piano accompaniment or to organ and piano duets. For smaller congregations or choir consider a simple guitar accompaniment.

Among those tunes lending themselves to duets are JESUS LOVES ME, AWAY IN A MANGER, and WORDS OF LIFE. Accompaniment for these types of tunes might include flutes or recorders on the SA parts and a trio registration on the organ (single part in each hand on different stops on different keyboards with light, perhaps only 8', pedal on the tonic note of each chord.) (See example 5-6.)

Many of the revival and Sunday school hymns were originally sung as "call/response" hymns (echoing the call of God and humanity's response). Soloists or quartets would sing the stanzas while the congregation responded with the refrains. Tunes like ASSURANCE, FAITHFULNESS, MARCHING TO ZION, THE OLD RUGGED CROSS, THE SOLID ROCK, and TO GOD BE THE GLORY lend themselves to quartets on the stanzas, with fuller accompaniment on the congregational refrains; for example, on the organ add a 2' or additional 8' stop on the refrain. HANKEY ("I love to tell the story") and HANSON PLACE ("Shall we gather at the river"—clearly a "question and answer" hymn) particularly lend themselves to soloists on the stanzas, again with congregational refrain and fuller accompaniment. THOMPSON ("Softly and tenderly"—UMH 348) is a hymn tune that lends itself to a duet in the stanzas; trio accompaniment for the stanza should be followed by full accompaniment on the refrain (note the "echo" effect in the refrain). "Just as I am" (WOODWORTH) is an example of a multi-stanza text that lends itself to beginning with a solo and then gradually adding voices on the stanzas—duet, trio, quartet, congregation.

Another performance practice of the camp meeting and revival is appending a refrain to a text, as in the refrain "I am bound for the promised land" with "On Jordan's stormy banks I stand." Thus the refrains retain a "free-floating" quality which enables them to be used with various texts or on their own in worship. The singing of a hymn with refrain may occasionally begin with the refrain in response to a sermon or prayer, then followed by the stanzas.

Tunes such as CONVERSE ("What a friend we have in Jesus"), FAITHFULNESS ("Great is thy faithfulness"), SHOWALTER ("Leaning on the everlasting arms") and WEBB (also known as MORNING LIGHT—"Stand up, stand up for Jesus") were meant to be sung in four-part harmony. If your congregation is inclined only to sing unison, feature the choir singing the stanza in four parts, or during a hymn sing or less formal service move the choir around the congregation to encourage part-singing. These tunes lend themselves to piano accompaniment as well as church orchestras or bands. Fill in any long notes on the piano, particularly on a tune that alternates rhythms as much as CONVERSE. (See example 5-7.)

example 5-7

Another performance practice particularly for the revival and Sunday school hymns is to alternate singers on the verses, while everyone joins on the refrain. Alternate men/women, girls/boys, children/adults, right side/left side, back/front, either with notation in the bulletin, by a song leader's direction, or on an overhead projector. Many of the refrains also lend themselves to brief alternation, again with direction, such as the opening words of the refrain "Great is thy faithfulness!" sung first by women, then by men, with all joining on the

next phrase. Hand clapping and toe tapping will be natural responses to these Sunday school and revival hymns as they become familiar to congregations.

As mentioned above, many of the shape note tunes have recent texts written for them, as well as being interchangeable with older texts to the same tune. Read the text carefully to help note its place in worship and also for clues to the tempo, whether stately, somber, or joyful. Unfamiliar tunes may be introduced with the many organ preludes based on them or with choral or instrumental interpretations.

Hymns from the revival and Sunday school movements do have a place in regular congregational worship. Many of them are based on scripture and therefore fit with particular readings or sermons. Because of the refrains, these hymns are a good way to involve children and developmentally challenged persons. These tunes tend to be energetic; even the more reflective of them, such as PILOT ("Jesus, Savior, pilot me"—LBW 334) or THE OLD RUGGED CROSS (UMH 504), should not be dragged out sentimentally but rather sung as faithful expressions of earlier generations. (See track 28.)

Pianists may delight in adding pianistic elements from the 1800s without losing sight of the primary goal of enabling congregational singing. These hymns helped bring many persons to faith, and they can still do the same today.

---

1. In contrast to many hymnic traditions, early North American tunes are often known independently of any particular text. For easier identification, however, we have provided for each the first line of a text set to that tune in some current hymnal.

2. A good source of information on yearly "sings" of shape note hymns is *Directory and Minutes of Sacred Harp Singing*, available from Sacred Harp Publishing Company, 1010 Waddell Street, Bremen, GA 30110.

That light, it's far off and you've got to wait to see it.

But it's there. It's waiting.

The spirituals, they're a way of seeing that light.

Sidney Bechet, Treat It Gentle

Hear the term "African American church music," and the image that comes to mind is probably the gospel choir—singing, clapping, commenting, swaying—in Charles Wesley's words, "lost in wonder, love, and praise." It is a tradition whose freedom makes many other Christians envious and whose influence is increasing in American church music. But how can this music best be incorporated into the worship of other cultures, borrowing it but not misappropriating it? One key is to respect it for what it is and let its voice assert itself. Don't try to "improve" it or force it into a European American mold. This chapter will provide some helps for authentic performance of this music.

Knowing and understanding the principles that undergird the performance of African American religious music is one thing, an important first step. Putting these principles into practice is quite another. Performances that look easy when executed by an experienced practitioner of spirituals and gospel music can be quite deceptive. The seemingly effortless melismatic passage or the brilliant display of polyrhythmic clapping comes not from mere spontaneous inspiration, but from years of persistent honing of cultural skills through careful listening, observation, and practice. Learning to perform songs indigenous to the African American religious experience may at first seem awkward: the key to success is to prayerfully keep trying.

For many church musicians, developing proficiency in African American music may pose a great challenge; after all, many of the principles of African American music performance are polar opposites of standard European American musical values. The first and perhaps biggest challenge is coming to terms with the role of the musical score in African American music. In western music, the score reigns supreme; for the most part, performers are expected to adhere to tempo and dynamic markings. Beyond that, tampering with the melodic line, the rhythm, or the meter may well be considered an act of heresy. In contrast, the significance of the score in African American music is determined by the genre or type of music that it represents.

6

As a music whose foundation rests in the oral rather than the written tradition, African American gospel choirs typically learn new repertoire by rote, having heard the chosen selection sung by another group, or having heard the recording on CD, radio, or television. Frequently, no transcription of the selection exists or at least the choir does not have scores. It is the choir director's responsibility to know and demonstrate every vocal line and ensure that the parts blend harmonically.

Even though gospel music is often referred to as a "composed" music (distinguishing it from the spiritual created during slavery whose specific composers are unknown), writers of gospel songs both expect and accept deviation from the score. This improvisational dimension of gospel music performance does not mean that "anything goes." On the contrary, there are boundaries and principles and broadly accepted music values to guide performers in deciding when, what, and how to do what they do. Only through the discipline of constant practice, generated by a sincere willingness and desire to learn, will the expression of African American music grow to assume personal and collective meaning in worship.

Performance Practice

Three primary areas of significance are identifiable in the performance of African American religious music regardless of genre: quality of sound (timbre); mechanics of delivery (manipulation of musical variables); and style of delivery (physical and visual dimensions of performance). Principles that govern African American religious music performance must not be viewed as inflexible rules which must be applied in the same way in every performance, for the underlying premise of African American music is fluidity, constant change. The intent of sharing these fundamental, practical applications is to spark interest and confidence in creating a wider and stronger embrace of African American music, African American culture, and with God's help, African American people.

Sound Quality

Singing in the traditional African American worship is an expression of jubilation, power, and praise. Even when the text of a spiritual communicates lament, the vocal quality of the singer remains strong. Vocalists are expected to convey their total sincerity and complete absorption in communicating both outward, to others present at the event, and upward to God. The vocal timbre in gospel solos may vary constantly, alternately utilizing moans, groans, shouts, wails, and growls. Similarly, in congregational singing the concluding verse or refrain may be hummed, allowing the assembly to experience the song's meaning through another timbral dimension. Whereas in the singing of spirituals the vocal timbre is more closely aligned with that of western music, maximizing the use of the head voice, in gospel music the commanding power of the chest voice is highly valued in women's singing, and male soloists frequently utilize falsetto.

Much congregational song takes the African-influenced form of call/response. The soloist, a strong and experienced singer, will issue the "call" in a firm manner that elicits an equally bold, full-voiced response from the congregation. It may take time and consistent use to develop the trust necessary for this assured back-and-forth song, but it is integral to African American worship.

A highly valued dimension of timbre, representing a continuing African tradition, is percussive delivery both in vocal and instrumental performance. Particularly in highly syncopated songs with faster tempos, short phrases are strongly punctuated to accent the rhythm. For example, in the opening line of "What a fellowship," breaks will commonly occur after "what" and "a." The line is

example 6-1

TRACK 29

not sung as a single continuing legato melodic phrase, but is instead chopped up into short, percussive fragments. The phrase is deliberately broken after the first word, adding rhythmic and timbral (percussive) interest.

Mechanics of Delivery

This broad category of performance defines the way time (rhythm, tempo, duration), text, and pitch are conceived in African American sacred music expression. This cate-

gory represents the technical aspects of performance that shape and define African American musical experience.

Rhythm. More than by any other factor, African American music is driven by its rhythm. Rhythm is preeminent in both vocal lines and instrumental accompaniment; rhythm establishes the character of the piece. Each beat must be clearly sensed and heard. The principal pulse, of course, is given a strong accent. However, frequently the weak beats (such as 2 and 4 in 4/4) are given an even stronger accent than the primary and secondary ones. To illustrate, look at the spiritual JESUS LIFTED ME (WOV 673). It has four quarter note beats per measure and it is played with the accents not only on beats 2 and 4, but on the eighth note offbeats (1 *and* 2 *and* 3 *and* 4 *and*). (See example 6-1; tracks 29 and 30.)

This sort of syncopation pervades all forms of African American religious music. It should never be rushed, always a temptation when you are anticipating the accent. Keep a firm sense of the tactus so that the syncopation can play off of it. As singers become more experienced in this style of music, they will often add layers of symmetrical and asymmetrical beat divisions over the basic pulse, contributing to the characteristic rhythmic complexity. Those less accustomed to the style, however, will be better off maintaining the basic rhythm. Above all, avoid smoothing out the rhythms; to do so will rob the music of its vitality and energy.

While rhythmic precision is critical to the performance of spirituals and gospel music, at the same time, rhythm must never be mechanical. Precision is one thing; rigidity is another.

In gospel music, the soloist must feel free to alter rhythms when so moved. Notes may be held longer than written, they may also be shorter than written, and notes may even be anticipated—coming slightly earlier than indicated in the score. The same is true for congregational singing in both spirituals and gospel. Each member of the congregation is free to personalize the singing experience—to make it one's own. In contrast, when the choir sings there is less latitude, for the presence of the director symbolizes greater structure and definition. Of course, all of these practices fall under the rubric of improvisation—a skill that can be learned, but only through diligent and regular practice. Improvisation is a dimension of performance without which African American music loses its defining character.

Duration. In traditional African American worship neither the length of service in general nor the length of the songs in particular is dictated by the clock. Depending upon the quality of the interaction between the performer (preacher or singer) and the working of the Holy Spirit, extemporaneous elements of the worship may be extended or shortened. In congregational singing it is common

for the final chorus of such well-loved hymns as "What a fellowship" to be repeated as directed by the song leader. Similarly, soloists frequently interject such textual phrases as "I believe I'll say that one more time" to signal repetition of a particular phrase or stanza. In neither of these instances is repetition viewed as boring or grandstanding; instead, repetition serves as an essential tool for generating and sustaining the spiritual fervor that has historically distinguished the worship of African Americans in the United States.

Text. Most spirituals and many gospel songs have very short texts, a feature which was helpful in committing them to memory. These brief texts are, however, repeated many times with improvised variations, the repetition helping to convey their message. Another way in which these texts are extended is through the interjection of "wandering," independent couplets and quatrains. Sometimes these are closely related to the text of the song, sometimes not. They are selected according to the spirit of the moment. Popular insertions include:

My Lord's done just what he said,
He healed the sick and raised the dead.
and
If you cannot sing like angels,
If you cannot preach like Paul,
You can tell the love of Jesus
And say he died for all.

INTERPOLATIONS Anyone who has experienced African American worship will be familiar with the freely spoken interjections such as "Yes, Lord," and "Hallelujah" throughout the service. These are also frequently inserted into songs. Notice, however, that they fall into the space between phrases and do not conflict with the rhythmic pulse of the song.

So influential is this variation on the oral tradition that at times the standard text will be replaced entirely by the wandering couplet or quatrain. The same situation may be found in gospel music where at times only the refrain text will remain, the rest having been displaced by the "oral" text.

As a form created during the period of slavery, the spiritual may be sung in dialect. Too often, however, in an effort to be authentic, dialect is overly stressed, resulting in an interpretation of the spiritual that sounds stilted and out of character. Song leaders should remember simply to soften hard consonant sounds at the beginnings and endings of words. To achieve an acceptable rendering of the word "dat" (that) in "Deep river," or "de" (the) in "Ezekiel saw de wheel," the singer should not think or sing a hard "d" but rather a soft "t." In addition, the vowel sound will change according to its position. "De" will have a short "e" sound before a word starting with a vowel ("Oh, de ol' ark's a-moverin'"), but a schwa sound before a consonant ("I jes come from duh fountain").

example 6-2

written:

1 Soon and ver - y soon
2 No more cry - in' there   we are goin' to see the King.
3 No more dy - in' there
4 Soon and ver - y soon

played:

Although rhythm is unquestionably preeminent in African American religious music performance, text—the message—must not be minimized. Spirituals and gospel songs are filled with rich biblical imagery and intense devotion. The text, regardless of its relative simplicity or profundity, must be given its due.

PLAYING PERCUSSIVELY The significance of the drum in African tradition continues in African American music by singing or playing nonpercussive instruments percussively. As Bernice Johnson Reagon has said, "You can take away the drums, but you can't stop the drumming." Because of its quick timbral response and potential for variation allowing the instrument to imitate the voice, or "talk," the Hammond organ has historically been associated with gospel music performance. The pipe organ simply does not produce the same effect; it can be used, but preferably in conjunction with other, more percussive instruments such as piano. Instruments of all kinds may be combined to provide accompaniment for gospel songs—piano, organ, drums (trap set, congas, African drums), tambourine, trumpets, vibraphone, saxophone—the possibilities are unlimited. In all of these, though, pay close attention to attacks and releases. Notes may be shortened for added percussive effect and placed on the offbeat to enhance the underlying rhythm. (See example 6-2; track 31.)

organum. Whatever style is used, both spirituals and gospel songs are almost always sung in harmony.

Pitch. The concepts of pitch that characterize African American religious music are distinguished in some rather marked ways. First of all, melodic lines in both spirituals and gospel music include a preponderance of blue notes—lowered third, sixth, and seventh degrees in the major scale. Just as rhythms should not be smoothed out, neither should pitches. Even if a flatted seventh in the melody conflicts with a diatonic seventh in the accompaniment, this is considered an acceptable dissonance. Slides, scoops, and bends are all so fundamental to gospel music performance that soloists and congregations alike employ these vocal techniques intuitively. They have learned to value how pitch is conceived in the African American tradition through the process of years of exposure and practice.

Pitch is also one of those key variables used to generate change in the midst of repetition. In repeating choruses at the close of a hymn or gospel song, raising the pitch by increments of a half step serves to sustain the musical and spiritual spark.

Harmony. Two styles of harmonization coexist with standard western harmony in unaccompanied singing. The first uses parallel thirds or sixths throughout the song, a constant parallel motion. In the second style, used especially with very slow-moving pieces, a parallel interval of a fourth or fifth predominates, creating an effect similar to

Meter and Tempo. Meter is another area in which oral tradition frequently takes precedence over what is written. Especially in the case of hymns borrowed from white sources, a piece written in 4/4 routinely will be sung in 12/8, with a swing. So, for instance, "What a fellowship" (WOV 780) is often written in 4/4, but played in 12/8. (See examples 6-3 and 6-4; tracks 32 and 33.)

example 6-3

written:

example 6-4

played:

Even songs that keep their 4/4 feel will often have a flexibility in the meter that will show a triple-meter influence. "Deep river" (LMGM 150), for example, is sung in 4/4, but the ♪. ♪ figure on "I want to cross over into campground" will most likely be softened into something approaching ♪ ♪ .

Tradition has come to dictate the tempos at which most African American songs are sung. Spirituals fall, for the most part, into either of two tempos. The sorrow song—such as "Go down, Moses" (WOV 670)—is sung at a slow tempo, while the jubilee song —such as "Ain-a dat good news?"(SZ 114)—is taken at a brisk walking tempo. Within the arena of the gospel song, the gospel waltz is often employed for slower songs like "What a fellowship" while shout songs like "I'm so glad Jesus lifted me" would be sung at a quick tempo.

Accompaniment. Whereas the choral arrangement of the spiritual is typically sung unaccompanied, the acoustic piano alone almost always accompanies the spiritual for solo voice. In gospel music, as well as gospel interpretations of hymns, piano is still the

basis, but instrumentation is unlimited. At minimum most African American churches in urban areas will routinely utilize piano, electric (not pipe, and preferably Hammond; see page 77) organ, drums, tambourine, and often add bass guitar. Dependent upon the talents within the congregation, accompaniment may also include instruments ranging from synthesizer or vibraphone, to trumpet, saxophone (often soprano), or flute. In virtually all forms of African American music, instrumental accompaniment functions to complement the voice; its role is not a secondary one, but rather one of equal importance to the voice. At the same time, instruments such as horns playing riffs or obbligatos should be careful to play on the "response" sections and not on the "calls" that are reserved for the leader.

example 6-5

IMPROVISATION   Clearly, in orally based music like African American sacred song, improvisation plays an important role. At least some basic filling in beyond the written notation is essential to accompanying or leading this music. In singing the solo part, the leader will freely add runs, riffs, or motives to make the line more expressive. The melody line itself may be altered; rubato or rhythmic alteration may be employed. The best way to learn such techniques is to listen to an experienced singer, either on recording or live, and then gradually, as you feel comfortable, add to your performance style. The more free you can be with the music (within the parameters of the style), the closer you will come to the spirit of this song.

A basic principle for accompanists is that open spaces in the gospel style are almost always filled in by the keyboard. At the very least this would require

repeating chords during longer, held notes.

Even more effective would be adding an arpeggiated figure; for instance, leading from one phrase to the next. It requires listening and practice, but such fills can add immeasurably to the song.

A next step could be to add a moving bass line as was done in the excerpt from the refrain of "I'm so glad Jesus lifted me." (See example 6-5; track 34.)

Few "upper limits" exist for the amount of improvising open to the keyboard player. Once the assembly is familiar with the hymn, even the melody is optional for the pianist. Arpeggios, scale passages, passing tones, upper and lower neighbor tones, even the occasional glissando are all possibilities within the style. Harmonic alterations that support the singing are also welcome. The player must sense when to "let loose" and when, especially when the vocalists are more active, to back off.

6

Style of Delivery

Perhaps the dimension of African American religious music that poses the greatest challenge for cross-cultural sharing is its style of delivery, or physical mode of presentation. This dimension of performance includes variables which, in the European American tradition, may be considered extraneous. In the African American tradition, however, the visual dimension—the expressive behavior that characterizes performance—is of equal significance to the sonic dimension. In other words, it's not just *what* is sung, but *how* it's sung that counts.

The most striking aspect of delivery in African American music is the incorporation of dance. Although "flat-footed" singers have always been a part of African American song tradition, movement in synchrony to the rhythm of the song has been a dominant aspect of worship since slavery. While singing, particularly during moderato or spirited, up-tempo selections, choirs move side to side together on beats 1 and 3 and clap on beats 2 and 4 following the cues of the director. Although clapping and dancing are important parts of the African American

worship experience, they should never assume dominance over the singing itself. In contrast to gospel music, when singing arranged spirituals ("Nobody knows the trouble I see" or "Deep river"), there should be no organized body movement.

Facial expression is equally significant in communicating the message of both spirituals and gospel songs. Whether the eyes are open or closed, facial expression is a powerful tool in helping to convey the spiritual message of the song. Neither soloist, choir, director, nor instrumentalist should hesitate to openly express the personal meaning the song holds. The face, hands, and feet are all tools which musicians must fully utilize to convey meaning.

Conclusion

These principles of African American musical performance are intended to serve as general guides toward developing musical facility and growth in these styles. The real mark of excellence in performing in ways characteristic of the traditional African American church will come when these principles have become internalized. That requires commitment and determination, but the end result can be a richly rewarding experience.

1. Al - le - lu - ia. Al - le - lu - ia,
2. He's my Sav - ior, He's my Sav - ior,
3. He is wor - thy, He is wor - thy,
4. I will praise Him, I will praise Him

The point of worship

is to experience the truth of God,

and in knowing the truth of God

we know the truth about ourselves.

Sally Morganthaler

CONTEMPORARY

Popular music. Contemporary music. We know what we're talking about, even if none of the labels are quite satisfying. This type of church music is certainly popular in many quarters—but so are other genres. And if "contemporary" is taken to mean "composed in the last few decades," then this qualifies—but so does some music covered in every chapter of this book. We will call it by its most common name, contemporary music—you know what we mean.

What is contemporary music? This term has been used to describe a host of diverse worship music styles developed within the last forty years. Among others, contemporary music embraces folk, country, rock 'n' roll, praise, alternative, and the eclectic music of the post-Vatican II Roman Catholic tradition. While each of these styles stands as a musical genre in its own right, some of them having numerous subgenres, all of them hold enough in common to come under the umbrella of "contemporary music." In particular, these genres share a common emphasis on strong accented rhythm, orally conceived melodies, roots reaching back to the African American spiritual and Appalachian folk traditions, and accompaniment styles based on the unique technical possibilities and limitations of the guitar. Contemporary music is also set apart from traditional music in that it is usually performed by an ensemble combination of keyboards, guitars, bass, drums, melody instruments, and vocalists.

History

Western culture has always been the hearth of a creative tension between the so-called "high art" music and more broadly popular music. Often individual composers wrote contentedly and creatively in both styles. Mozart composed operas *(Singspiele)* for both the nobility and the common people. Brahms wrote beer-drinking songs as well as sophisticated symphonic works. However, at the beginning of the twentieth century, with the advent of twelve-tone music and other sophisticated aleatory styles of music, those with less investment in the nuances of art music became increasingly uninterested in it. They went their own way, and a chasm opened between the two forms of music. One of the first indications of this rift was the rise of Dixieland, ragtime, and other early forms of jazz.

Initially the church was insulated from this split because of the simplicity and accessibility of its traditional worship music. However, in the late 1950s, as a general cultural suspicion of all institutions and traditions arose, pressure increased on the church to adapt its musical language. Church musicians began introducing elements of jazz and folk music into their worship services as a way to satisfy the changing tastes of their congregations. Contemporary music became prominent within the Roman Catholic tradition through the Second Vatican Council's initiation of liturgical renewal.

In the sixties and seventies this trend was accelerated by the rise in popularity of country, rock 'n' roll, pop, and related styles of music. Furthermore, as North American primary and secondary schools began to drop music from their curricula, people found it increasingly difficult to access styles of music removed from their everyday experience. People began to ask for worship music that sounded more like what they heard on their radios, televisions, and stereos.

Kinds of Contemporary Music

As mentioned earlier, contemporary music is actually an umbrella for many different styles of newer worship music. It is very important to distinguish between the various kinds of contemporary music and how they function with different kinds of people. Here is a short list of prominent styles.

Praise and Worship

Praise and worship music is the largest subgroup within contemporary music. Generally speaking, it appeals particularly to suburban baby boomers of northern European background, born between 1940 and 1960. Praise music, which has its roots in the West Coast Jesus Movement as well as in charismatic and Pentecostal renewal, draws primarily from gospel, country, folk, and pop music for its inspiration. Its melodies can sound like Broadway tunes, country ballads, smooth jazz, and pop jingles, or even simple Taizé-like mantras. Likewise, its harmonies are rich and varied. Although piano or guitar alone can be used, ensembles that use praise music typically consist of two acoustic or electric guitars, an electric bass, two to three keyboards,

---

ONE SIZE DOESN'T FIT ALL   One common mistake made by people who plan worship is to assume that contemporary music generally sounds all the same and reaches the same kinds of people. As a result, many worship planners have chosen music that completely mismatches the musical languages of those they intend to reach. For example, urban and suburban postmodern communities (people born between 1960 and 1980) may not be turned on by baby-boomer praise music. At the same time, the rough-edged nature of younger adults' postmodern alternative music is perceived by their older boomer siblings (born between 1946 and 1960) as depressing, aggressive, and "whiny."

assorted solo instruments, drums and percussion, and a small group of vocalists. In some situations a choir and small orchestral ensemble may be employed as well. The primary task of leadership usually falls to one or two lead vocalists within the ensemble.

Alternative

Springing from the hopes, fears, and stories of the generation that followed the baby boomers (often referred to as Generation X) and others of the postmodern community, alternative music sounds a lot like the music of the Beatles, the Dave Matthews Band, U2, the Verve, R.E.M., or the Gin Blossoms. It is the most recent genre to find itself within contemporary worship music. Unlike praise music, this style makes almost no use of keyboards. Typically an alternative music worship team consists of two or three guitars (both acoustic and electric), electric bass, a drum set, Latin hand percussion of all kinds, and a small vocal ensemble. On occasion solo instruments such as violin, cello, harmonica, accordion, sax, or trumpet might be used as well. Like folk music, alternative music can also be played "unplugged" using just one guitar and a single vocalist. In many ways, alternative worship music is a reaction to the highly styled and layered sound of praise music. Alternative music is very simple, making use of extremely long melodic lines and sparse diatonic harmonies. Also, most alternative music is composed for local worship settings as opposed to a "mass market." Presently, worship teams within several growing Generation X congregations have produced CDs and melody scores with chords, but no major publishing house carries any of this style.

Contemporary Liturgical

Contemporary liturgical music is in large part the contribution of Roman Catholic composers and authors, whose task beginning in the 1960s was to create a vernacular singing tradition in the context of liturgical renewal. Much of this work had the official encouragement and support of bishops and liturgical scholars. This allowed Roman Catholic church musicians to work more from inside their institutional structures than their Protestant counterparts. As a result, they worked less at innovating new liturgical forms than at serving the needs of existing ones. For this reason contemporary liturgical music often has an easier "fit" than other kinds of contemporary music within congregations that value the traditional expressions of historic patterns of worship.

Composers within this style have written hundreds of musical settings for Holy Communion, Morning and Evening Prayer, as well as numerous settings of the psalms and many independent songs. The "sound" of contemporary liturgical music has been influenced predominantly by Gregorian chant, American folk music, and, most recently, multicultural and European art music. It is different from praise and alternative in that it makes significantly less use of pop and rock rhythms. Also, while this style shares many elements essential to contemporary music—strongly accented rhythm, orally conceived melodies, and guitar-based harmonies—there is more reliance on harmonies found in European art music.

Major composers in this style include Marty Haugen, David Haas, Jeremy Young, and Bernadette Farrell. Worship ensembles that play this kind of music use instruments as diverse as piano, pipe organ, synthesizer, dulcimer, recorder, harp, and electric guitar. The "average" ensemble consists of two to three acoustic guitars, synthesizer and/or pipe organ, solo instruments of all kinds, one or two cantors, and a small vocal ensemble.

Rock 'n' Roll

Although this style is less commonly employed within mainstream contemporary worship music, it has been kept alive by youth ministry leaders within Lutheran and many other denominational traditions. Typically the sound of this music relies heavily on blues chord progressions and driving rock rhythms. It is often performed with guitars, bass, keyboards, drums, and several vocals, although a piano or guitar alone with solo voice can also work.

Jazz and Blues

Although used rather widely in the sixties and seventies, jazz and blues styles in their pure forms are less common today in congregational music. Most likely this has to do with the fact that these styles have been superseded in mainstream culture by rock, pop, and rhythm and blues. Also, these styles do not easily lend themselves melodically to congregational singing. When they are now performed, pure jazz and blues

forms are usually found within pieces used for preludes, anthems, and postludes. Recently, however, the forms have been making their way back into the worship of congregations that minister within the postmodern community.

Country

Increasing in popularity in cities as well as rural areas, sacred country music has grown so large that it is almost as diverse as the whole category of contemporary music itself. While some country songs sound like mainstream pop, others sound like bluegrass or southern gospel; there is even alternative country. Initially, country music branched off of early rock 'n' roll by maintaining its stress on acoustic instruments, downplaying the roll of drums, and stressing themes from rural experience.

Another characteristic of early country music was the simplicity of chord progressions as well as vocal style. As the level of musicianship increased among its performers, country music began to borrow from other musical styles and, thus, increased in complexity and variety. At present there are as many "types" of country music as there are artists. Interestingly enough, the country music found in most congregations is still based on its earlier manifestations: bluegrass and southern gospel. It is also common for worship leadership ensembles to perform more "pop"-sounding worship songs in classic country style. Only in the last ten years have the more mainstream country styles found their way into congregational singing.

Finding Contemporary Music

Major sources publishing contemporary praise and worship music at this time include Maranatha! Music, Word/Integrity Music, Inc., and Mercy Publishing, Inc. (Vineyard Music Group). In addition to individual pieces, these publishers all offer collections as well as CDs and tapes.

Two denominational Lutheran houses, Augsburg Fortress and Concordia (CPH), publish a selected amount of music in contemporary styles. Changing Church Forum in Burnsville, Minnesota, publishes music primarily composed by Handt Hanson and Paul Murakami. Fellowship Publications of Phoenix, Arizona, publishes a variety of resources that include praise and worship music, as well as music from the Lutheran pietist tradition. Musicians and bands such as John Ylvisaker, Jay Beech, and Dakota Road publish their own music primarily in rock 'n' roll and folk styles.

COPYRIGHT ISSUES A major copyright licensing agency for contemporary music is listed:

Christian Copyright Licensing Inc.
17201 N.E. Sacramento
Portland, OR 97230-5941
Phone: 503-257-2230 or 800-234-2446
Fax: 503-257-2244

Congregations may rent a copyright license on a sliding fee scale which is determined by average annual worship attendance. Typically a congregation with worship attendance of 300 could expect to pay about $150.00 per year. Remember, congregations must gain permission to reproduce copyrighted music or text in any form, including overhead projection.

Major sources for music with a Roman Catholic contemporary sound include GIA Publications, Oregon Catholic Press (OCP), and World Library Publications. All three publishing houses offer a wide variety of eucharistic settings, psalm settings, and songs for the liturgical year and for various parts of the liturgy. They also provide CDs and tapes that model various styles of performance.

As with any hymnal or song book, congregations will find about twenty to twenty-five percent of the music published to be useful for their situation. One of the best ways to sort out the music useful for your congregation's setting would be to gather your worship planning team for a two-day retreat and sing through the various songbooks that you've collected. Here are some basic criteria for song selection.

● Does the text of the song articulate a biblical view of reality?

● Does the music match the overall tone of the text?

● Is the music easy enough for a congregation to learn after singing one or two verses?

● Is the music interesting enough to motivate the congregation to learn it in the first place?

● Is the music durable enough to be sung several times over the course of a year?

Performance Practice

In most cases, praise and worship music for congregational singing is led by a band or "worship team." These come in all sizes and shapes. As mentioned earlier, the most typical configuration for a worship team consists of one or two keyboards, a rhythm and a lead guitar, a bass, a drum set, and several vocalists. Sometimes there may be one or two obbligato instruments as well. A good resource for a more detailed exploration of performance practices in relation to the various styles within contemporary music is *Contemporary Music Styles: The Worship Band's Guide to Excellence* by Bob Barrett. Much of what follows is derived from the information found in this very useful book. Here are the functions of each instrument and their relation to the typical worship team as a whole. Later we will discuss how to lead contemporary worship with piano or guitar alone.

Keyboards and Pianos

There are three basic ways electronic keyboards (synthesizers) and pianos function within a typical worship team. The first way is as a solo instrument reinforcing the melody along with the vocalists. In small ensembles with weak vocalists this is absolutely essential for effective leadership in congregational singing. Taking the song "Lord, I lift your name on high" as an example, we first hear the piano alone emphasizing the melody. (See example 7-1; track 35.) When using a synthesizer, often the performer has several life-like and useful sounds at his or her disposal. The most important thing to remember when choosing solo

sounds is to make sure they fit with the character of the song as well as blend acoustically with the rest of the ensemble.

The second way keyboards and pianos function within a typical worship team is by providing a harmonic "pad" which serves as a

example 7-1

Lord, I lift your name on high,
Lord, I love to sing your
prais - es.
I'm so glad you're in my life,
I'm so glad you came to save us.
You came from heav - en to earth to show the way,

foundation for the rest of the worship team. A pad is usually a middle-range (centered around middle C) accompaniment of sustained or repeated chords, or a repeated pattern of arpeggios. This rounds out the team's sound and provides support for the vocalists and other solo instruments such as lead guitar. Some possibilities for "Lord, I lift your name on high" are in example 7-2.

The third way keyboards and pianos function within the team is by serving as a bass or rhythm instrument, either alone or by doubling the lines of other bass and percussion instruments. In most worship teams keyboards and pianos serve in at least two of these capacities. In larger ensembles their role becomes simplified and more confined to avoid a cluttered and confusing sound.

Copyright © 1989, arr. © 1997 Marantha! Music, admin. The Copyright Company. Used by permission.

What kind of keyboard player should you look for? The ideal keyboard player for a worship team is able not only to read music, but to improvise as well. Many high school musicians share these twin talents. The ability to improvise is important because most music scores for contemporary music consist of only melodies, words, and chords. Most newer alternative music scores have only words and chords. If your keyboard players do not know how to improvise it will be important that you support them by providing them with lessons. Often a high school or college music teacher can provide such lessons. The good news is that learning to improvise is not as difficult as it looks, and most people like the notion of being able to make up their own music. For circumstances where this is not possible, publishing houses such as Maranatha, Hosanna, GIA, and OCP all provide keyboard versions of their music. However, because of the improvisatory nature of this genre, keyboard scores often sound a bit wooden.

example 7-2

Rhythm and Lead Guitars

Guitars have two primary functions within a worship team: (1) providing harmonic foundation through comping (strumming chords) or picking (playing repeated arpeggiated patterns); and (2) providing embellishment and ornamentation through different kinds of melodic lines.

When a guitar provides a harmonic foundation it is playing the role of *rhythm* guitar. This role is primarily one of undergirding and supporting the rest of the ensemble. (See track 36.)

When a guitar is filling the *lead* role, playing a melodic line, it may be:
- soloing out the melody to support the vocalists and congregation
- playing descants and counter melodies (fills) to increase musical interest

- playing improvised solos between verses or refrains.

Again the function is support, no matter how predominant the instrument may be at any given time.

There are also two basic types of guitars: acoustic and electric. Acoustic guitars are more often found in bands that play Roman Catholic contemporary, country, and "unplugged" alternative styles. Electric guitars are found in ensembles that play more mainstream praise, rock 'n' roll, aggressive alternative, and pure jazz and blues. Guitarists with a high level of proficiency often have both at their side to increase their worship team's flexibility in presenting diverse musical styles. Both can fulfill the roles of lead and rhythm.

What kind of guitarist should you look for? At the very least guitarists should be able to play in tune. This would seem to be obvious but experience has taught that often it is not

---

BUYING A KEYBOARD   If you need a keyboard for your band, what should you look for? Because of rapid advances in digital technology, congregations are confronted with a dizzying array of selections for electronic keyboards. Obviously, if the money is available, a high-quality grand piano should always be considered as an option. When considering electronic keyboards, either as a substitute for the piano or as a complement to it, two criteria come into play: (1) the keyboard must be easy enough to use so that the widest possible variety of people can play it; and (2) the sounds must be as true to life as possible. The best way to find this out is to have your worship leaders try out each keyboard you are considering purchasing. Often music store owners are happy to loan you a keyboard so that you can listen to it in the worship space intended for its use. If you don't have an appropriate amplification system (the church PA system is usually an unwise choice), make sure they supply you with one. In regard to ease of play, the best way to discern whether an electronic keyboard is simple enough for your use is to try it out. Additionally, ask around and learn from the experience of other congregations and performers. As with all instruments, there will be a learning curve involved in becoming proficient with an electronic keyboard.

the case. Guitarists should also be able to perform the chords found in most contemporary music or be able to learn new chords quickly. In some cases the worship team leader can assist medium-skill-level guitarists by substituting. For instance, more complex chords like Amin7 and CMaj7 can be simplified to chords such as Amin and C. Another way to assist guitarists is by providing for guitar lessons. This honors the commitment of the guitarist as well as raises the overall quality of the worship team.

Bass Guitar

The bass guitar comes in four-, five-, and six-string models. We will focus on the four-string bass since most bass players in congregational settings play this type of instrument. Four-string basses are tuned just like the bottom four strings of the guitar except they sound one octave lower. Likewise, the bass sounds its notes one octave lower than the music written for it. Although a bass player may encounter written-out parts from time to time in more sophisticated music, he or she typically reads from the same lead sheet (melody and chord score) as the guitarist. Sometimes on such scores there will be chords with non-root inversions as well as polychords. When this happens the bass player always plays the lowest note implied. For example, if the score reads CMaj7/F the guitarist and keyboard player may play the CMaj7 but the bass player always plays the F.

In this example from "Lord, I lift your name on high," the bass player, reading from the score, would play something like this (example 7-3):

Normally the role of the bass is twofold: (1) to work in consort with the drums in providing a rhythmic foundation for the worship team—often they will play the same rhythm as the kick (bass) drum; and (2) to increase musical interest by improvising ostinato patterns throughout any given song. Occasionally the bass will be called on to play an extended melodic phrase. When that happens one of the keyboards will need to provide the foundation normally assigned to the bass. As with guitarists, most bass players read chords better than they read notes. Their flexibility increases greatly, however, when they learn to read notes, especially when encountering jazz and soft rock. This is another reason why congregations should consider providing encouragement and financial support for lessons as well as continuing education experiences for their musicians.

Percussion

One of the most significant components of any worship team is the percussion section. The primary role of percussion is to provide rhythmic stability to the music. At times this means holding the rest of the worship team back from rushing. At other times the team will need to be pushed so not to drag the tempo. Well executed and reliable percussion also allows other members of the worship team to be rhythmically creative and flexible without risking instability or loss of momentum. This helps the congregation feel more confident in its singing because the tempo

example 7-3

remains comfortable and predictable. Within a worship team the most common percussion section is a drum set or "trap set." Most drum sets consist of:

- **Bass (or kick) drum.** This acts as the cornerstone of the rhythmic ostinato patterns so common to contemporary music percussion. Usually it is played on beats one and three.
- **Snare drum.** This works in tandem with the bass drum to complete the rhythmic ostinato pattern. Usually it is played on beats two and four in 4/4 time and on beats two and three in 3/4 time. Metal wires under the bottom drum head cause the characteristic sharp "white noise" sound associated with snare drums.
- **Mounted and floor toms.** These drums provide various kinds of rhythmic augmentation (fills) between phrases, periods, and other major sections. Often toms help signal the beginning or end of an introduction, verse, or refrain.
- **Cymbals.** Usually there are three kinds of cymbals used in a drum set: the crash cymbal, the ride cymbal, and the hi-hat. The main job of the crash cymbal is to accent phrase beginnings as well as underscore the major divisions within a given piece. Usually some kind of fill provided by the toms precedes such accents. On the other hand, both ride and hi-hat cymbals almost always play a constant ostinato pattern of quarter, eighth, or sixteenth notes. Whereas the crash cymbal and the bass and snare drums emphasize certain beats within

a measure, the job of the ride and hi-hat cymbals is to bring out the rhythmic flow of a measure. This gives the listener a sense that the music is dynamic and moving beyond itself.

The following example shows how bass drum, snare drum, and cymbals would commonly combine in rhythmic patterns for 4/4 and 3/4 time. (See example 7-4; track 37.)

example 7-4

Other percussion instruments found in worship teams are the ones used in Latin and Afro-Caribbean music. These include such instruments as:

- congas, timbales, bongos (drums of various sizes)
- claves (two wooden bars struck against each other)
- tambourines of various types
- guiros (hollowed-out gourds, notched on the sides and scraped by a stick)
- cowbells of various sizes
- finger cymbals.

These can be used in combination with a drum set or alone. Often when a drum set is unavailable, one or more of these instruments can provide the rhythmic pulse and stability so necessary for confident congregational singing. (See track 38.)

Vocalists

The primary role of vocalists is to guide and support the congregation in its singing. This may be done by simple hand gestures or short instructions at the beginning of a song. But the most common way they accomplish this is by unison singing. Even in very large congregations, where the vocalists on their worship teams are at professional level in their technique, almost seventy percent of what they do is unison singing. Now and then, when the congregation is confident with a particular song, the vocalists will add some simple harmonies to the melody. In some cases one of the sopranos or tenors may embellish a final refrain with a gospel-style improvised descant.

Solo Instruments

Within a worship team, instruments such as trumpet, sax, violin, or flute perform much the same functions as lead guitar. That is, they reinforce the melody, play descants and counter melodies, and improvise embellishments between verses and refrains. Many congregations have several moderately skilled musicians who play solo instruments. One of the best ways to introduce them to worship leadership (and to motivate them to improve their skill level) is to have them play simple, slow moving descants or counter melodies during one or two songs per service. This allows them a "front door" into your worship team while not sacrificing the overall quality of your team's sound.

Working with a Smaller Ensemble

In many congregations it is difficult to find all the musicians that make up a typical worship team. This does not mean that you cannot make use of contemporary music. It just means that you need to be a little creative! The minimum ensemble necessary to lead contemporary music is one keyboardist or guitarist and one moderately-skilled singer. In many cases where there is a second keyboard player on hand (or a guitarist and a keyboard player), one person might play the piano (or guitar), while the other would play the synthesizer where the left hand functions as the bass player and the right hand functions as a string section. Since almost all synthesizers have the ability to divide their keyboards into two or more different types of sound, such a strategy can easily be accomplished. Add one or more people to play some simple hand percussion such as bongos and tambourine and your congregation has almost all the components of a typical praise team—just in a simplified form. (See track 39; also example 7-1.)

Leading the Congregation's Worship with Contemporary Music

In traditional European worship music, the organist or pianist leads the congregation by maintaining a steady beat (tactus) throughout the hymn, as well as employing slight rhythmic articulations or "lifts" at the beginning of each verse or refrain. Much of this is present within contemporary music as well. That the entire ensemble keeps a steady beat is essential to the proper execution of all contemporary music styles. But the primary task of leading the congregation falls to the vocalists. Typically, vocalists on a worship team guide the congregation in three ways. The most obvious way vocalists lead is by singing the melody. This is especially crucial in contemporary music where instruments such as piano and synthesizer are unable to articulate all the vocal embellishments so common to this genre. (See example 7-5.) Another way vocalists lead contemporary music is by literally conducting the congregation. This is done through the use of small but clear hand gestures at the beginning of a song or after an extended interlude. Finally, vocalists also lead the congregation with their breathing. An obvious breath right before an entrance makes it clear when the congregation should begin to sing.

Although not as central as the vocalists' role, the drummer also helps the congregation to know where to sing. Usually the drummer will play fills (rhythmic augmentation) on the toms and/or cymbal crashes of various sorts right before the congregation needs to start singing. Together with the vocalists' leadership, these cues make it very easy for the congregation to know when to begin singing. (See track 40.)

Recruiting Musicians for Your Worship Team

When assembling a worship team it is good to look for certain qualities, such as:
- a passion for quality and integrity in worship
- an eagerness for constant learning

- an openness to all kinds of music styles
- a basic level of competence on their instrument
- an ability to work as team players and subordinate their own taste desires to the larger mission of the worship team.

example 7-5

Lord, I lift your name on high, Lord, I love to sing your prais-es.

Where can you find these musicians? Finding musicians for a contemporary music worship team is often easier than it appears. Many times musicians can be found in the congregation. At first glance this may appear not to be the case because many musicians who play contemporary music were led to believe that their music was not wanted in the church. In fact, when they first begin to play, they often need to be reassured that they are not doing something disruptive or improper. Other places to look for musicians, or for people who might have connections to musicians are:
- music stores
- bars (especially with country music musicians; often they are practicing Christians looking to use their craft to glorify God)
- local high school and college music departments
- large evangelical congregations which often have more musicians than they can use.

Another key issue for worship teams and their leaders is continuing education. Several large congregations across the country, as well as publishing houses such as Maranatha! Music, GIA and OCP Publications, offer one- to three-day clinics and seminars for everything from proper vocal technique to rehearsal strategies to operating sound systems. Other resources for continuing education are music directors of large congregations doing contemporary music, and high school and college band or choral directors, particularly if they are comfortable with jazz, rock, and pop music. Many of them would be willing, for a modest honorarium, to spend four to six hours on a Saturday with a congregational worship team improving their musicianship and leadership skills. In some cases several smaller congregations could sponsor such an event, thus lowering the cost for all involved.

Conclusion

As with any area of worship, if you have decided that contemporary music is worth doing, then it is worth doing well. Don't undercut it before it has a chance. Rather, make a commitment of time, talent, and resources. Decide ahead of time that you will keep at it for a good period of time—at least a year. Work to get the congregation's entire leadership team behind the effort. Talk through ways in which you can make this an integral part of the congregation's entire worship life, something that will enhance, not divide. In many ways, contemporary music is the common musical language of our day, and it certainly deserves a place in the church. It is another way we answer the call to sing to the Lord a new song.

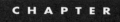

Cantemos al Señor un himno de alabanza

que exprese nuestro amor,

nuestra fe y nuestra esperanza.

En toda la creación pregona su grandeza;

así nuestro cantar va anunciando su belleza.

¡Aleluya! Cantemos al Señor. ¡Aleluya!

Carlos Rosas

LATINO

One of the fastest growing segments of the population in the United States today is the community known as Latino, sometimes called Hispanic. As a cultural designation, "Hispanic" is a very broad term, incorporating many lands and ethnic groups. The term itself comes from the word *España* (Spanish for "Spain"), the country that led the conquest of the New World. Major categories include:

- persons of European descent, especially Spain and Portugal
- persons of African descent (especially those from eastern Nigeria, the Gold Coast, and particularly the Congo basin) who were brought to the West as slaves and who later intermarried and adopted Spanish as their language
- American Indian persons (Aztec, Maya, Inca, and other indigenous language groups)
- persons who are genealogically as well as culturally a mix of two or more of these groups.

Although there is considerable discussion about the proper use of these terms, "Latino/a" is a word often used to designate people of Latin American heritage born or raised in the United States and Puerto Rico. In this chapter we will attempt to share a bit of the richness and *sabor* (flavor) of this multicultural music known as *Hispanic* or *Latino*.

As we think about worship music from this tradition it is useful to take into account its historical context. The gospel has been a part of Latin American life and history for over 500 years. Roman Catholic priests formed a part of the entourages that accompanied Columbus and successive conquistadores. Because congregational singing was not a part of Roman Catholic worship practices during those 500 years, music in public worship was often provided by people in religious orders or, in some cases, persons who made their living as professional musicians. Participation by the congregation was initiated only recently, in the 1960s, as a result of the reforms of the Second Vatican Council (1962–65), when Rome began encouraging the use of the vernacular in the celebration of the public eucharistic rite. Hymns and songs giving expression to the thoughts and needs of worshipers sprang into being. This initiation coincided with profound social changes that challenged all forms of traditional authority. In Latin America, Spain, and Portugal the Bible, as well as the liturgy, became available to people in their own tongue. People began using all forms of vernacular expression in public worship. This included musical styles and tunes that were indigenous, already a part of their daily lives.

Singing always played a significant role in the non-Roman churches of Latin America.

The repertoire was largely limited to hymns and songs imported by missionaries from the North or, in the case of immigrant churches, from Europe. These, of course, were translated into Spanish (or Portuguese where necessary). There had been some timid venturing into creative areas involving local composers and authors, but this was not by any means extensive. In the 1960s the same social revolution that shook the Roman church touched the Protestant churches. Folk, popular, and dance idioms were grafted to the music of Christian worship.

In recent decades the music of Latin America has become more and more familiar to non-Hispanic *norteño* communities due to the increased interest and availability of recordings (especially in the area of "world music"), the growing number of Spanish-speaking residents in the United States and Canada, as well as the development of greater interdependence in nations of the Western Hemisphere. This has also affected the availability of musical resources in the church. Many recent denominational hymnals contain at least a few, if not several, texts and tunes from the Hispanic tradition. Hymnals produced by mainline Protestant denominations in the early 1960s for their "sister" churches in Latin America were primarily collections of European hymns and liturgies translated into Spanish. Only a small percentage of the hymns were composed by Latin Americans. Newer Spanish hymnals (*Mil*

Voces Para Celebrar published by the United Methodist Publishing House, *Flor y Canto* by Oregon Catholic Press, and *Libro de Liturgia y Cántico* by the Evangelical Lutheran Church in America, Augsburg Fortress, Publishers, to name a few) exhibit a more balanced stylistic selection with a majority of the hymns coming from various Latino musical sources.

Because the designation "Hispanic" or "Latino" includes such a broad spectrum of peoples, traditions, cultures, and cross-influences, it is difficult to speak of Latino music as a generic whole. Latino music is, in fact, extraordinarily diverse. Think for a moment of the variety of traditions included in the category: the mariachi tradition of Mexico, the Tejano of southern Texas, the stunning Afro-Cuban tradition with its multi-layered rhythms, the Dominican merengue, and the Caribbean calypso. There is also the ethereal sound of Andean

example 8-1

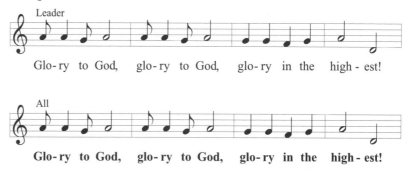

example 8-2

F B♭ C7   F B♭ C7

I Se - ñor,   ten pie - dad.
O Lord,   have . . mer - cy.
                            Have

II Se - ñor,   ten pie - dad.
O Lord,   have . . mer - cy.

F B♭ C7 Dm B♭ C7

I Cris - to, ten   pie - dad.   I Se -
mer - cy on   us, Christ.   *O*

II   Cris - to, ten   pie - dad.
Have mer - cy on   us, Christ.

example 8-3

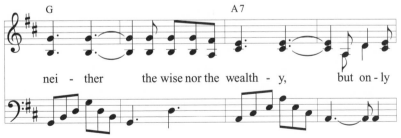

D   A7   D

You   have come down to the lake - shore   seek - ing

G   A7

nei - ther   the wise nor the wealth - y,   but on - ly

pipes that color the music shape of tunes from Peru and Ecuador, the influence of dances like the tango in the music of Argentina, the flamenco of Spain, the fado of Portugal, and the cross-pollination of it all that takes place in geographically central places like Costa Rica.

Caribbean music is often characterized by binary rhythms in combinations of syncopated patterns. The music of the native peoples, frequently accompanied by drums or rattles according to its function, tends to be single-line melody, often descending in shape. (See example 8-1.)

Call/response patterns are characteristic of African-Latin music, which is often accompanied by drummers improvising various patterns over a rhythmic ostinato. (See example 8-2.)

In contrast, the music born of European influences is characterized by a melody commonly set in triple meter which is derived from either major or minor scales and modes. Accompaniment is frequently provided by the guitar or harp, augmented by various melody instruments. (See example 8-3.)

Characteristics of Latino Congregational Song

Refrain

The refrain, or *estribillo*, is one of the most characteristic elements in Latino song. Because Latino congregations generally sing with the aid of materials including only text,

8

ease in learning and memorizing the tune is desirable. An unchanging, tuneful refrain after each stanza can quickly be taught by a leader and easily learned by the congregation. As the congregation becomes more familiar with the *estribillo* there may be some improvisation or enrichment of the melodic line, usually with parallel harmony moving along below or above the melody in thirds.

Dance Forms

Much of Latino music is based on dance. In Texas and much of Mexico the polka is extremely popular in its own unique form called *ranchera, norteña,* or "Tex-Mex." Variations of the waltz *(vals)* are heard virtually throughout Latin America. The mazurka *(mazurca)* is a favorite among the peasant farmers of northern Nicaragua. Although it may seem strange, the media played a vital role in the dissemination of Latino music to the general North American public. In the 1930s and 1940s, Xavier Cugat, a Spanish band leader who lived in both Mexico and Cuba, as well as stars like Carmen Miranda brought

CULTURAL DIFFERENCES IN LATINO MUSIC In her writing on Hispanic hymnody, Raquel Gutiérrez-Achón has summarized some of these basic musical differences in the major cultural Latino groups:

The music from the Caribbean countries has a very strong African influence. The well known "cross-rhythm pattern" is nothing but the polyrhythmic sound of the African drums. I can remember in Cuba listening to the black people playing their music, where each drum played a different rhythm but nevertheless there was a "central beat," so to speak, common to them all. This is common too in the music which comes to us from Brazil. Hispanic musicians have adopted some other rhythms such as, for example, the calypso from the Virgin Islands.

The Andean countries—Peru, Bolivia, and Ecuador—reflect much of the indigenous element. Many of their melodies use minor scales. It could be that they still identify somewhat with Gregorian melodies, which were the first with which they became acquainted, or perhaps they do want to express the mysticism that church music was always meant to express. Nevertheless, all the resurrection hymns are in major keys. For the most part, the hymns from Peru are pentatonic.

Brazil and Argentina reflect more variety in style. They use folk songs, popular North American music, European four-part harmony (almost classical). In Brazil, they emphasize the descending melodic line. Much of their church music is more sophisticated musically than that of other countries. The same may be said also of Argentina. Venezuelan music uses more complex rhythms, and often they change from major to minor, or from minor to major.

Central America, except Guatemala, has produced only a few Hispanic hymns. Their cultural influence tends to be Mexican or South American. Mexicans, as well as Texan-Mexicans, have a great affinity with North American music. They are, generally speaking, very conservative, using simple melodies and simple repeated patterns of melody and harmony, but fewer elements of the indigenous folk song. Melodies are often harmonized in parallel thirds, which is the sound of the style known as mariachi.

There is also music which comes from Spain. It is rich in melody and harmony, nevertheless having characteristic Hispanic cadences. Sometimes one finds simple melodic lines which reflect the Moorish element of Spain's history.[1]

Afro-Latin rhythms to the Hollywood screen. During the 1950s, Desiderio Alberto Arnaz y de Acha (Desi Arnaz) and his band played regularly on the "I Love Lucy" television sitcom. Incidently, Arnaz's famous "Babaloo" is, in reality, a song to the Yoruba (African) deity Babalú, a saint in the *santería* religion. Latin Jazz artists like Tito Puente, Rubén Blades, and Willie Colon made *salsa* one of the most popular musical styles in the world. These rhythms and dance forms also play an important role in Latino music used in the context of worship.

Rhythm

Ask anyone to name a major characteristic of Latino music as a whole and the answer will undoubtedly have something to do with rhythm. Most music of Latino traditions involves complex layered rhythmic patterns often played on a large battery of instruments: congas, timbales, bongos, claves, guiros, maracas, and so on.

Performance Practice

As with many other ethnic forms of church music, most North Americans have a vague sense of how Latino music sounds, but not many firm ideas on how to arrive at such a sound in their own practice. There is, for instance, a certain stereotype about Hispanic music that seems to inspire non-Latino worship leaders to hand out a dozen or so small percussion instruments to members of the choir or even the congregation and ask them to play along with no prior preparation. In these cases it is almost inevitable that chaos will result. How *does* one begin to gain an understanding of how to do music from the Latino tradition in an authentic way?

The "Rhythm Section"

Rhythm is a huge part of Latino music, of any music, but people with an instrument thrust into their hands can't be expected to "feel" it straight away. While skilled percussionists

---

PERCUSSION   A word about percussion. Don't get worried about complex percussion notations. If there are people in your community with the requisite training and the instruments to be able to play the percussion parts "authentically," that's great. This will not always be the case. There are a number of options. First, you can see this as an opportunity to invite Latin American or other percussionists to help out at worship. You might also train some interested people in your own congregation. One congregation, for example, invited a Latin American guitarist (who also knew how to teach people to play many Latin American percussion instruments) to be the guest soloist for Ariel Ramirez' *Missa Criolla*. This musician led a mini

workshop in percussion with members of the choir who did a fine job with the aid of simple percussion parts in the score.

The best place to look for potential percussionists is among those who are studying percussion as a part of a school band program. While most percussion training in this country is based on the use of mallets and sticks (to play snares, bass drum, tom-toms, and the like) as opposed to open hand conga and bongo techniques, the basic premise is easily adapted. Modern bands and drum and bugle corps demand a high level of proficiency regarding percussionists as do jazz bands (often versed in Latin rhythms as well). So, people *are* out there.

trained in Latin rhythms would undoubtedly add a degree of integrity to any song, their talents may not be available to the "average" Anglo congregation. What's to be done? Begin simply. If you are able, familiarize yourself with various types and aspects of Latino music through recordings. The Mexican-American music of Los Lobos or the Texas Tornadoes and the mariachi recordings of Linda Ronstadt will help you hear some of the connections between this music and the various country music traditions of North America. "Guantanamera" and "La Bamba" are two of the best-known Latin American songs in the English-speaking world. They are examples of popular Caribbean *guajira* and *son* dance rhythms. Various dance styles on page 109 (*bolero, guajira, son, cha cha,* and *mambo*) have similar rhythmic underpinnings that have made their way into mainstream North American rock 'n' roll. Listening to recordings will help you appreciate the richness of the various musical traditions of Latin America: Colombia's Carlos Vives, Argentina's Mercedes Sosa, the Dominican Republic's Juan Luis Guerra, Cuba's Albita Rodríguez, and Gloria Estefan. The music of these artists is truly distinctive and listening to them helps the musician (even the church musician) get some idea of how related pieces might be performed.

After listening to the recordings, though, start perhaps with only one percussion instrument, then two, three, and even four. Contrary to some preconceived notions, not all percussion instruments need to play all the time. Faster tempos do not always require more percussion. Some gentle layered rhythmic patterns (egg shakers and hand drum on a delicate waltz, for example)

example 8-4

TRACK 41

You are the seed that will grow a new sprout; you're a

star that will shine in the night,

JUST DO IT! Ángel M. Mattos de Jesús, director of the project that culminated with the publication of *Libro de Liturgia y Cántico,* is often asked, "How can primarily Anglo music leaders bring integrity and high quality of 'performance' to Latino music?" He responds,

"The most important thing to keep in mind is not to feel intimidated by Hispanic music. Just do it! But, is this doing it with integrity and high quality of performance? Listen, as long as you do it with expressiveness, it will have integrity, and as long as you do the best you can, it will have a high quality of performance. Let the music speak to you. See how you can be expressive through the song you have in front of you!"

might be used to accompany melodies cast in slower tempos.

What percussion patterns does one play? A table of rhythmic possibilities might prove helpful. One such table appears in an appendix to the aforementioned *Libro de Liturgia y Cántico* (Augsburg Fortress, 1998); it contains suggested styles for a majority of the songs included in that resource. Some of these rhythmic notations are written for guitar, some for piano, some for both. In cases where percussion suggestions are not given, the rhythms of the piano/guitar can easily be translated to various percussion instruments as well. (See the appendix to this chapter on page 109.)

example 8-5

TRACK 42

Id, a-mi-gos, por el mun-do, a - nun-cian-do el a -

example 8-6

TRACK 43

Can - tad al Se - ñor un cán - ti - co nue - vo

*T ↓ ↓ T ↓ ↓ T ↓ ↓ T ↓

Em B

* Thumb (or pick) bass note
↓ - downward strum

Certain songs are readily identified with specific rhythmic forms. Other songs lend themselves to a variety of rhythms. A common practice among Latino musicians is to change the rhythmic pattern, hence the very character of the piece, in the course of singing the song. This is a concept of freedom many non-Latino musicians find both surprising and challenging. It is rather uncommon for the average church musician on any given Sunday to take a piece written in 4/4 meter (which might be considered a *marcha* in the Latino world) and adapt it to another rhythmic structure, say 6/8 (for example, a *balada*). Latino musicians, however, do this all the time, often employing various rhythmic structures in the course of several stanzas. Think for a moment how J. S. Bach did the same thing when he rhythmically transposed chorale tunes (changed the meter) in his cantatas.

The Spanish hymn "Sois la semilla" ID Y ENSEÑAD ("You are the seed"—WOV 753, LLC 486) is usually performed as a polka in Mexico and Central America. (See example 8-4; track 41.)

It also sounds great done as a relaxed *bolero ranchero* or *paso doble*. One possibility, sometimes employed by Latino musicians, is to make use of a simple duple rhythm (pick, strum, pick, strum) on the stanzas, and a brighter structure *(bolero ranchero/paso doble)* on the refrain. (See example 8-5; track 42.)

Note the totally different effect on each of the following examples of CANTAD AL SEÑOR (WOV 795, LLC 598):
- as a *vals* (example 8-6; track 43)
- cast in a pattern of two against three (sometimes called *seis por ocho*, a compound

103

8

meter, but notated here in 3/4) (example
8-7; track 44)

● as a modified *zamba* (notated in 6/8)
(example 8-8; track 45)

● and even cast into a 4/4 rhythm as a modified *guaracha simplificada* (example 8-9;
track 46)

Keyboard

Most Latin American pianists think of their
instrument as a percussion instrument. When
accompanying a song or hymn the pianist
generally does not play the melody line, leaving it to another instrument (flute, violin,
trumpet, accordion). By doing this the pianist
is able to achieve a strong rhythmic effect, the
left hand playing the bass line (sometimes
doubling it in octaves), the right hand playing
chords on non-accented beats. In this way the
keyboard player becomes a part of the percussion section and drives the beat, thereby providing rhythmic leadership.

As noted above, it is not uncommon for
the pianist or other keyboard player to
employ the concept of rhythmic "theme and
variations" in the course of the execution of a
song. This adds spice and interest to repeated
sung stanzas and *estribillos*. The ability to
substitute rhythmic patterns depends on the
keyboard player's ability to learn "stock"
accompaniment styles (such as those given in
the rhythmic index and the examples above)
and transpose them to the specific key and

example 8-7

*↓ downward strum

↑ upward strum

↕ downward percussive string hit

example 8-8

*↓ downward strum

〜 downward finger fan from beat 2 through beat 3.

LOOKING FOR HELP? One resource mentioned in this chapter is *Libro de Liturgia y Cántico (Book of Liturgy and Song)* from Augsburg Fortress. It is a worship book by and for Spanish-speaking Christians, and therefore Spanish is the primary language throughout. It is, however, also immensely useful as an aid for the neophyte in the world of Latino worship. It offers hundreds of hymns and songs from throughout the Spanish-speaking world. In addition, though, it presents an "Apéndice de ritmos" (Appendix of Rhythms) in both Spanish and English giving basic information on how to accompany this music as well as thirty-five rhythmic patterns written out for appropriate instruments. See page 109 for a selection of these rhythms; also example 8-10.

chord structure of a given piece. This is much like following a chord chart comprised of melody line and chord names above to indicate where chord changes occur. The keyboard player familiarizes himself or herself with the desired (or prescribed) rhythmic pattern and adapts it to each of the chord changes as the song progresses. This is, in fact, the way virtually all Latin American keyboardists play these tunes.

Begin with a Latin American polka or waltz—at heart, very simple songs that can be accompanied quite adequately by musicians even with limited training. The downbeat (bass/root note of the chord) is followed by two weaker beats that employ the full triad (usually in root or first inversion). Pick a song that might easily be paired with this structure (CANTAD AL SEÑOR, for example). Practice the pattern (boom-chick-chick or root-chord-chord) for each tone of the scale (for CANTAD this would be E minor). Practice the tonic (E minor), dominant (B major), subdominant (A minor), and so on. Actually, those three chord patterns, plus a minor seventh added to the dominant (B chord) for color, are all that are necessary. Either follow the chords listed above the music in most editions, or use your ear. It's surprising how good one can become at anticipating chord changes with a minimal amount of practice. Next, select another rhythmic structure that would fit; for example, a *pasillo ó criolla*. (See example 8-10.)

example 8-9

TRACK 46

Can - tad   al   Se - ñor   un

↓ ~ ↑ ↓ ↑ ↓ ↑ *etc.*

Em

cán - ti - co   nue - vo

B

*↓ downward strum

↑ downward strum

~ downward finger fan from beat 2 through beat 3.

example 8-10

example 8-11

*↓ downward strum
↑ upward strum
↟ downward percussive string hit

etc.

example 8-12

TRACK 47

[L] Se - ñor, ten pie- dad.

[C] Se -

F   B♭   C7

ñor, ten pie- dad.

F   B♭   C7

*↓ downward strum
↑ upward strum
⇓ downward percussive string hit

Again, practice the rhythmic pattern with each chord structure (E minor, B major, A minor), then wed it to the song, singing the melody yourself if necessary.

In this type of music, virtuosity is experienced not in the fluency of the keyboard player, but rather in the instrumentation and layering of it, the improvisation of bass lines, guitar runs, little keyboard or accordion flourishes (such as trilling the notes of a chord), and two- and three-part simple vocal harmonization. These elements are, however, frosting on the cake and the cake itself suffices without the additional toppings!

Guitar

Perhaps the greatest musical contribution of Spain to Latin America is the classical-style flamenco guitar. Impassioned flamenco technique includes strumming in a fan pattern (using all fingers across the strings which may be employed in both directions), tapping the bottom of the instrument, and striking the fingerboard to produce percussive sounds. While this is most appropriate for solo performances, the style, combined with rhythmic forms like the *cha cha*, the polka, and other dances, has had a profound effect on the music of Latino culture in general.

The guitarist usually employs a mixture of different types of strumming (either up or down) as well as picking (a single note), striking the strings, and striking then holding for a percussive muting effect. (Anyone who has heard or even mastered playing Creedence Clearwater Revival's rendition of "Proud Mary" knows exactly what is meant by the last statement!) (See example 8-11.)

Also, Latino musicians take advantage of various possibilities arising from the material with which their guitars are strung: nylon or steel. An upward strum on a steel-string guitar has a far different (brighter, crisper, more percussive) sound than the same movement on a guitar with nylon strings.

example 8-13

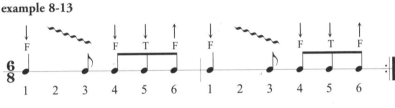

*↓ downward strum

〜 finger fan

F finger strum

T thumb pick

DARING TO PLAY To use musicians' vernacular, what kind of "chops" does it take to play Latino music? William Dexheimer Pharris, a former pastor in El Salvador and a member of the subcommittee on music which edited the Spanish language hymnal *Libro de Liturgia y Cántico*, comments,

"I am a guitarist of modest ability. Still, I feel comfortable accompanying most of these hymns. It's more a matter of understanding the *spirit* of the music than one of having a virtuoso technique. This doesn't deny the place of virtuosity in regard to music, that's not the point here. A great way to come to an understanding of this music is through listening. Go hear concerts of Latin American music. Buy some recordings or get some from your local library. Attend worship at the nearest Hispanic congregation and join in the singing even if you don't understand the words. You'll start to soak up the deep and wonderfully varied spirit of this music!"

To get an idea of some performance possibilities, again begin with an easy form. When a guitarist is accompanying a polka or a waltz, the downbeat (bass, root of the chord) is played with either the thumb (on a nylon string classical guitar) or a pick (on a steel string guitar). The two weaker afterbeats are comprised of descending strummed chords—a basic bluegrass accompaniment. (See example 8-6 of CANTAD AL SEÑOR.) It should be noted that somewhat of the same effect can also be achieved on a synthesizer or keyboard. The strong downbeat might be played in the octave below middle C (or lower) using a string bass sound in the left hand while experimenting with different sounds for the afterbeats in right hand treble clef chords (in root position or first/second inversion). Marimba, piano, or accordion sounds in addition to those of the guitar would be appropriate.

Here's an example of strumming patterns for José Ruiz's setting of the Kyrie, SEÑOR, TEN PIEDAD (WOV 605, LLC 188), which is basically identical to the rhythmic pattern for both the popular "La Bamba" and "Twist and Shout." (See example 8-12; track 47.)

Here's an example of the fanning technique (from the traditional flamenco style) used with the third example of CANTAD AL SEÑOR (a modified *zamba* or *jota*). (See example 8-13.)

Instrumental Groupings

In the realm of instrumental accompaniment there is no one authentic way to perform Latino music as a whole. The availability of instruments and musicians

8

who can play them is certainly a place to begin. The creativity of a single musician or a group of instrumentalists working together can lead to a variety of possibilities as is often the case with Latino groups themselves. A solo guitar or piano can prove quite adequate in many cases. Percussion and solo instruments add variety and color. Common "bands" in the polka tradition consist of keyboards, trap set, brass, woodwinds, bass, and accordion. Other instrumental groups might consist of guitar, fiddle, mandolin, and various percussion instruments. The possibilities are endless. Group singing may be facilitated by a group of individual singers or soloist singing various stanzas; but, in the end, it's *always* the people's song. (See track 48.)

Language

The use of the original language (in speaking of Latino or Hispanic music this would of course be Spanish) certainly lends authenticity to the piece. However, in an Anglo community it is not very likely that people will want to join in singing in Spanish for the entire song. They may, however, find it very interesting to sing a short simple refrain in Spanish, providing they are able to discern the meaning (either through familiarity—"El Señor es mi pastor," for example—or by means of a translation in the bulletin). This often works quite well due to the fact that many Latino songs for worship are refrain

based. Some interesting bilingual combinations might prove satisfying and even fun. The congregation might sing the simple refrain in Spanish and the stanzas in English. Songs like "Cuando el pobre" EL CAMINO ("When the poor ones"—UMH 434, LLC 508) and the popular ALABARÉ (WOV 791, LLC 582) are often done in this way. Another possibility is to have a soloist or choir sing the stanzas in Spanish and the congregation the refrain (also in Spanish). A written translation might be provided for the congregation to read while the stanzas are being sung, thereby actively participating as well. Another possibility is to have the congregation sing the refrain or other selected sections in English, the soloist or choir sing other sections in Spanish, and so on.

Conclusion

Why should Anglo congregations sing Latino music, or any "foreign" music, for that matter? Music reflects culture. Language reflects culture and the thought processes that have given birth to that culture. The experience of singing another's song, of letting images, by means of words, pass through both mind and body, is a unifying experience for the *whole* people of God. The sensation of forming the words of another's language binds us together as a people of God. In singing together, in sharing our songs and our insights, we broaden who we, ourselves, are. We broaden our understanding of each other, our understanding of God. *¡Cantad al Señor!*

---

1. See, *Hymnal: A Worship Book*, Accompaniment Handbook. Elgin, IL: Brethren Press; Newton, KS: Faith and Life Press; Scottdale, PA: Mennonite Publishing House, 1993. Used by permission.

A selected listing of Latino rhythms from *Libro de Liturgia y Cántico* (see pages 630–39: Apéndice de ritmos).

2 Cueca

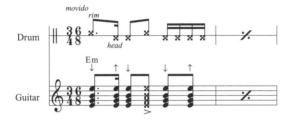

4 Zamba

9 Mazurca

10 Vals

12 Danza

13 Guaracha simplificada

17 Calypso

19 Guajira

25 Bolero rítmico

31 Tango

Masi thi!

Amen, siakudumisa!

Masi thi!

Amen, bawo. Amen, siakudumisa!

South African traditional

How do we make African music part of our worship? Typically, we western, classically trained musicians read the page of written music and turn it into a musical event. There is, of course, another way—the way by which most Africans still learn and pass on their music—and that is the aural/oral method by which one sings or plays back what one first hears. This method assumes freedom in delivery and invites improvisation, two key characteristics of African song. Can western worshipers achieve such freedom, even after the music has been committed to the page? Yes, and it isn't that difficult. This chapter presents some ways to "get inside the music," as Africans say.

To begin, we need to gain a sense for how Africans approach and understand music. Much more than in the United States and Canada, music is woven through all of life. To illustrate, Mark Bangert tells of an incident on a study trip he and his wife Kristi were taking in Africa.

The assembly of nearly three hundred people, mostly between the ages of 17 and 21, became silent and with somber faces, listened to Principal Akyoo announce that the concert by the choir, scheduled for 2:30 P.M. that November day in 1988, would instead occur at 7:30 P.M. Meanwhile, he continued, the entire student body of the Mwika Bible School, seated before him in the chapel, would be mobilized to search for my tape recorder which had been stolen from the principal's own office. Commissioning for this activity took the form of a lengthy prayer.

My wife and I had just arrived a few hours earlier for a five-day stay at this school located on the lush foothills of Mount Kilimanjaro. Our purpose was to hear yet another choir sing the music of Africa and to learn how its conductor, Pelangyo, carried out his vocation as church musician. Our luggage had been placed in the principal's office for retrieval later in the day. Two bags were very important to us; one carried cameras, the other my tape recorder. Usually these bags were never out of sight. But, given the location and the assurances of the principal, we parted ways with these precious tools.

After lunch I sought out the tape recorder for the concert that had been set up just for us and discovered that it and its blue bag were gone. Some reported having seen the "crazy lady" walk off campus with the bag. She was known to wander on to campus from one of the nearby villages and pilfer the belongings of others for her brothers who were rumored to be thieves.

By dusk the students returned from their assigned scouting missions with no information and no tape recorder. The concert went on—never taped. It was at that concert that I first heard "Christ has arisen, alleluia."

The principal had missed the concert. Together with about six others, trusted students and some faculty, he drove to the nearby village to involve the police. Unaware of his plans, we settled into our lodging, a vacated faculty home, and began to plan what it would be like to visit all the remaining places on our itinerary without recording capabilities and without cameras.

About 9:30 P.M. we heard singing and cheering coming from the distance. It came nearer and finally entered the spacious front yard of our "home." Going out we could see in the African night the blue bag held by one of the search party; we were pulled into a quickly organized round dance and together we sang and cheered a hymn of praise. The recorder had come back to life.

A lengthy rehearsal of events revealed that the "crazy lady" had in fact stolen the bag, but since the tape recorder had no external speakers she figured it was of no value. Instead she left the bag and its contents on the porch of the village's mayor.

I learned at least two things: (1) keep the blue bag at my side, and (2) where there is music in Africa, something else is usually going on. To separate music from liturgical behavior, from faith, from acts of mercy, is to dismember it. This music begs for involvement, it begs for participation, it begs for manifestations of the Christian life.

example 9-1

Christ has a - ris - en, al - le - lu - ia.

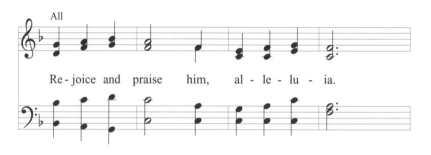

Re - joice and praise him, al - le - lu - ia.

For our re - deem - er burst from the tomb,

e - ven from death, dis - pel - ling its gloom.

Haya and Beyond

T he Tanzanian hymn "Christ has arisen, alleluia" (example 9-1) probably comes from the folk tradition of the Haya nation. This is one of eight musical territories identified by ethnomusicologist Gerhard Kubik[1] as comprising the country of Tanzania. Tanzania is one of fifty-three countries on the continent of Africa, which in turn is three times the size of the United States and which has a population of about 700 million people. Christianity has fared well in Africa, especially in countries such as Tanzania. The vastness of the continent and the broad success of Christianity make it very difficult to describe and to understand the many repertoires of Christian music currently in use across Africa.

Because the music of countries north of the Saharan desert seem to have characteristics linking them with the Middle East and the Mediterranean areas, but more because these countries have smaller populations of Christians, the focus on church musics of Africa is here sub-Saharan.

Development of African Church Music

M usical influences on Africa and within Africa are manifold. External forces, from missionary hymns to the introduction of the guitar by the Portuguese, account for one kind of influence. Another shows up in the common characteristics shared across large parts of the continent and reflects the exchange of techniques, understandings, and instruments across African nations. Employing the skills of the finest musical detectives, scholars have traced migratory patterns of various tunings, for instance, and have uncovered patterns of lively cross-fertilization and the impressive inventiveness of the African peoples.[2]

Sometimes continental developments show distinct similarities to, if not influences from, other global sources. Just what if any

9

connections exist between the equidistant pentatonic tunings of Indonesia and eastern Africa, for instance, is unclear.[3] But such tunings persist in many of the Tanzanian xylophones and Zimbabwean "thumb pianos" *(mbira)*, and suggest that cross-cultural dynamics are more than continental.

Surges of British and German missionaries disembarked on the shores of both western and eastern Africa in the 1850s. They brought with them those worship materials they knew best. Musically that meant isometric hymns in simple four-part settings. If oral tradition is to be believed, and it usually holds for about

two hundred years, these hymns were sung very slowly, providing time to savor both text and harmony. Contemporary hymn singing practices on the European continent support that observation. Accompaniment for these hymns was provided by hand-pumped field organs, local pianos, or brass bands. In many areas Africans adapted to this new repertoire easily and quickly since local musical practices already included singing in thirds and fourths. When translated into local languages, however, especially by those who were amateurs, the hymns evolved into contorted exercises in nonsense and poetic unattractiveness.

From the very beginning the missionaries taught the converts what they knew about music. The locals were eager to learn another musical system. Those showing promise were enrolled in correspondence courses offered

---

AFRICAN SCHOOLS OF MUSIC Among schools that have been preeminent in the study of African church music are:
• The School of Music at the University of Ghana. This prestigious institution was founded in the mid-1950s and continues to be a center where musicians can develop their skills for composing music for the church.
• Bulawayo's Kwanongoma College of Music in present-day Zimbabwe. Supported by the Church of Sweden, researchers here investigated regional music and that of South Africa, and arranged for the publication of several volumes of songs entitled *Sjung med Afrika*, edited by Anna Sjögren.[4] Some of these songs were later translated into English and published under the title *Freedom Is Coming*.[5] Recent political changes in Zimbabwe have resulted in the curtailing of the scope of activity at Kwanongomo. The college currently only trains musicians for the national schools.

• Ruhija School of Music in Tanzania, a few kilometers outside of Bukoba. Established by the local diocese of the Evangelical Lutheran Church of Tanzania, the school for music here, under directors W. Both, first, and later, Joas Kijugo, set out to train musicians for the parish and for academic institutions. Students from this school, taught to lead and write music in western and African styles, have contributed significantly to the growing collections of hymns with traditional tunes and newly composed texts. Foremost among these books of hymns is *Tumshangilie Mungo*,[6] edited by Howard S. Olson, former professor at the magnet seminary in Arusha, Tanzania. This volume contains 152 hymns from all over Tanzania, many translated into English, and is one of the major sources for that body of African hymnody contained in contemporary western hymnbooks. Currently the Ruhija school attracts students from over a dozen countries in eastern and central Africa.

by English schools of music. Some few had the privilege of going away for study either in England or in Germany. Many of these pedagogical patterns persist into the present, especially among those given the vocation of leading the church's song in Africa.

Even with the reverence and admiration African Christians held for their missionary mentors, indigenous musical impulses could not be quieted forever. By the turn of the century there were signs of discontent among those Christians given a solid diet of European hymnody. To break free from such musical bondage (somewhat unintentionally placed on the nationals) meant that local Christians were given an opportunity to reevaluate their own music and dance, long proscribed by their revered teachers and pastors. That called for internal fortitude and reorientation.

Such struggles led to a variety of developments. In Nigeria, for instance, members of the African church movement sought ways to

remold Christianity to meet the cultural needs of the African. They baptized their children with Yoruba names, and they inserted African dance, poetry, and music into their liturgies. Eventually, these stirrings birthed several new denominations and a series of hymnbooks. Elsewhere in Africa, a linking of European and African practices led to the founding of schools in which African music was studied.

The Spectrum of African Song

Even accounting for the hymns that Tom Colvin has collected for the church in Ghana,[7] the pieces published by the Iona community,[8] the songs show up in collections printed by the World Council of Churches[9] or the Lutheran World Federation,[10] westerners see only a minuscule part of African church music. Parishes deeper "in the bush" create and sing music that rarely finds its way into publication.

Choirs learn new pieces from each other at choir festivals. True to the characteristics of such transmission the music often changes when handed from one group to another. Because resources for publication are not readily available in most cases, a strong aural/oral tradition is still at work. This makes impossible both "definitive" editions and stringent pronouncements about performance practice.[11]

For example, a hymn such as NJOO KWETU, ROHO MWEMA ("Gracious Spirit, heed our pleading"—WOV 687) likely began its life as a unison song, but may have been given improvised harmony soon after its inception. (See refrain in example 9-2.)

example 9-2

Nowadays it is presented with complex parts for rattles, bell, and drums, and, following well-beaten paths, may even show up as a solo song with *mbira* (finger piano) accompaniment only.

While local characteristics and differentiations are noticeable to the expert, the African repertoire of hymns available to the average western parish, when taken as a whole, comprise a body of music quite homogenous. Texts, especially in translation, are poetically simple and display a kind of theological naïveté that is biblically rooted, compelling, anchored in experience, and strikingly similar to the early Lutheran chorales. Just as some of the chorales were modeled on subgenres such as pilgrimage songs and songs to

carry the current news, so the African repertoire relies on models provided by praise songs (lauding an individual for some achievement), litigation songs (public announcement of social disruptions), and work songs. The latter gave birth to the so-called hardship songs, secular and sacred. Then, inspired by the African American spirituals that found a home in South Africa in the early part of the century, these hardship songs evolved into the apartheid protest and freedom songs.

Tunes for African hymns often derive from folk songs. Sometimes tunes are newly composed or assembled in a kind of group improvisational setting. Depending upon

example 9-3

Hush, lit- tle Je- sus boy, Al- le- lu- ia. Hush, lit- tle Je- sus boy, Al- le- lu- ia.
Ye- su, u- la - le, Ha- le- lu- ya.   Ye- su, u- la - le, Ha- le- lu- ya.

AFRICA, UNHOMOGENIZED The bulk of African hymnody available through western hymnbooks is from Ghana, Nigeria, South Africa, and Tanzania; as indicated, a few altruistic brokers have made that possible. But the body of existing vocal music is much larger than collections of hymns, for it includes liturgical music such as that prepared by Roman Catholic musicians in Zimbabwe, Tanzania, and Kenya. Because the continent is so vast, representing hundreds of cultures, it is important to understand that local music differs in significant ways. For instance, not all cultures use drums as the mainstay of their musical systems. One of the most important instruments in Zimbabwe is the *mbira* or finger piano. In South Africa the musical bow has had

an important role in the formation of musical thinking. These few examples are meant to caution recipients of African musical gifts against making it all sound alike. Some songs are still best sung as unison pieces without percussion, such as the delightful carol "Hush, Little Jesus Boy" in *Set Free* (Augsburg Fortress, 1993). The first line is shown in example 9-3.

On the other hand, many African Christians are increasingly using and writing music that employs electric guitars and drum sets—all in imitation of what they believe to be the most current western developments. Larger and more experienced choirs also regularly sing standard European choral literature, including Handel's *Messiah* complete with orchestra.

the point of origin, a typical tune originates as a unison piece, usually undergoes presentation with heterophony (simultaneous vocal or instrumental variations of the melody), will often receive improvised harmony in parallel thirds or fourths, or simply be invented along with full four-part hymnbook harmony.

Contemporary editions of these hymns sometimes include harmonizations far more complex than what one would hear in African parish settings.[12] Yet one should not assume that African church music is always and idiomatically simple. Concurrent with the development of indigenous hymnody, African composers, many of whom at first gained their skills through church involvement or sponsorship, have begun to create a sizable body of sophisticated religious art music. Most of this awaits discovery, but promises wide-ranging successes at writing in African, European, and hybrid styles.

Performance Practice

How might North American congregations best enter into the wealth of African sacred music? Three steps might be helpful: know the text, know the music, and join the heartbeat.

Know the Text

To know the text usually means to memorize it, especially the refrains. Such memorization frees one *from* books and *for* clapping and other movements. But to know the text also means to know something about it. Despite our warnings about generalizations, some are nevertheless here offered. Commonly across Africa, songs intended for group singing are arranged in what is known as the call/response form. There are three variations of this process:

• A solo or small group sings through an entire strophe of a song, and then the whole group repeats it. See, for example, HALELUYA! PELO TSO RONA ("Hallelujah! We sing your praises"—WOV 722); the hymn was likely meant to be sung in this fashion. (See refrain in example 9-4.)

• A lead singer begins a phrase and after a few notes the others join in. NENO LAKE

example 9-4

Hal - le - lu - jah! We sing your prais- es, all our hearts are filled with glad - ness. Hal - le - lu- jah! We sing your prais- es, all our hearts are filled with glad - ness.

example 9-5

Leader: Je-sus gave his man-date: All: share the good news

MUNGU ("Listen, God is calling"—WOV 712) is an example. (See example 9-5; track 49.)

● A lead singer, or singers, sings simultaneously with the others though with different text and/or music creating a kind of descant (this form is rare in hymns but prevalent in choral music).[13]

When African hymns are sung giving attention to the call/response form, the leader or leaders might sing without accompaniment, vocal or instrumental, so that the responsive character of the hymn (unison/harmony) is made very clear. One rhythm instrument might play to keep the motion going. Note that the call/response form permits easy memorization of the song by most people. In addition, the form further brings to life the pattern of dialogue inherent to all liturgy, indeed to the nature of the church.

For a case study in "knowing the text," we look at MFURAHINI, HALELUYA ("Christ has arisen, alleluia"—WOV 678), shown at the beginning of this chapter as example 9-1. The text was written by Bernard Kyamanywa from Tanzania. For this text he selects scriptural commentary on the resurrection and puts it into the mouth of an Easter angel (stanzas 3 and 4). To surround that message the poet offers a general Easter pronouncement and an exhortation to praise. Each stanza then ends with an outburst of praise. With that, by the way, the hymn takes its rightful place alongside the texts of Luther

and Watts, for a common pattern in all these hymns is the simple but bold proclamation of the gospel which prompts expressions of praise. To praise God means first of all to know and rehearse what God does.

Each stanza of the hymn ends with the refrain. The form suggests that the first page (the stanza) be sung by a soloist, or female/male duet in octaves. In either case this should happen without accompaniment. Then only the leader or the leader group needs text. The goal is that the refrain then would be sung by all others from memory. Strong, convincing, bold voices are needed to deliver the leader part.

Know the Music

Melodies for African hymns come from a variety of sources. Some are newly composed in a western style. Others are newly composed in an African style, and still others are versions of folk melodies that have been transmitted via aural/oral tradition. Most harmonizations have been added to please western ears or to honor the European harmonic tradition. Finding your way to the more traditional African sound, and learning to internalize it, can occur by attending to these observations:

- African tunes characteristically begin on high notes and descend as the phrase progresses
- traditional tunes are often hexatonic, that is, they employ only six of the notes from the octave implied (e.g., "Jesu, Jesu, fill us with your love"—WOV 765, UMH 432, PH 367; see example 9-6), sometimes are pentatonic, using five notes (e.g., "Listen, God is calling"—WOV 712), or tetratonic, using four notes (e.g., "Gracious Spirit, heed our pleading"—WOV 687)

example 9-6

- any note of an implied octave can be the final note of the tune
- excursions within a tune to another key usually do not occur and are not recognized even if European ears hear them
- melodies progress via a kind of internal, spiraling process.

Some of these characteristics are more noticeable in that layer of hymnody currently deemed a little too strange for current parish consumption. For instance, the Nyaturu tune which goes with the text "Jesus, Jesus Has Conquered Death,"[14] if considered apart from its harmonization, begins above, is hexatonic, and ends on the dominant of an implied (to western ears) F major.

Also in *Set Free* is another hymn which demonstrates a tune trait more common to secular music. The Meru tune used for the text "Shout Alleluia to the Savior"[15] concludes with three measures of "hocket," or momentary breaks in the melodic flow. This tendency manifests an important aspect of African musical sensibility. Hocket provides space for another voice to enter the musical experience, thus creating dialogical musical community, a key concept for all of African musical undertakings.

To return to our case study of "Christ has arisen, alleluia," we have seen that the tune probably comes from the folk musical traditions of the Haya nation. Like other Haya tunes the form of the melody is AABA. Half of the refrain is sung two times by the leader before the people even need to sing. Repetition is at the heart of much of African people's music.

While keyboards are also used in Africa to help the people sing and are useful here to teach both melody and harmony, hymns like this are meant to be sung chorally without accompaniment. Note how the structure makes such a task quite easy if a leader alone sings the stanza. For the refrain the people can sing the tune or add the harmony as indicated.

Join the Heartbeat

Rhythm in Africa, it is said, is closely linked to speech, language, signaling, and the dance.[16] Since Africans dance their identity as it relates to all of life, rhythm is therefore at the heart of existence.

Basic rhythmic "lines" are shaped from two principles: (1) rhythmic division, achieved by the subdivision of larger pulses (a quarter value divided into two eighth values—illustrating a principle very common to western music); (2) rhythmic addition, achieved when the basic eighth value, for instance, is not divided but is compounded by eighth-note increments that form units not alike: two plus two plus three, plus five, plus two, etc. This latter characteristic is similar to the "twos and threes" we have seen operating in Gregorian chant and Genevan Psalter tunes. Even though few of the African tunes imported so far into American worship make use of rhythmic addition, it surely would be stylistically faithful to accompany one of them with a rhythmic counterpoint constructed in this way. (See the suggested bell part in example 9-9 for "Christ has arisen, alleluia.")

This brings the discussion to a core understanding about African music: It takes at least two rhythms to bring a piece of music to life. Traditionally, the compounding of rhythms, or more clearly, the layering of rhythms, was accomplished by the addition of more people. Hence rhythm by definition includes at least two people. You need community to make music.

The density or complexity of layered rhythms is sometimes constructed or recognized by differentiating those rhythms that are slow, those moderately fast, and those fast. Inside these three groups is an underlying pulse, usually signified or implied by the moderately fast rhythmic layer. This would be a good rhythm to bring out by hand clapping.

To illustrate how the layering of rhythms works and functions as the heartbeat of the music, we will once again look at "Christ has arisen, alleluia." Rhythm is at the heart of this music. Haya people live life rhythmically

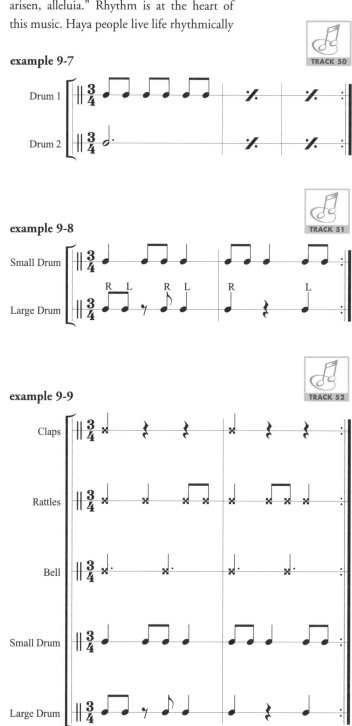

example 9-7

TRACK 50

example 9-8

TRACK 51

example 9-9

TRACK 52

and understand the drum to be the voice of ancestral and royal wisdom. This music cries out for rhythm instruments, all the more so since these instruments will keep the music going in the absence of keyboard.

As this music is brought into being in Africa, rhythm instruments usually begin first, the (lowest, if more than one) drum setting the pace. In the same way these instruments sometimes go beyond the vocal conclusion to add a kind of coda.

Pulse for hymns of this kind is related to normal heartbeat (here, ♩.=58–60) and comprises an entire measure. Quarter notes should be felt as subdivisions of the pulse.

Though at least two rhythms are needed to bring a piece to life, there is in theory no upward limit. Example 9-7 (track 50) shows a minimal approach; a slightly more complex suggestion could be something like example 9-8 (track 51).

> It takes at least two rhythms to bring a piece of music to life.

The moderate rhythmic pattern (such as that suggested above for the large drum) helps to determine at what point the rhythmic patterns begin to repeat themselves. Such repetition is also dependent upon the phrase structure of the song. For the hymn "Christ has arisen, alleluia," the pulse is most strongly felt on the first quarter note of each measure, thus inviting claps at those points. Phrases are four measures long, which suggests a rhythmic grouping of either two measures (as above) or of four measures. As a rule, the length of a pattern comprises from two to six claps (six relates to pieces in 9/8 time).

Slow patterns, such as that for the bell below, are almost like a "drone," and generally introduce a contrary rhythm of some sort (here, two against three). The fast patterns are subject to improvisation, which then partly obliterates the sameness of repetition, making the entire rhythmic presentation an evolving experience.

Example 9-9 is a two-clap, and example 9-10 a four-clap, rhythmic accompaniment for "Christ has arisen, alleluia," built with additional instruments and more complex rhythms. (See also track 52.)

Theoretically, just as the community always makes room for another individual, any piece of music with its layered rhythms can always make room for another rhythm. Sometimes this is achieved (in more complex situations) by the introduction of "apart playing." That is, another drummer might take the rhythm assigned to the large drum and play it beginning one pulse later. This is not suggested for beginners.

example 9-10

It should be clear that drum sets and drum machines torpedo the foundation of African rhythmic purposes for they ignore the importance of the individual in rhythmic compilation, and make no room for a community of "heartbeats."

In one sense rhythms are understood to exist "from eternity," that is, they are thought to be always sounding somewhere. Their incarnation at any given time or place means simply that *this* group is joining the rhythm for awhile only to disengage until another opportunity for its incarnation comes around. There are deep connections to the wider community of ancestors (or the communion of saints) in this approach to rhythm.

There are also some implications for performance. Typically the rhythm instruments begin a piece, usually one by one, before the voices commence. Once everyone is engaged in the ensemble's praise, the rhythms and tempo continue onward without alteration, that is, without ritards or fermatas. At the conclusion, rhythm instruments trail off one by one after the voices have concluded their participation, or some "tag" formula fills the last measure of the piece leading to a single strong pulse on the first beat of the next measure—a kind of farewell to the rhythm.

Instruments

While chordophones (instruments with strings, such as zithers,[17] lutes, and harps) are very common in most parts of Africa, their use in African church music is rare, though theoretically welcomed. Should someone with expertise on these instruments (or perhaps even western equivalents) be available, the melodies of the African songs could be reinforced or embellished with a chordophone.

Aerophones (wind instruments, such as flutes, double reeds, and trumpets) are also common in Africa, but too are rarely used for African church music. As with the chordophones, performance practice would suggest that these instruments accompany the melodies, adding improvisatory embellishments.

Idiophones (self-sounding instruments such as gourd rattles, other shakers, bells, or xylophones) are very common in all parts of Africa and are used in African church music.

IMPROVISATION As is true of the music of many cultures, the information on the page is only a rough outline of what might actually happen. Improvisational outbursts add color and a certain existential quality to the praise that comes from the page. They range from variations of drum patterns (as described in this chapter), to ululations (a kind of yodeling effect), to alternative clapping patterns, to foot stomping, or to descants from talented voices. Freedom and ability to generate these additions come with experience and repetition.

Membranophones (instruments with a membrane of some sort, such as drums) are used all over Africa, though their relative importance in local music varies from nation to nation.

> Christian community means that everyone participates; no one can just sit and listen.

African inventiveness shows up in the variety of designs for drums: slit drums made from hollowed-out logs, drums with a single head, drums with double heads, so-called hour-glass drums (which change pitch as the head is stretched tight), and sets of drums that parallel family structure. Symbolism of drums is quite profound among certain peoples.

Issues abound here as western church musicians in the European/American tradition seek to bring African church music off the page into actual praise. The recording industry has helped to give us jitters about performing Bach cantatas unless "period" instruments are used. What does one do with African pieces from places as diverse as western Tanzania, Ghana, and Zimbabwe?

The use of genuine African instruments brings the experience of African church music a little closer to its origins. But such concerns are ultimately peripheral. Of more importance to the spirit of African church music is the distribution of the rhythmic parts among several people, for the layering of individual parts is a deliberate manifestation of relationship within the community and a sign of the bonds rhythm creates even across cultures.

AUTHENTIC INSTRUMENTS   If you want to try for a more authentic sound, you can purchase shakers and rattles in African specialty shops scattered across North America. You should know, though, that most of these instruments come from larger supply houses that import them directly from entrepreneurs who also supply the souvenir stalls like those in the alleyways of Nairobi. Several local suppliers, such as Spirit Drum World[18] or Dove Music[19] have a wide variety of African drums for sale at sizable prices. Their origin is uncertain. A trip to Africa will yield a multitude of "souvenir" drums, but the finer instruments are, like Bösendorfer pianos, few and difficult to find. So, what difference does it make whether one uses drums and rattles made by professional drum makers from Africa, or instruments from a local supplier, or equivalents? Probably very little. Congas of various sizes work very well, as do some of the deeper "toms" of drum sets. In any case it is useful to remember that African drummers play with and without sticks. Rattles from a specialty shop serve well, as do maracas—a Latin American version of rattles. African double bells are plentiful in well-equipped percussion shops, and a set of claves can be substituted for the bells.

Leadership

It is worth stressing again that African church music is vocal and essentially unrelated to the keyboard. Therefore leadership from the keyboard is uncharacteristic and tends to rob the music of its charm.

How then, does this music come into being? First, at least one percussion instrument makes it possible to maintain tempo and to offer a rhythm complimentary to, but different from, the rhythm of the song. Like a master drummer, the church musician would be the obvious person to play and lead the percussion. Second, a choral ensemble should be placed close enough to the people in order to provide leadership as well as harmony. Behind these suggestions let it be known the hands are to be understood as a primary percussion instrument, and people should be invited to enter the clap patterns of the songs.

Not all songs require percussion. Some, in a more western lyrical style, can be sung like conventional hymnody. But even these songs fare best when they are supported by a choral group alert to keeping the tempo moving.[20]

As a last resort in all of these and similar examples, the keyboard (preferably piano, because of its percussive qualities) could be used to support and encourage the singing of the people. The goal in such cases would be to wean the people away from such dependence as quickly as possible.

Conclusion

Entering African church music provides an opportunity for church musicians, choral groups, and the Christian assembly to discover for the first time, or once again, the way musical presentation can be a manifestation of the baptismal community. Africans offer the rest of the church this challenge: Christian community means that everyone participates; no one can just sit and listen. There is always room for another rhythm, a clap, or a heterophonous rendition of the melody. In Africa there are no monotones.

Then too, the more we are led into that arena where there is always room for the voice or rhythm of yet another baptized individual, the more we might sense our mutual dependence and responsibility. In other words, praise and the grace-filled life are of the same fabric, they constitute a single musical idea. The "concert" heard at Mwika didn't end until the late night hour when the tape machine was returned. This musical linkage of liturgy and life, a centuries-old prophetic concern, sometimes lost through the singular pursuit of beauty, now through African church music presents itself anew for serious allegiance in our own time.

1. Peter Cooke, "East Africa: An Introduction," *Africa*, Ruth Stone, ed., vol. 1 of *The Garland Encyclopedia of World Music* (New York: Garland, 1998), p. 599.

2. Gerhard Kubik, "Intra-African Streams of Influence," *Africa*, pp. 295ff.

3. Mireille Rakotomalala, "Performance in Madagascar," *Africa*, pp. 781ff.

4. See, A. B. Stockholm, *Carl Gehrmans Musikförlag*, 1982 ff. Vols. 2 and 3 contain work songs and other non-liturgical material.

5. Anders Nyberg, ed., (Fort Lauderdale: Walton Music Corp., 1984).

6. 6th ed. (Nairobi: Lutheran Theological College, 1987)

7. Tom Colvin, ed., *Fill Us with Your Love* (Carol Stream, IL: Agape, 1983).

8. John Bell, ed., *Many and Great*, vol. 1 of *Songs of the World Church* (Chicago: GIA, 1992) and *Sent by the Lord*, vol. 2 of *Songs of the World Church* (Chicago: GIA, 1992).

9. I-to Loh, ed., *African Songs of Worship* (Geneva: World Council of Churches, 1986); *In Spirit and In Truth* (Geneva: World Council of Churches, 1991); and Per Harling, ed., *Worshipping Ecumenically* (Geneva: World Council of Churches, 1995).

10. *Supplement to Laudamus* (Geneva: Lutheran World Federation, 1990).

11. The accuracy of transcriptions varies as well. "We thank you, Father," a hymn originating with the Bena peoples of Tanzania appeared in *Lead Us, Lord* (Minneapolis: Augsburg, 1977) and in *Songs of the People* (Minneapolis: Augsburg, 1986) as a tune in 3/4 meter; while in Africa in 1988 Mark Bangert heard it consistently sung in 6/8, which provides the hymn with interesting syncopations.

12. See, e.g., "Hear Us, Abba Father," in *Set Free*, Howard Olson, ed. (Minneapolis: Augsburg Fortress, 1993), p. 44.

13. See, J. H. Kwabena Nketia, *The Music of Africa* (New York: Norton, 1974), pp. 140–43.

14. *Set Free*, p. 14.

15. See, "I Truly Am the Vine," *Set Free*, p. 28.

16. Barbara Hampton, "Identities: Music and Other African Arts," *Africa*, pp. 105–106.

17. Information, identification, and illustrations of the African zither and all the other instruments named in this section are available in Curt Sachs's, *The History of Musical Instruments* (New York: Macmillan, 1940), in the *New Groves Dictionary of Music*, and in *The Music of Africa*, pp. 67–110.

18. Catalog available from 15445 Ventura Blvd., Suite 31, Sherman Oaks, CA 91403.

19. Catalog available from P.O. Box 08286, Milwaukee, WI 53208.

20. *The Music of Africa*, p. 33.

CHAPTER *10*

Sound a mystic bamboo song;

raise a changing lyric voice;

Beat the drum and play the flute;

let the Asian church rejoice.

Bill Wallace

ASIAN

The church music of Asia is as broad and diverse as the region. It includes the complex and the simple; the traditional and the newly composed; unaccompanied song and that incorporating the sounds of flute, plucked strings, drums, cymbals, and more. At times, a completely authentic sound is not easily notated in western systems, and the original interrelationship between text and tune may be lost in translation. Yet for all of that, here is hymnody that is well worth learning and leading in our churches. In contrast to other forms of hymnody, Asian song is focused much more on the melody, though not to the exclusion of other facets. The melody, often cyclical in form, both supports and takes its shape from the text. One will frequently notice a deliberate holding back of musical language and resources, a spareness that helps to heighten attention to that which is present. This music is a fresh addition to our congregations' repertoire, and can greatly enrich our worship when presented with sensitivity.

Upon entering a home in Taiwan, a guest removes her shoes as she crosses the threshold at the front door. The host gives the guest a pair of sandals to wear while in the home. These sandals are like the ones the host also wears in the home. Guest and host alike use these comfortable sandals as we would use slippers. The sandals at the door are a sign of welcome for the guest and a gesture of equality between guest and host. The sandals are a sign of hospitality; they also serve to remind the guest that she is not at home.

This distinction between guest and host offers a helpful way for a non-Asian to consider Asian song. It is important to put on the guests' sandals, to learn about and respect

10

lations of the English hymns. Now Asian tunes that reflect the culture and languages of Asian Christians are being sought and cultivated.

The work of the Asian Institute for Liturgy and Music and the Christian Conference of Asia produced the hymnal *Sound the Bamboo* in 1990. This significant collection brings together 280 hymns and liturgical responses from every region of Asia. With a new second edition now in preparation this hymnal has served to collect the music of a diverse area in one resource. Together with *All Nations Praise*, a Taiwanese hymnal published in 1996, it is now possible to find Asian hymnody for the seasons of the church year, for themes like culture and creativity, and for portions of the liturgy like the Kyrie.

Hymns from *Sound the Bamboo* are finding their way into North American hymnals. "God created heaven and earth" (UMH 151), "Jaya ho" (UMH 478), "Sing with hearts" (PH 484), and "When twilight comes" (WOV 663) all appeared first in that resource.

I-to Loh has spawned a generation of Asian church music composers through his own ethnomusicological work. Seeking out indigenous tunes from all over Asia, Loh has adapted and arranged tunes and provided texts for a multitude of new congregational songs. Speaking about his work, Dr. Loh says, "I develop a new song out of a motive of a folk song. I never use the whole song. This retains the original color without transferring the whole meaning of a previous song."[1]

what one can about another's culture, to try them on for size. At the same time, one remembers that these are not her shoes, she remains a guest in another's home, the song is a piece of another's culture. The shoes of hospitality welcome the stranger. Receive the songs of this region as a gift and sign of hospitality. "Remember the sandals from your feet, for the place on which you are standing is holy ground" (Exod. 3:5).

The Asian church is finding its own lyric voice. Today indigenous tunes of Asia are beginning to enter worship in Christian Asian churches. Asian melodies are taking their place alongside the western tunes that the missionaries brought to Asia from the west. Through the work of the schools like the Asian Institute for Liturgy and Music in Manila, Philippines, and Tainan Theological College and Seminary in Tainan, Taiwan, church musicians from all over Asia receive training in indigenous composition and performance practice. Through the work of composers and ethnomusicologists like Dr. I-to Loh and Dr. Francisco Feliciano, folk tunes and original melodies are finding a new home in Christian worship.

Asian texts and tunes are coming together in new musical languages. Until recently, most Asian Christian hymns used western tunes introduced by the Scottish, British, or later, American missionaries. These tunes were simply fitted with texts that were trans-

I-TO LOH   I-to Loh is currently the President of Tainan Theological College and Seminary (Presbyterian) in Tainan, Taiwan. He is an ethnomusicologist who has done extensive research on the instruments and musical styles of many Asian regions. Born in 1936, Dr. Loh is a Taiwan native. He is a hymn writer and composer, arranger, and hymnal editor. He was professor at the Asian Institute for Liturgy and Music in Manila, Philippines, before his appointment in Taiwan. He was the general editor of *Sound the Bamboo* (1990) and *All Nations Praise* (1995). Loh is currently working on the second edition of *Sound the Bamboo*.

I-to Loh shares with Martin Luther a pastoral sensitivity about cultural change and a sense of the importance of the compatibility of text and tune. In making changes that would allow the German parishioner to understand and participate in the Mass, Luther found that changes in musical form necessarily followed. In using poetic texts that translated the portions of the Ordinary of the Mass into German, Luther sought a new musical form which matched the declamation of the German language. The Latin chant was not an appropriate vehicle for the German language. The rhythmic chorale is the result of Luther's insistence on new musical clothing for the German text.

So, too, Dr. Loh sees the need to bring Asian texts and Asian tunes together. He, like Luther, seeks out poets and composers who write in Asian idioms. He encourages the development of an Asian voice from the cultural traditions of Asia's varied regions.

In looking at an Asian text with an Asian tune it is important to consider the relationship between them. In many cases there is a particularly close connection between Asian speech and song. Many Asian languages have a tonal nature. Pronouncing a word with tonal characteristics demands attention to its characteristics of pitch. A word can have different meanings depending on whether its pitch rises or falls as it is pronounced.

Thus, the music in an Asian tune can be an extension of tonal patterns already present in the hymn's text. "Music can be developed through natural speech."[2] In ways that English cannot render, there is an interrelationship between such Asian texts and tunes, which serve as mutual enhancement. Here there is a possibility of a symbiotic relationship between text and tune, which an Asian text and a western tune can simply not provide.

This close connection between spoken word and melody is a key to the performance of this music. When approaching an Asian hymn, melody is of primary importance and demands first consideration. "Asians treasure the beauty of singing through their unique timbre, melodic shapes and subtle ornaments."[3] Melody is the building block upon which other musical elements may be added. Sometimes melody and text alone may constitute a hymn's delivery.

There are two cautions to consider when a western-trained musician approaches Asian music. The first is a tendency to overlay western harmonic patterns on an Asian melody. Harmony is not necessarily implied for an Asian tune, and even less seldom is functional western harmony implied. By adding a chordal structure to an Asian melody, a western musician may set up a harmonic form to the tune which was not originally intended.

10

Unison, octave doubling, or open intervals more often characterize accompanying lines than does a chordal structure.

A second caution is a tendency to generalize about Asian music. Asia is a group of regions and countries with greatly diverse musical cultures. In the context of this book, the term *Asian* encompasses an area roughly from China south and east to Indonesia. From the complex raga of the music of India to the simple beauty of a Taiwanese pentatonic melody there is wide melodic expression. From the multi-layered sound of a gamelan orchestra to the singular beauty of the bamboo flute there is a wealth of timbre. While there are certain trends and values that tend to recur in music of many Asian countries, it is important not to overgeneralize or apply musical principles randomly from one region to another.

The hymns considered in this chapter can all be found in the Asian hymnal *Sound the Bamboo*, and most are also in one or more of the North American hymnals *With One Voice*, *The Presbyterian Hymnal*, or *The United Methodist Hymnal*. It is important to note that the written notation is usually a transcription from an oral tradition. In some cases, Asian hymn tunes are adapted from folk and traditional songs of a country or region. Not only is the written notation already a reduction of an oral tradition, the musical score also freezes in time a melody that may adapt and change through its various presentations.

In addition, while melodies are presented in western written notation, the original melodies are not always based on a twelve-note chromatic scale. Pentatonic scales and equidistant five- and seven-note scales are only some of the varieties of scales found in various Asian regions. "Traditional Asian melodies use intervals of various sizes larger or smaller than major or minor seconds or thirds."[4] Such variations cannot be represented in standard western notation.

In capturing a melody in a written form and presenting it in standard western score, some of the rhythmic and melodic subtleties are lost. It is important to see the score as a reflection, not a perfect representation, of an Asian song.

Performance Practice

In preparing to present an Asian hymn, consideration should be given to issues of melody, monophony and polyphony,

> In Asian hymns it is melody that is of primary importance and demands first consideration.

ASIA It is important to remember that "Asia" is a western term for a collection of regions, cultures, languages, and countries. While it is helpful to be able to speak about this region as a conglomeration, there may be very little that can be said about music in Asia as a whole. The rhythmic drive of the Korean drum is completely different in style from the gentle melody of the Pakistani nose flute. The complex scale of a Bangladeshi song is a world away from the seven-note equidistant scale of some Thai songs. Many Asian languages are tonal. This gives a musical character to some Asian cultures. While music from Asia will differ from western music in significant ways, finding that difference will not mean that all Asian music will follow. The parts of the whole within Asia contain great diversity.

SOUND THE BAMBOO This 1990 hymnal is a joint project of the Asian Institute for Liturgy and Music in Manila and the Christian Conference of Asia. Dr. I-to Loh is the general editor. The hymnal contains 280 hymns, liturgical songs, and canticles from many regions of Asia. Malaysia, Burma, Bangladesh, Korea, and Thailand are just a few of the cultures represented here by hymnody. Especially helpful are the editor's notes in the beginning of the hymnal. These give helpful performance practice suggestions for pronunciation, singing, and accompanying the hymns. There are also suggestions for selecting the western instruments best suited to accompany Asian song. This hymnal is available through Dove Music and the Hymn Society Book Service, among other sources.

rhythm and the use of instruments, other instrumentation, vocal range, and text. None of these elements alone is sufficient. A hymn should be approached in a way that considers all of these elements, both individually and in their relationship to each other. The following sections will consider each aspect individually and demonstrate it with a musical example.

Melody

Consider the Pakistani Kyrie KHUDAYA, RAHEM KAR (SB 120). Here is a melody that is complete when sung by a single voice, choir, or congregation, and needs no instrumental support. (See example 10-1; track 53.) In fact, an instrumental accompaniment may obscure the nature of the melody.

The melody has a haunting, modal character in its opening phrases. The / sign in front of a note indicates a vocal slide from the previous note to the one indicated. The syllable changes as the slide to the new note begins. This is a deliberate slide with time taken before arriving at the new pitch. This slide adds to the emotional character of the melody and conveys the meaning of the text "Lord, have mercy."

The \ sign in back of a note, on "rahem" in the next to the last line, indicates that the slide to the next note takes place before the change in text to the new syllable. The written grace notes are treated in a similar fashion. They are not hurried, but added as the text changes to the new syllable. These ornaments have the effect of softening the rhythmic pulse. Unlike music from other parts of the globe, here the pulse does not

example 10-1

TRACK 53

10

example 10-2

Lone - ly the boat, sail - ing at sea,

tossed on a cold, storm - y night;

drive the melody. Rhythm rather becomes responsive to the slight changes in time that the ornaments naturally create. *Sound the Bamboo* suggests a quarter-note pulse of about 88.

Another feature of this Pakistani style is the singing of the "m" sound on "rahem." The "m" is closed into a hum upon reaching the syllable "hem." This close should occur no later than the second eighth note of duration (♪ ♪). The hum is sustained in the singing through the length of the note rather than the sustaining of the preceding vowel. This is repeated wherever "rahem" recurs.

The melodic high point is reached on "Christ, have mercy." Here the melody rises to a high D and is sustained there through-out a measure. This marks the place of greatest melodic and emotional intensity. Sung in full voice with a *forte* dynamic, this line carries the impassioned plea of the singer to Christ. The melody gradually falls back to its opening range as the emotional pitch also falls. The melody returns to its opening motive with its humble request, "Lord, have mercy."

Bringing out the melodic enhancements serves to emphasize the pleading nature of this piece. Keeping the pulse flexible and responsive to the melody allows the melody to breathe and speak without a rhythmic drive. A light percussion stroke with a triangle or

example 10-3

Voice I
Lift up your eyes and see God's face full of

Voice II
Lift up and see God's face full of

grace for - ev - er; may the Lord,

grace for - ev - er; may the Lord,

might - y God, bless and keep you for - ev - er.

might - y God, bless and keep you for - ev - er.

finger cymbal may be added at the interval of every eight beats. This adds a larger cycle of rhythm to the melody.

KAHM KAHM HAHN BOM SANAOON ("Lonely the boat"—PH 373) is a Korean melody. (See example 10-2.) This is a rather somber, lyrical hymn. *Sound the Bamboo* suggests ♪=126 for this hymn. The 6/8 meter seems to convey the constant rolling of the sea, which is the hymn's theme. Here the hymn conveys the deep loneliness, fear, and despair that comprise a suffering life. The tempo is slow, pondering, and mournful. The melody reflects the pleading nature of the hymn's text.

A monophonic treatment of an Asian tune keeps the focus on the beauty of the melody. It also signals the importance of the

relationship between text and tune. Even though the connection with tonal language is lost when sung in English, a single-line melody allows for focus on the text without other complicating musical factors.

Monophony and Polyphony

Not all Asian tunes are rendered monophonically and unaccompanied. "May the Lord, mighty God" (PH 596) is a two-voice Mandarin hymn of Benediction. (See example 10-3.) The second voice enters as the first voice begins a second stanza, and provides counterpoint to it. Open fourths and fifths characterize the intervals between the two voices. *Sound the Bamboo* suggests that a few female voices sing the second voice. The open character of the harmonies created by the two voices renders a nonwestern flavor. These voices do not imply functional western harmony. Rather, their spareness should be left, creating a feeling of openness and transparency, and a lack of harmonic drive.

JAYA HO (UMH 478) is another hymn that uses independent vocal parts. (See example 10-4; track 54.) The opening refrain is set against a melodic ostinato, sung by the basses. In the verses there is a call/response pattern between the leader and the people. Here the congregation sings in three-part harmony in its responses. The harmonies created form major chords and open fifths. This homophonic treatment centers around a B♭-major chord. There isn't any harmonic motion away from that B♭ center. Rather, it serves as a centering harmony for the melodic variation of the leader's part. This hymn will be considered further in the next section.

example 10-4

*Ja-ya ho ja-ya ho ja-ya ho ja-ya ho ja-ya ho ja-ya ho

Leader
We come be-fore thee, O Great and Ho-ly,
Te - re sa - na mukh ham hain . . a - te.

O Great and Ho- ly.
Ham hain . . a - te.

*pronounced Jáhee-ya

10

Rhythm and the Use of Instruments

In some Asian hymns a steady rhythmic pulse is intrinsic to a hymn's performance. The hymn JAYA HO is a well-known hymn of victory in India. The hymn uses a traditional Hindi melody. "Jaya ho" means "victory be to you." The bass voices set a steady eighth-note pulse singing "jaya ho" throughout the refrain. In India the tabla, a pair of pitched drums, would provide a typical rhythmic accompaniment to such a hymn. While tabla playing is a complex art requiring intensive training, a simple drumbeat played with the hands could be added to create the flavor of the tabla. A rhythmic pattern like ♪ ♫ ♪ ♪ ♫ ♫ ♪ ♪ would undergird the hymn's rhythmic character and would complement the bass singers without duplicating their singing rhythm.

This is a lively, energetic hymn, which requires a rhythmic singing style. *Sound the Bamboo* suggests a tempo of ♪=c. 200 for this hymn. The eighth-note rests in the bass ostinato are a clue to the articulation. Singing should be separated with a marcato style. Phrases are short, and all rests should be observed.

The drum is also used widely in Korean song. The *changgo* is a Korean double-headed drum shaped like an hourglass. It employs a variety of striking techniques, with a padded mallet, a bamboo stick, and hands. This adds rhythmic complexity and interest to Korean song. The *changgo* is one of the chief percussion instruments of Korea and is used in folk and traditional Korean song. A rhythmic pattern under the melody of ♪ ♪ ♪ ♪ ♫ ♫ would be typical for the *changgo*. The drum fills out the measure where the vocal line slows and rests, propelling the singer into the next phrase. "Joy in truth will set the world free" (SB 66) is an example of a Korean song that typifies this style. The meter is 6/8, alternating with 9/8 in the refrain. (See example 10-5.)

Korean song is typified by an aggressiveness of spirit. This spirit is found in the singing style, which uses a large range of dynamics, and in the drumming technique, which adds rhythmic interest and complexity.

example 10-5

CHING

A small cymbal commonly used in east Asian music.

Gongs, ching, and cymbals are often used in Asian melodies for rhythmic color. Such sounds give the impression of rhythmic points of light, which punctuate the melodic line. Rather than adding a rhythmic accent on a downbeat, a gong or ching might be added at the end of a phrase, or in between two phrases, as a sort of interspersed timbre. In a cyclical melody, such a sound serves as a signal of the melodic cycle's return. "Amen, hallelujah" (WOV 792) is based on a Javanese melody. (See example 10-6.) A small gong could be sounded on each dotted half note and a large gong on the last note, with the melody

beginning immediately again. Such a technique is used in a gamelan orchestra, where the large gong signals a return to the beginning of the melody.

Small cymbals, called *ching*, accompany Thai song alternating a ringing and damped technique. SOI SON TUD ("Come, all of you"—UMH 350) is an example of a Thai folk song. Cymbals and gongs add punctuation to the melodic line, often in an unaccented portion of a measure. Acceptable substitutes would be finger cymbals and a triangle.

Other Instrumentation

Other instruments may be added to an Asian melody. The bamboo flute is found in many forms throughout Asia. It is most commonly found as a transverse flute with the blow-hole about one third of the way along its body. The bamboo flute has a distinct and beautiful tone color. The sound is reedier than the western flute and less breathy than a recorder. However, either a recorder or flute would be an adequate substitute and an appropriate way to introduce or accompany many Asian melodies.

A Chinese instrument called the *erh-hu* is a two-stringed instrument played like a cello. Its range is similar to the viola, and its sound has a stronger presence than the viola. The *erh-hu* is often used to play the melody in the tenor range as an accompaniment to the melody. The viola or cello could be an acceptable substitute for the *erh-hu*. The advantage of a stringed instrument for Asian song is the possibility of showing the slides and lengthened grace notes that the vocal

example 10-6

A - men, hal - le - lu - jah!   A - men, hal - le - lu - jah!

We praise your name, O Lord.   A - men, hal - le - lu - jah!

GAMELAN ORCHESTRA   A gamelan orchestra is part of the traditional music of Indonesia. The orchestra is a collection of metallophones of five bars each, pitched gongs, and assorted percussion instruments, including a drum. There are often twenty or more players in an orchestra. The music, built on a pentatonic scale, is based on a series of patterns that different instruments play in cycles. The largest gong is used to signal a return to the beginning of the cycle. The complexity of the music is based on the number of different patterns going on at one time and the length of the cycle. Gamelan technique is used in Christian churches as a performance group for the playing of hymns and other literature.

character often demands. "Since most of these (melodic) features cannot be reproduced by western keyboard instruments, they are not ideal instruments for accompaniment. However, flutes of any type, lutes (bowed or plucked) and/or drums may greatly enhance the singing and reinforce the beauty of ethnic styles."[5]

A guitar may sometimes function well as an accompanying instrument. It can replicate the sound color of a plucked lute with a picking, rather than a strumming, style. The Maundy Thursday hymn "When twilight comes" (WOV 663) demonstrates the use of guitar for accompaniment. (See example 10-7; track 55.) Francisco Feliciano wrote the melody, indicating two guitars for accompaniment. One guitar is strummed while the other is plucked. *The Presbyterian Hymnal* (547) includes the two-guitar accompaniment. The effect of the accompaniment is an undulating, undergirding support for the melody. Such an accompaniment does not obscure the melody but allows it to continue to take a leading place in the sound.

For this hymn the addition of an instrument to double the melody would be helpful to reinforce congregational singing. A flute or stringed instrument could play the melodic line, which is not present in the guitar parts. A song leader could also facilitate leading the melody for the congregation. *Sound the Bamboo* recommends ♪=**160** for this hymn.

example 10-7

Text: Moises Andrade, tr. © James Minchin
Music: © Francisco Feliciano, admin. Asian Institute for Liturgy & Music. Used by permission.

VOCAL RANGE Many Asian hymns employ a vocal range of well over an octave. Such a large range may at first appear to be a block for a congregation accustomed to melodies that lie within the octave. However, if the piece is learned in melodic units, a phrase at a time, with the high points noted, congregations may be surprised to find that the melodies are quite accessible. Led to the high point in a melody, a congregation can learn to build intensity and release into its singing style. In this process they will also learn about the construction and delivery of an Asian vocal line.

Piano and organ are not the best choices for leading Asian song. The keyboard is unable to render many of the subtleties of this song, especially the ornaments and slides. There is also the temptation to add a harmonic structure as a left-hand accompaniment on a keyboard. When a keyboard is the only choice, use it sparingly, and treat it mainly as a melodic instrument. (See track 56.)

The accompaniment for "Lord, your hands have formed" provided in *With One Voice* gives an example of the discreet use of piano for accompanying an Asian hymn. (See example 10-8.) The accompaniment is spare and does not force the melody into western functional harmony. The piano part adds some of the rhythmic pulse that will help keep a congregation together without becoming rhythmically driving. The piano accompaniment should always allow for the flexibility and dominance of the vocal line. A few guidelines to keep in mind when using the piano or organ with an Asian melody:

- Use the right hand to lead the melody. Try the melody an octave higher on the piano for variety. On the organ, try various solo stops. Try a 4' flute only on the melody.
- Use the left hand (and pedal on the organ) sparingly. Less can be more here. Open fifths, repeated and varied slightly at a slow rhythmic pulse (every half note or whole note), may be enough to undergird the melody.
- Avoid harmonies that form a western harmonic progression (e.g., I–IV–V–I). Leave harmonies open. Use open fourths and fifths rather than complete triads.
- Let the piano be a strictly melodic instrument at times, doubling the melody. It isn't always necessary to add any harmony.

Vocal Range

DAPIT HAPON ("When twilight comes"— example 10-7) exemplifies the cyclic nature of many Asian melodies. The melody begins, as it ends, on E. The first half of the piece gradually

example 10-8

1 Lord, your hands have formed this world,
2 Yours the soil that holds the seed,
3 Like a mat you roll out land,

ev - 'ry part is shaped by you—
you give warmth and mois - ture, too.
space to build for us and you

wa - ter tum - bling o - ver rocks, air and
Sprout-ing blos - soms, crops and buds, trees and
earth - ly homes and, bet - ter still, homes for

sun - light: each day's signs that you make all things new.
plants: the sea - son's signs that you make all things new.
Christ: the tru - est sign that you make all things new.

Text: © James Minchin, admin. Asian Institute for Liturgy & Music. Used by permission.
Music: Ikalahan (Philippines) traditional; arr. © 1995 Augsburg Fortress

rises to the high point of B on the word "nest." From the halfway point the melody gently falls back, with melodic stress points at B, A, G, F♯, and coming to rest on E. This rising and falling motion of the melody also creates the tension and release that the voice naturally follows. As the melody rises, the vocal intensity does also. As the melody descends, the voice relaxes. The melody ends as it begins, in repose, in the lower register of the voice.

This creation of a gradually ascending melodic line, composed of the accumulation of smaller melodic phrases and reaching a melodic climax at the highest note, is a basic building block of Asian song. Describing this hymn, Francisco Feliciano likens this phenomenon of a musical phrase to a bird that comes to rest on a branch. The branch bends as the bird lights upon it, then comes to rest. Then the bird flies on to another branch.[6] This collection of melodic units often creates a rather large vocal range for the song. It is not unusual to find the range of an eleventh (an octave plus a fourth) for an Asian hymn. "When twilight comes" employs the range of a tenth.

Text

A final musical example, which employs such undulating melodic contours, is "Lord, your hands have formed" (WOV 727). (See example 10-8.) The piece begins and ends with the melodic fragment B–C♯–E. From this low B, the melody rises to G♯, then B, then finally

reaches the E, an octave and a fourth above the starting note. From this high mid-point the melody begins its descent, pausing briefly on B, then E, and finally repeating the opening B–C♯–E motive.

The images in the text convey a movement similar to the melody. "Water tumbling over rocks," "sprouting blossoms, crops and buds" seem to be musically depicted in the melody's rising and falling. This text shows a God who participates in the work of creation with human hands. The image of God rolling out the land like a mat would be a familiar image in traditional Asian homes. Parents roll out their mats each

agogic accent	A durational accent, usually effected by shortening the previous note while keeping the accented note on the beat, thus creating a brief lift before the accented note.
functional harmony	Harmony built around the tonic (I), dominant (V), and subdominant (IV), in which the western-trained ear expects to hear a progression, as I–IV–V–I. This harmonic language is not the norm in all parts of the world, and the western musician should beware of imposing it where it is alien.
scale	A collection of pitches arranged in order from high to low or low to high. In western music, the seven-note diatonic scale is predominant, in which the octave is divided into two half steps and five whole steps. In other regions of the world, other scales may be more common. Among them are the pentatonic (employing five notes of the diatonic scale), tetratonic (four notes of the diatonic scale), or various equidistant scales, in which the octave is divided evenly into five, seven, or other number of intervals. These equidistant scales will usually result in intervals other than half or whole steps, and therefore will sound odd to western ears.

evening for their children. This loving human action is like God's divine action in creating the land for all humans.

This traditional tune from the Northern Luzon of the Philippines could be accompanied with a flute. The text is based on Psalm 24, making it useful for liturgical worship, or simply as a song of praise. *Sound the Bamboo* recommends a pulse of ♩=112.

Conclusion

In rendering an Asian song in a western context it may be helpful to consider some of the distinguishing marks of Asian tunes. While serving as guides, they are not uniform standards that can be applied to every case. They serve as reminders that the Asian musical palette has some different items from a western musical palette.

A first mark is the interest in spareness in Asian art. The deliberate limiting of the musical palette serves to heighten the experience of the inherent beauty of the music. We noted this in the attention to the musical line and its fluid ornamentation without a complicating harmonic structure. Beauty is found in the simple, unadorned melody sung by the human voice. The use of a five-note scale also shows the choice of limiting the musical language. Such limitations are not less developed musical forms. Rather, in the expression of a confined musical form, the beauty within that form may emerge from it.

Another mark is the cyclical character to many melodies, which end as they began.

There can often be a cyclical character to a melody which simply begins again as soon as it finishes. There is often not a functional harmonic movement that drives a melody to a conclusion. We noted this in the use of a gong to signal a return to another cycle of the melody. We also noted this in the undulating character of a melody that ends with the same motive with which it began.

A third value is the importance of symbol. The symbolic character of Asian song appeared between the text and tune of "Lord, your hands have formed." The ability of a musical phrase to render a visual image was shown in this hymn. Feliciano's comments about the musical phrase resembling a bird landing on a branch points to this same symbolic relationship between a musical phrase and a visual image. Images of creation are often portrayed in the texts of Asian song, and their reflection may be portrayed in the melodic line.

I-to Loh, in the World Council of Churches worship resource *Worshipping Ecumenically*, notes some overarching qualities of Asian song. "Asian music treasures diversified tone colours, melodic shapes, subtle ornaments and rhythmic force. Harmony as understood in Western music is almost totally absent."[7] Awareness of these qualities informs the presentation of an Asian hymn in a western context.

Performance practice of Asian hymns should allow these qualities to be clearly presented. Simple instrumentation, highlighting string and flute sounds, can provide a rich and expressive tone color. Attention to the rising and falling character of melodies can provide shape to the larger melodic line.

10

Listening and experimenting with vocal ornaments, like the vocal slide, can add an important nuance to many melodies. Careful use of the drum can add a rhythmic force important to some singing styles. Keeping a melody free from an obscuring harmonic structure can bring the singer to focus on its singular melodic beauty.

Within the tremendous variety of Asian melody there is consistent attention to the beauty of a single melodic line. Within the wide range of expression found in hymn texts there is still a close relationship between text and tune. Within the various ways a melody unfolds there is still a sense of the cyclic nature of a melody which comes back to itself.

As North Americans begin encountering Asian hymnody, there are surprises that await the guest. Here is the beauty of attention to the spareness heard in the beauty of the bamboo flute; there is the sound of the ching punctuating the end of the vocal phrase. Here is the notion of the human connection to all of creation; there is the plaintive call of the Kyrie. The landscape of Asian song offers to North Americans new sounds and new texts of peoples rooted in Jesus Christ expressed through an Asian context. As we North Americans put on our Asian sandals we open ourselves to receive the hospitality of Christians from across the globe. We experience our unity in diversity as we find praises of the same God in others' cultural expressions. As we marvel at the diversity of God's creation we open ourselves to the variety of ways God works through all cultures and peoples. These diverse songs reflect a common theme: praises of the God made known to us in Jesus Christ. Let the songs begin!

---

1. I-to Loh "Contextual Worship—The Role of Music," workshop on Contextual Liturgy and Music, Tainan Theological College and Seminary, Tainan, Taiwan, February 1997.

2. Ibid.

3. See I-to Loh, ed., *Sound the Bamboo*, (Manila: Asian Institute for Liturgy and Music and the Christian Conference of Asia, 1990), p. 17.

4. See, Per Harling, ed., *Worshipping Ecumenically: Orders of Service from Global Meetings with Suggestions for Local Use* (Geneva: World Council of Churches, 1995), p. 14.

5. Ibid., p. 17

6. Francisco Feliciano. "Conducting Workshop," workshop on Contextual Liturgy and Music, Tainan Theological College and Seminary, Tainan, Taiwan, February 1997.

7. See, Harling, p. 14

So many ways of singing a new song to the Lord! We parish musicians read a book like this and become inspired to broaden the scope of song in our congregation. But then we remember what it's really like on Sunday morning. We remember the comments, the looks accompanying the smallest of changes. It takes so much work and can be so draining of the spirit to lead the song in new directions. And people are seemingly comfortable with the status quo, so why not take the easy way out?

But consider your calling. You are a leader of the *church's* song—in this particular place and time, to be sure, but are these parishioners well served by being limited to only a tiny fragment of the loaf that is the body of Christ in all times and places? Don't they deserve—even if they don't know what they are missing—to encounter the unfamiliar spices of "ethnic" song, the transcendence of chant, the immediacy of contemporary song? Is it not worthwhile to take a fresh look even at familiar hymnody?

Yes, it is worth the effort, the looks, the comments. But how do we put it into practice? Look again at the beginning of this book—many valuable ideas there can help you get started. And then, prepare . . . practice . . . present.

Prepare. If you just throw something new at an unprepared congregation, it will fail, and they will resent it and you. Instead, help them get ready to receive something new. Whatever the genre you are introducing, get it into their ears ahead of time. Use it as prelude, voluntary material, or during communion. You might play recordings during Sunday school and adult forums—maybe even do a presentation about music from that time or place. By all means, have the choir sing the music for the congregation before the congregation tries to do it. Then some people, at least, will be looking forward to trying out that new song for themselves.

Practice. Another formula for disaster is to lead the song—any song—when the leaders aren't ready. If they are fumbling around, the message that is communicated is "This music is too hard for them—it must be way beyond me!" So make sure that you and the choir, and any instrumentalists involved, are absolutely secure. And that means going over it as many times as necessary, making the rough places plain—you know the routine. Then when you stand up to lead the song, the congregation will sense your ease, and they will think "This doesn't seem so hard!" And it isn't.

Present. Give careful thought to the manner in which the new song will be done. Give the people as much help as you can, in the form of words and music, support from the choir, and leadership. Many songs from around the world take the form of call and response—and there's a lesson there for us. Musically, ours too is a largely illiterate society, so if the leaders can sing the music and have the people immediately repeat it, the chances of success are greatly enhanced. Where that is more difficult to do (for example, chant), have the choir—so the congregation can hear a group of voices—sing a stanza or, better, two, and then help them to find their own voice in the song. It will be halting at first. Remember that any new song needs to "pitch a tent" among the people for a few weeks before it will be accepted. Then gradually spread out the number of weeks between repetitions. Don't throw too much new at the people at one time. All these are common-sense suggestions, but we need reminders from time to time.

Most of the decisions regarding how the church's song is led in your congregation are ones that you—and other members of the worship leadership—are best equipped to make. Must you segregate each genre into a separate service? In most cases, no. In fact, the people will gain a better sense of the inclusive household of God if they sing various styles within one service. Yet it is undeniable that some abrupt transitions from one type of song to another can be jarring. (Imagine, for instance, going from Gregorian chant right into a contemporary praise song.) Your judgment is called into play. Again, with music from African, Asian, or Latino traditions, must the accompaniment be authentic, or is it more important that the song be heard, however it is presented? Within those boundaries, you must make the nuanced decision of how much effort to put into letting the song appear in its native garb.

The questions continue: How much weight do we give to lectionary relationships when we are trying to introduce a piece over time? Where in the worship will a given song best function? Those necessary questions are moot if we do not first decide that the church's song, from familiar to exotic, is worth doing, and doing well.

In the end, one recommendation remains, and for us leaders this may be the hardest part: get out of the way. It is, finally, the church's song, the song of the people of God. In a sense, even to speak of leading it is too strong. We facilitate it. We enable the people to make it happen. We can prepare, enlighten, encourage, train, lead, and all the rest, but when the worship begins, it is the song of God's people of every time and every place, and we are privileged to be among them.

> Lo, the apostolic train
> Join your sacred name to hallow;
> Prophets swell the glad refrain,
> And the white-robed martyrs follow;
> And from morn to set of sun
> Through the Church the song goes on.[1]

---

1. Tr. Clarence A. Walworth; from *Lutheran Book of Worship* #535.

HYMNALS, HYMNAL SUPPLEMENTS, AND SONG COLLECTIONS

A. M. E. C. Bicentennial Hymnal. Nashville: The African Methodist Episcopal Church, 1984.

All Nations Praise. General editor I-to Loh. Tainan, Taiwan: Department of Church Music, Tainan Theological Seminary, 1995.

Baptist Hymnal, The. Nashville: Convention Press, 1975, 1991.

Borning Cry: Worship for a New Generation. Compiled by John Carl Ylvisaker. Waverly, IA: New Generation Publishers, 1992.

Cantad al Señor! St. Louis: Concordia Publishing House, 1991.

Celebrate! Songs for Renewal. Whittier, CA: Praise Publications, 1998.

Celebration Hymnal: Songs and Hymns for Worship, The. Nashville: Word/Integrity Music, 1997.

Chalice Hymnal, The (Disciples of Christ). St. Louis: Chalice Press, 1995.

Come and Worship. Mobile, AL: Integrity Music, 1994.

Come Celebrate! Praise and Worship! Music for Contemporary Worship. Compiled by Cathy Townley. Nashville: Abingdon Press, 1997.

Come Celebrate! Jesus! Compiled by Cathy Townley. Nashville: Abingdon Press, 1997.

Covenant Hymnal, The. Chicago: Covenant Press, 1973.

Dancing at the Harvest. Ray Makeever. Minneapolis: Augsburg Fortress, 1997.

Flor y Canto. Portland, OR: OCP Publications, 1989.

Freedom Is Coming: Songs of Protest and Praise from South Africa. Uppsala, Sweden: Utryck; Ft. Lauderdale: Walton, 1984.

Gather Comprehensive. Chicago: GIA Publications, Inc., 1994.

Global Songs II: Bread for the Journey. Minneapolis: Augsburg Fortress, 1997.

Global Songs—Local Voices. Minneapolis: Bread for the Journey, 1995.

Glory and Praise 2nd ed. Portland, OR: OCP Publications, 1977.

Hymnal: A Worship Book. Elgin, IL: Brethren Press, 1992.

Hymnal Supplement 1991. Chicago: GIA Publications, Inc., 1991.

Hymnal Supplement 1998. St. Louis: Concordia Publishing House, 1998.

Hymnal: The United Church of Christ. Cleveland: The Pilgrim Press, 1974.

Hymnal 1940, The. New York: The Church Pension Fund, 1940.

Hymnal 1982, The. New York: The Church Pension Fund, 1985.

Hymns from the Four Winds: Supplemental Worship Resources 13. General Editor I-to Loh. Nashville: Abingdon Press, 1983.

Hymns of Praise. rev. ed. Hong Kong: Taosheng Publishing House, 1994.

In Spirit and in Truth: Hymns and Responses. Geneva: WCC Publications, 1991.

Journeysongs. Portland, OR: OCP Publications, 1994.

Lead Me, Guide Me: The African American Catholic Hymnal. Chicago: GIA Publications, Inc., 1987.

Lead Us, Lord: A Collection of African Hymns. Minneapolis: Augsburg Publishing House, 1977.

Liber Usualis, The. Tournai, Belgium: Descle & Co., 1947.

Libro de Liturgia y Cántico. Minneapolis: Augsburg Fortress, 1998.

Lift Every Voice and Sing II: An African American Hymnal. New York: The Church Hymnal Corporation, 1993.

Lutheran Book of Worship. Minneapolis: Augsburg Publishing House; Philadelphia: Board of Publication, Lutheran Church in America, 1978.

Lutheran Hymnal, The. St. Louis: Concordia Publishing House, 1941.

Lutheran Worship. St. Louis: Concordia Publishing House, 1982.

Maranatha! Music Praise; Hymns and Choruses. Laguna Hills, CA: Maranatha! Music, 1998.

Mil Voces Para Celebrar: Himnario Metodista. Nashville: The United Methodist Publishing House, 1996.

Mission Praise. London: Marshall Pickering, 1990.

Moravian Book of Worship. Bethlehem, PA: Moravian Church in America, 1992.

Music from Taizé. Vols. I and II. Chicago: GIA Publications, Inc., 1978–1984.

New English Hymnal. Norwich: The Canterbury Press, 1986.

New Century Hymnal, The. Cleveland: The Pilgrim Press, 1995.

O Blessed Spring: Hymns of Susan Palo Cherwien. Minneapolis: Augsburg Fortress, 1998.

Other SongBook, The. Compiled by Dave Anderson. Phoenix, AZ: The Fellowship Publications, 1971.

Praise and Worship Songbooks. Mobile, AL: Hosanna/Integrity Music, 1987–1998.

Praise Chorus Books. Continuing series. Mobile, AL: Hosanna/Integrity Music, 1987–1998.

Praise Hymns and Choruses. 4th ed. Laguna Hills, CA: Maranatha! Music, 1997.

Presbyterian Hymnal, The. Louisville: Westminster/John Knox Press, 1990.

Psalter Hymnal. Grand Rapids, MI: CRC Publications, 1987.

Remembering the Promise: The Work of the People. Vols. I and II. Sioux Falls, SD: Dakota Road Music, 1989.

Renew! Songs and Hymns for Blended Worship. Carol Stream, IL: Hope Publishing Co., 1997.

RitualSong. Chicago: GIA Publications, Inc., 1996.

Rock Hymnal, The. Vols. I and II. Compiled by Jay Beech. New London, MN: Baytone Music, 1988, 1991.

Sacred Harp, The. 3rd ed. 1859. Reprint. Nashville: Broadman Press, 1968.

Set Free: A Collection of African Hymns. Arranged by Howard Olson. Minneapolis: Augsburg Fortress, 1993.

Songs for Praise and Worship: Chorus Book. Nashville: Word Music, 1992.

Songs for the Congregation. Laguna Hills, CA: Maranatha! Music, 1991.

Songs for the People of God. Whittier, CA: Praise Publications, 1994.

Songs of the First Light. Burnsville, MN: Changing Church Forum, 1996.

Songs of Zion. Nashville: Abingdon Press, 1981.

Sound the Bamboo. Edited by I-to Loh. Manila: Christian Conference of Asia, 1990.

Source, The. Compiled by Graham Kendrick. Rattlesden, Great Britain: Kevin Mayhew Ltd., 1998.

Southern Harmony, The. Edited by Glenn C. Wilcox. 1854. Reprint. Murray, KY: Pro Musicamericana, 1966.

Spirit Calls, Rejoice. Burnsville, MN: Prince of Peace, 1987.

Spirit Touching Spirit. Burnsville, MN: Prince of Peace, 1987.

This Far By Faith: An African American Worship Resource. Minneapolis: Augsburg Fortress, 1999.

Thuma Mina: International Ecumenical Hymnbook. Munich: Strube Verlag, 1995.

United Methodist Hymnal, The. Nashville: The United Methodist Publishing House, 1989.

United Methodist Hymnal Music Supplement, The. Nashville: Abingdon Press, 1991.

Vietnamese Specialized Ministries of C. & M. A. Hoi Thanh, Tin-Lanh, Viet-Nam, 1983.

Voices: Native American Hymns and Worship Resources. Nashville: Discipleship Resources, 1992.

Voices United. Etobicoke, Ontario: The United Church Publishing House, 1996.

We Celebrate: Worship Resource. Schiller Park, IL: World Library Publications, 1997.

With One Voice: A Lutheran Resource for Worship. Minneapolis: Augsburg Fortress, 1995.

With One Voice: A Lutheran Resource for Worship. Accompaniment Edition. Minneapolis: Augsburg Fortress, 1995.

Wonder, Love and Praise. A Supplement to the Hymnal 1982. New York: Church Publishing, Inc., 1997.

Wonder, Love and Praise. Leader's Guide. Edited by John Hooker for the Standing Commission on Church Music. New York: Church Publishing, Inc., 1997.

World Praise. London: Marshall Pickering, 1993.

Worship III. Chicago: GIA Publications, Inc., 1986.

Worship & Praise. Minneapolis: Augsburg Fortress, 1999.

Worship Him: Scripture Songs for Worship. Vols. I, II, and III. Leawood, KS: Tempo Music/Intrada, 1995.

Worship Songs of the Vineyard. Continuing series. Anaheim, CA: Vineyard Music Group, 1994–1998.

Worshiping Church: A Hymnal/Worship Leaders' Edition, The. Carol Stream, IL: Hope Publishing Co., 1990, 1991.

Worshipping Ecumenically: Orders of Service from Global Meetings with Suggestions for Local Use. Geneva: WCC Publications, 1995.

HYMNAL COMPANIONS

Christian Worship: Handbook. Edited by C.T. Aufdemberge. Milwaukee: Northwestern Publishing House, 1998.

Come Sunday: The Liturgy of Zion. (Companion to Songs of Zion). Edited by William B. McClain. Nashville: Abingdon Press, 1990.

Companion to the United Methodist Hymnal. Edited by Carlton R. Young. Nashville: Abingdon Press, 1993.

Historical Companion to Hymns Ancient and Modern. Edited by Maurice Frost. London: William Clowes and Sons, Ltd., 1962.

Hymnal Companion to the Lutheran Book of Worship. Marilyn Kay Stulken. Philadelphia: Fortress Press, 1981.

Hymnal 1982 Companion, The. Vols. I, II and III. Edited by Raymond F. Glover. New York: The Church Hymnal Corporation, 1990.

Lutheran Worship Hymnal Companion. Edited by Fred L. Precht. St. Louis: Concordia Publishing House, 1992.

New Century Hymnal Companion: A Guide to the Hymns. Edited by Kristen L. Forman. Cleveland: The Pilgrim Press, 1998.

Presbyterian Hymnal Companion, The. Edited by Linda Jo McKim. Louisville: Westminster/John Knox Press, 1993.

Presbyterian Hymnal Complete Concordance and Indexes, The. Judith L. Muck. Louisville: Westminster/John Knox Press, 1997.

Psalter Hymnal Handbook. Edited by Emily R. Brink and Bert Polman. Grand Rapids, MI: CRC Publications, 1998.

Worship Third Edition Companion. Edited by Catherine Salika and Marilyn Kay Stulken. Chicago: GIA Publications, Inc., 1998.

BIBLIOGRAPHY

GENERAL WORKS ABOUT CONGREGATIONAL SONG

Bangert, Mark. "Welcoming the Ethnic into our Church Musical Diet." *Cross Accent: Journal of the Association of Lutheran Church Musicians* 5 (January 1995).

Blume, Friedrich. *Protestant Church Music.* New York: W. W. Norton, 1974.

Bradley, Ian. *Abide With Me: The World of Victorian Hymns.* Chicago: GIA Publications, Inc., 1997.

Cherwien, David M. *Let the People Sing! A Keyboardist's Creative and Practical Guide to Engaging God's People in Meaningful Song.* St. Louis: Concordia Publishing House, 1997.

Day, Thomas. *Why Catholics Can't Sing: The Culture of Catholicism and the Triumph of Bad Taste.* New York: Crossroad, 1991.

Engel, James. *An Introduction to Organ Registration.* St. Louis: Concordia Publishing House, 1986.

Eskew, Harry, and Hugh T. McElrath. *Sing with Understanding: An Introduction to Christian Hymnology.* 2nd ed. Nashville: Church Street Press, 1995.

———. "Shape-Note Hymnody in the Shenandoah Valley, 1816-1860." doctoral diss., Tulane University, 1966.

Fishell, Janette. *But What Do I Do With My Feet? The Pianist's Guide to the Organ.* Nashville: Abingdon Press, 1996.

Gleason, Harold. *Method of Organ Playing.* 7th ed. Englewood Cliffs, NJ: Prentice-Hall, 1988.

Glover, Raymond F. "What Is Congregational Song?" *The Hymnal 1982 Companion.* Vol. 1. New York: The Church Hymnal Corporation, 1990.

Halter, Carl, and Carl Schalk, eds. *A Handbook of Church Music.* St. Louis: Concordia Publishing House, 1978.

Heller, David. *Manual on Hymn Playing.* Chicago: GIA Publications, Inc., 1992.

Hustad, Donald P. *Jubilate II: Church Music in Worship and Renewal.* Carol Stream, IL: Hope Publishing Co., 1981, 1993.

Julian, John. *Dictionary of Hymnology,* Vol I and II. London: J. Murray, 1907. Reprint. Grand Rapids, MI: Kregel Publications, 1985.

Keiser, Marilyn J. *Teaching Music in Small Churches.* New York: The Church Hymnal Corporation, 1983.

Lawrence, Joy E. "Developing the Art of Creative Hymn Playing." *Journal of Church Music,* 28, no. 8 (November 1986).

Lawrence, Joy, and John Ferguson. *A Musician's Guide to Church Music.* New York: The Pilgrim Press, 1981.

Lovelace, Austin. *The Organist and Hymn Playing.* rev. ed. Carol Stream, IL: Agape Press, 1981.

Luther, Martin. *Luther's Works.* Vol. 53. *Liturgy and Hymns.* Edited by Ulrich S. Leupold. Philadelphia: Fortress Press, 1965.

Marshall, Madeleine Forell, and Janet Todd. *English Congregational Hymns in the 18th Century.* Lexington: University Press of Kentucky, 1982.

McCann, Forrest M. *Hymns and History: An Annotated Survey of Sources.* Abilene, TX: ACU Press, 1997.

Music, David W. *Hymnology: A Collection of Source Readings.* Metuchen, NJ: The Scarecrow Press, 1996.

Parker, Alice. *Creative Hymn-Singing.* Chapel Hill, NC: Hinshaw Music, 1976.

———. *Melodious Accord: Good Singing in Church.* Chicago: Liturgy Training Publications, 1991.

———. "Yes, We'll Gather! Singing Hymns with Alice Parker." Video. Chicago: Liturgy Training Publications, 1997.

Proulx, Richard. *Tintinnabulum: The Liturgical Use of Handbells.* rev. ed. Chicago: GIA Publications, Inc., 1997.

Ragatz, Oswald G. *Organ Technique: A Basic Course of Study.* Bloomington, IN: Indiana University Press, 1979.

Riedel, Johannes. *The Lutheran Chorale: Its Basic Tradition.* Minneapolis: Augsburg Publishing House, 1967.

Routley, Erik. *The English Carol.* New York: Oxford University Press, 1959.

———. *The Music of Christian Hymns.* Chicago: GIA Publications, Inc., 1981.

Schalk, Carl. *God's Song in a New Land: Lutheran Hymnals in America.* St.Louis: Concordia Publishing House, 1995.

———. ed. *Key Words in Church Music: Definitive Essays on Concepts, Practices, and Movements of Thought in Church Music.* St. Louis: Concordia Publishing House, 1978.

———. *Source Documents in American Lutheran Hymnody.* St. Louis: Concordia Publishing House, 1996.

Smith, C. Howard. *Scandinavian Hymnody from the Reformation to the Present.* Metuchen, NJ: The Scarecrow Press, 1987.

Sydnor, James Rawlings. *Hymns and Their Uses: A Guide to Improved Congregational Singing.* Carol Stream, IL: Agape Press, 1982.

Watson, J. R. *The English Hymn: A Critical and Historical Study.* Oxford: Clarendon Press, 1997.

Westermeyer, Paul. *The Church Musician.* rev. ed. Minneapolis: Augsburg Fortress, 1997.

———. *Te Deum: The Church and Music.* Minneapolis: Fortress Press, 1998.

CHANT

Apel, Willi. *Gregorian Chant*. Bloomington, IN: Indiana University Press, 1958.

Arnold, J. H. *Plainsong Accompaniment*. London: Oxford University Press, 1964.

Berry, Mary. *Plainchant for Everyone*. Handbook No. 3. Croydon, England: Royal School of Church Music, 1979.

Fenwick, Mary. "Anglican Chant." *Music* (August 1977).

Fleming, Michael. *The Accompaniment of Plainsong*. Handbook No. 11. Croydon, England: Royal School of Church Music.

Gajard, Joseph. *The Solesmes Method: Its Fundamental Principles and Practical Rules of Interpretation*. Translated by R. Cecile Gabain. Collegeville, MN: The Liturgical Press, 1960.

Hiley, David. *Western Plainchant*. Oxford: Clarendon Press, 1993.

Marier, Theodore, and Justine Ward. *Gregorian Chant Practicum*. Washington, DC: The Catholic University of America Press, 1990.

Murray, G. *Gregorian Chant according to the Manuscripts*. London: L. J. Cary, 1963.

Rayburn, John. *Gregorian Chant: A History of the Controversy Concerning Its Rhythm*. 1964. Reprint. New York: Greenwood Press, 1981.

Smith, Huston, ed. *Gregorian Chant: Songs of the Spirit*. San Francisco: KQED Books, 1996.

Tortolano, William, tr. and ed. *Beginning Studies in Gregorian Chant*. Chicago: GIA. Publications, Inc., 1988.

Vollaerts, J. M. A. *Rhythmic Proportions in Early Medieval Ecclesiastical Chant*. 2nd ed. Leiden, Netherlands: E. J. Brill, 1960.

AFRICAN AMERICAN

Barnwell, Ysaye M., and George Brandon. *Singing in the African American Tradition*. Woodstock, NY: Homespun Tapes, 1989.

Boyer, Horace. "Contemporary Black Music" *Black Perspective in Music* (1979).

Burnim, Mellonee V. "The Black Gospel Music Tradition: Symbol of Ethnicity." doctoral diss., Indiana University, 1980.

Burnim, Mellonee V., and Portia K. Maultsby. "From Backwoods to City Streets: The Afro-American Musical Journey." *Expressively Black*. Edited by Geneva Gay and Willie Baber. New York: Praeger, 1987.

Costen, Melva Wilson. *African American Christian Worship*. Nashville: Abingdon Press, 1993.

Heilbut, Anthony. *The Gospel Sound: Good News and Bad Times*. New York: Limelight Editions, 1985.

Riedel, Johannes. *Soul Music Black and White: The Influence of Black Music on the Churches*. Minneapolis: Augsburg Publishing House, 1975.

Southern, Eileen. *The Music of Black Americans: A History*. 2nd ed. New York: W.W. Norton, 1983.

Spencer, Jon Michael. *Black Hymnody: A Hymnological History of the African-American Church*. Knoxville, TN: University of Tennessee Press, 1992.

———. *Sing a New Song: Liberating Black Hymnody*. Minneapolis: Fortress Press, 1995.

CONTEMPORARY

Ballou, Glen, ed. *Handbook for Sound Engineers: The New Audio Cyclopedia*. New York: Howard W. Sams & Co., a Division of Macmillan, Inc. 1996.

Barrett, Bob. *Contemporary Music Styles: The Worship Band's Guide to Excellence*. Mission Viejo, CA: Tailor Made Music, 1996.

———. *Reading and Writing Chord Charts*. Mission Viejo, CA: Tailor Made Music, 1997.

———. *Synthesizers in Praise and Worship*. Mission Viejo, CA: Tailor Made Music, 1996.

Benedict, Daniel, and Craig Kennet Miller. *Contemporary Worship for the 21st Century*. Nashville: Discipleship Resources,1994.

Brandt, Donald M. *Worship and Outreach: New Services for New People*. Minneapolis: Augsburg Fortress, 1994.

Callahan, Kennon. *Dynamic Worship: Mission, Grace, Praise and Power*. New York: Harper Collins, 1994.

Dawn, Marva J. *Reaching Out without Dumbing Down: A Theology of Worship for Turn-of-the-Century Culture*. Grand Rapids, MI: William B. Eerdmans, 1995.

Doran, Carol. "Popular Religious Song." *The Hymnal 1982 Companion*. Vol. 1. New York: The Church Pension Fund, 1990.

Haugen, Marty. *Instrumentation and the Liturgical Ensemble*. Chicago: GIA Publications, Inc., 1991.

Joncas, Jan Michael. *From Sacred Song to Ritual Music: Twentieth-Century Understandings of Roman Catholic Worship Music*. Collegeville, MN: The Liturgical Press, 1997.

Kallestad, Walt. *Entertainment Evangelism*. Nashville: Abingdon Press, 1996.

Kroeger, Karl. *Music of the New American Nation: Sacred Music from 1780 to 1820*. Vols. I–VII. New York: Garland, 1995–1997.

Morganthaler, Sally. *Worship Evangelism*. Grand Rapids, MI: Zondervan, 1995.

Sandell, Elizabeth J. *Including Children in Worship*. Minneapolis: Augsburg Fortress, 1991.

BIBLIOGRAPHY

Schattauer, Thomas, Karen Ward, and Mark Bangert. *Open Questions in Worship*. Vol. 7. *What does "multicultural" worship look like?* Minneapolis: Augsburg Fortress, 1996.

Searle, Mark. *Liturgy Made Simple*. Collegeville, MN: The Liturgical Press, 1981.

Sykes, Sheri. "Christian Contemporary Music: Another Performance Practice." *The American Organist* 32 no.1 (January 1998).

Townley, Cathy, and Mike Graham. *Come Celebrate! A Guide for Planning Contemporary Worship*. Nashville: Abingdon Press, 1995.

Westermeyer, Paul., Paul Bosch, and Marianne Sawicki. *Open Questions in Worship*. Vol. 2. *What is "Contemporary" Worship?* Minneapolis: Augsburg Fortress, 1995.

Wright, Timothy. *A Community of Joy: How to Create Contemporary Worship*. Nashville: Abingdon Press, 1996.

Younger, Barbara, and Lisa Flinn. *Boredom-Busting Ideas to Involve Children in Adult Worship*. Loveland, CO: Group Publishing, 1996.

LATINO

Broughton, et al. *World Music—The Rough Guide*. New York: Penguin Books, 1994.

Celebremos. Prima Parte, Colección de Coritos, and *Celebremos. Segunda Parte, Salmos y Cánticos*. Nashville: Discipleship Resources, 1979, 1983.

Chávez-Melo, Skinner, ed. *Albricias*. New York: National Hispanic Office of the Episcopal Church, 1987.

Díaz-Stevens, Ana María and Anthony M. Stevens-Arroyo. *Recognizing the Latino Resurgence in U.S. Religion*. Westview Press, 1998.

González, Justo, ed. *¡Alabadle! Hispanic Christian Worship*. Nashville: Abingdon Press, 1996.

Hawn, C. Michael. "The *Fiesta* of the Faithful: Praising God in Spanish." *The Chorister* 49 no. 7 (January 1998).

Lockwood, George F. "Recent Developments in U.S. Hispanic and Latin American Protestant Church Music." doctoral diss., School of Theology, Claremont, CA, 1981.

Robb, John Donald. *Hispanic Folk Music of New Mexico and the Southwest: A Self-Portrait of a People*. Norman, OK: University of Oklahoma Press, 1980.

Tirabassi, Maren C., and Kathy Wonson Eddy. *Gifts of Many Cultures: Worship Resources for the Global Community*. Cleveland: United Church Press, 1995.

AFRICAN

Bangert, Mark. "Dynamics of Liturgy and World Musics: A Methodology for Evaluation." *Worship and Culture in Dialogue*. Edited by S. Anita Stauffer. Geneva: Lutheran World Federation, 1994.

———. "Songs from Africa in *Lead Me, Guide Me*." *GIA Quarterly* 3 no. 1 (Fall 1991).

Bebey, Francis. *African Music: A People's Art*. Translated by Josephine Bennet. New York: Lawrence Hill & Co., 1975.

Chernoff, John. *African Rhythm and African Sensibility*. Chicago: University of Chicago Press, 1979.

Hope, Anne. *Torch in the Night: Worship Resources from South Africa*. New York: Friendship Press, 1988.

Jais-Mick, Maureen. "Multicultural Resources for Worship: An Annotated Bibliography." *Cross Accent: Journal of the Association of Lutheran Church Musicians* 5 (January 1995).

Kazarow, Patricia. "Contemporary African Choral Art Music: An Intercultural Perspective." *Cross Accent: Journal of the Association of Lutheran Church Musicians* 5 (January 1995).

Locke, David. Drum Gahu. *The Rhythms of West African Drumming*. Crown Point, IN: White Cliffs Media Company, 1987.

Nketia, J. H. Kwabena. *The Music of Africa*. New York: W. W. Norton, 1974.

Olson, Howard. "Singing Our Theology." *Currents in Theology and Mission* 14 no. 1 (February 1987).

Stone, Ruth, ed. *Africa*. Vol. 1. *The Garland Encyclopedia of World Music*. New York: Garland, 1998.

ASIAN

Rowell, Lewis. *Thinking About Music: An Introduction to the Philosophy of Music*. Amherst, MA: University of Massachusetts Press, 1983.

Song, C. S. *Jesus, the Crucified People*. Minneapolis: Augsburg Fortress, 1990.

———. *Jesus and the Reign of God*. Minneapolis: Augsburg Fortress, 1993.

———. *Jesus in the Power of the Spirit*. Minneapolis: Augsburg Fortress, 1994.

Stauffer, S. Anita, ed. *Worship and Culture in Dialogue: Reports of International Consultations; Cantigny, Switzerland, 1993; Hong Kong, 1994*. Geneva: Lutheran World Federation, 1994.

Takenaka, Masao, and Ron O'Grady. *The Bible Through Asian Eyes*. Auckland, New Zealand: Pace Publishing and Asian Christian Art Association (Distributed by Friendship Press), 1991.

TUNE INDEX

A NOTE ABOUT THE SELECTED TUNE INDEX   This index of selected hymntunes is provided to guide your exploration of leading congregational singing; however, these lists are not definitive. Several chapters in this book may offer valuable assistance for many tunes listed. Musical techniques from particular historic or geographic sources may be applicable to tunes in various genres. Some tunes may be paired with additional English texts. There is no perfect tempo for any hymn in every setting. Generally, the tempo markings are given for a note value which is the suggested tactus. With some slower tempos, a quarter note metronome marking is given, although the tactus is either a half note or dotted half. It is crucial to understand that notation can vary between books. A quarter note in one source may be notated as a half note in another. Use this information carefully and critically.

TUNE NAME	COMMON ENGLISH TITLE	CHAPTER	TEMPO	WORSHIP BOOK
A la ru	Oh, sleep now, holy baby	8	♩=48–54	WOV 639, H82 113, PH 45
A va de	Come, let us eat	9	♩=92–96	LBW 214, UMH 625
Abbot's Leigh	God is here! Lord of light Lord, you give the great commission	4	♩=90–102	LBW 405, WOV 719, WOV 756, H82 379, H82 511, H82 523, W3 667, W3 470, NCH 70, PH 132, PH 425, PH 429, PH 461, VU 104, VU 260, VU 443, VU 512, UMH 584, UMH 660
Aberystwyth	Savior, when in dust to you Jesus, Lover of My Soul	4	♩=52–62	LBW 91, LW 93, LW 508, H82 349, H82 640, H82 699, NCH 103, PH 20, PH 131, PH 303, PH 409, VU 196, VU 669, UMH 479
Adelaide	Have thine own way, Lord	5	♩=48–60	NNBH 125, AME 345, UMH 382
Adeste fidelis	Oh, come, all ye faithful	4	♩=50–60	LBW 45, LW 41, H82 83, W3 392, LMGM 20, NCH 135, PH 41, PH 42, NNBH 59, VU 60, AME 106, UMH 234
Allein Gott in der Höh	All glory be to God on high	4	♩=50–58	LBW 166, LW 181, LW 215, LW 456, H82 421, W3 527, VU 870
Amazing Grace	*see* New Britain			
Amin haleluya	Amen, hallelujah	10	♩=52–60	WOV 792
Ar hyd y nos	Day is done For the fruit(s) of all (this) creation Go, my children with my blessing God, who made the earth and heaven	4	♩=40–48	LBW 281, LW 492, WOV 721, WOV 760, W3 677, NCH 82, NCH 92, NCH 425, PH 544, VU 227, VU 433, UMH 688
Argentina	*see* Central			
Arlington	Am I a soldier of the cross?	4, 5	♩=72–76	NNBH 388, VU 591, AME 169, AME 171, AME 312, AME 330, AME 410, UMH 511
Assurance	Blessed assurance	5	♩=52–62	WOV 699, LMGM 199, NCH 473, PH 341, NNBH 27, VU 337, AME 450, UMH 369
Aurelia	O Christ, the great foundation O Father all-creating The church's one foundation	4	♩=50–56	LBW 197, LBW 369, LW 251, LW 260, LW 289, H82 525, W3 618, W3 744, NCH 386, NCH 387, NCH 388, PH 442, PH 443, NNBH 377, VU 331, AME 519, UMH 545
Aus tiefer Not	Out of the depths I cry	4	♩=46–52	LBW 295, LW 230, H82 151, PH 240, UMH 515
Austrian Hymn/Austria	Glorious things of thee are spoken	4	♩=44–52	LBW 358, LBW 540, LW 294, H82 522, NCH 307, NCH 565, PH 285, PH 446, NNBH 42, VU 687, AME 521, UMH 731
Away in a Manger	Away in a manger	4	♩=72–84 (♩)	LBW 67, VU 6, AME 113, UMH 217

TUNE NAME	COMMON ENGLISH TITLE	CHAPTER	TEMPO	WORSHIP BOOK
Azmon	Awake, O sleeper Oh, for a world Oh, for a thousand tongues to sing	4	♩=78–88 (♩)	LBW 559, LW 350, WOV 745, H82 493, W3 586, NCH 42, NCH 383, NCH 575, PH 386, PH 466, NNBH 17, VU 326, VU 697, AME 1, AME 23, AME 63, AME 278, UMH 57, UMH 59, UMH 422, UMH 608
Bai	Lonely the boat	10	♪=120–130	PH 373, UMH 476
Balm in Gilead	There is a balm in Gilead	6	♩=50–54	WOV 737, H82 676, W3 608, LMGM 157, NCH 553, PH 394, VU 612, AME 425, UMH 375
Beach Spring	Lord, whose love through humble service Wash, O God, our sons and daughters	4, 5	♩=66–80	LBW 423, WOV 697, NCH 332, PH 422, VU 115, VU 374, VU 442, VU 457, UMH 581, UMH 605
Beecher	Love divine, all loves excelling	4, 5	♩=50–58	NCH 43, NNBH 44, AME 455, UMH 384
Bethany	Nearer, my God, to thee	5	♩=44–54	LW 514, LMGM 143, NCH 606, NNBH 283, AME 332, UMH 528
Borning Cry	see Waterlife			
Bradbury	Savior, like a shepherd lead us	4, 5	♩=45–54	LMGM 47, NCH 252, PH 387, NNBH 247, AME 379, UMH 381
Bunessan	Baptized in water Morning has broken Praise and thanksgiving	4	♩=45–54	LBW 409, LW 403, WOV 693, H82 8, W3 674, W3 682, W3 720, PH 469, PH 492, VU 409, AME 575, UMH 145
By and By	We are often tossed and driven	5	♩=45–53	NCH 444, NNBH 325, AME 394, UMH 525
Cantad al Señor	O sing to the Lord (our God)	8	♩=44–54	WOV 795, VU 241
Caribbean Refrain	Halle, halle, hallelujah	8	♩=58–68	WOV 612, NCH 236, VU 958
Central	Christ is risen (Cristo vive)	8	♩=98–112 (♩)	NCH 235, PH 109, VU 424, UMH 313
Chereponi	Jesu, Jesu, fill us with your love	9	♩=58–67	WOV 765, H82 602, W3 431, LMGM 33, NCH 498, PH 367, VU 593, UMH 432
Christ ist erstanden	Christ is arisen	4	♩=62–69	LBW 136, LW 124, H82 184, PH 112
Christ lag in Todesbanden	Christ Jesus lay in death's strong bands	4	♩=56–62	LBW 134, LW 123, H82 185, H82 186, PH 110, UMH 319
Cleansing Fountain	There is a fountain filled with blood	5	♩=55–64	NNBH 84, AME 255, UMH 622
Conditor alme siderum	Creator of the stars of night	3	♩=52–63	LBW 323, LW 17, H82 60, W3 368, PH 4, UMH 692
Converse	What a friend we have in Jesus	5	♩=40–50	LBW 439, LW 516, LMGM 214, PH 403, NNBH 340, AME 323, UMH 526
Coronation	All hail the power of Jesus' name	4, 5	♩=52–60	LBW 328, LW 272, H82 450, W3 494, LMGM 88, NCH 304, PH 142, NNBH 2, AME 4, UMH 154
Cradle Song	Away in a manger	4, 5	♩=76–86 (♩)	LW 64, WOV 644, H82 101, W3 378, PH 24, VU 69, AME 114
Crucifer	Lift high the cross	4	♩=60–68	LBW 377, LW 311, H82 473, W3 704, NCH 198, PH 371, VU 151, UMH 159
Crusader's Hymn	see Schönster Herr Jesu			
Cwm Rhondda	God of grace and God of glory Guide me, O thou great Jehovah	4	♩=46–58	LBW 343, LW 398, LBW 415, LW 220, H82 594, H82 690, NCH 18, NCH 436, PH 281, PH 420, NNBH 107, VU 651, AME 52, AME 62, AME 181, UMH 127, UMH 577

TUNE INDEX

TUNE NAME	COMMON ENGLISH TITLE	CHAPTER	TEMPO	WORSHIP BOOK
Dapit hapon	When twilight comes	10	♩=74–78	WOV 663, PH 527
Dennis	Blest be the tie that binds	4, 5	♩=88–104	LBW 370, NCH 393, PH 438, NNBH 359, VU 602, AME 522, UMH 557
Diadem	All hail the power of Jesus' name!	4, 5	♩=88–106 (♩)	W3 495, LMGM 89, PH 143, NNBH 523, AME 5, UMH 155
Diademata	Crown him with many crowns	4	♩=52–60	LBW 170, LW 278, H82 494, W3 496, LMGM 68, NCH 301, PH 151, VU 211, AME 174, UMH 327
Divinum mysterium	Of the Father's love begotten	3	♩=52–63	LBW 42, LW 36, H82 82, W3 398, NCH 118, PH 309, VU 61, UMH 184
Down Ampney	Come down, O love divine	4	♩=54–60	LBW 508, LW 162, H82 516, W3 472, NCH 289, PH 313, VU 367, UMH 475
Duke Street	From all that dwell below the skies I know that my Redeemer lives! Jesus shall reign	4	♩=62–76	LBW 352, LBW 530, LW 264, LW 312, H82 544, W3 445, W3 492, W3 521, LMGM 63, NCH 300, PH 423, NNBH 436, VU 330, AME 69, AME 96, UMH 101, UMH 157
Easter Hymn	Jesus Christ is risen today	4	♩=54–62	LBW 151, LW 127, H82 207, W3 442, LMGM 58, NCH 233, PH 123, NNBH 99, VU 155, AME 156, UMH 302
Eat This Bread (Berthier)	Eat this bread (Taizé)	7	♩=42–54	WOV 709, LMGM 130, VU 466, UMH 628
Ein' feste Burg	A mighty fortress is our God	4	♩=44–50 (metric) ♩=86–94 (rhythmic)	LBW 228, LBW 229, LBW 239, LW 297, LW 298, H82 687, H82 688, W3 575, W3 576, W3 616, NCH 439, NCH 440, PH 259, PH 260, NNBH 15, VU 262, AME 54, UMH 110
El Camino	When the poor ones (Cuando el pobre)	8	♩=50–60	PH 407, VU 702, UMH 434
Engelberg	We know that Christ is raised When in our music God is glorified (Engelberg)	4	♩=50–56	LBW 189, WOV 802, H82 296, H82 420, H82 477, W3 549, W3 721, NCH 561, PH 264, PH 495, VU 448, VU 533, UMH 68, UMH 610
Es ist das Heil	All who believe and are baptized Salvation unto us has come	4	♩=56–60	LBW 194, LBW 297, LW 225, LW 355, H82 298
Es ist ein Ros	Lo, how a rose e'er blooming	4	♩=52–58	LBW 58, LW 51, LW 67, H82 81, W3 374, LMGM 24, NCH 127, NCH 600, PH 48, VU 8, UMH 216
Faithfulness	Great is thy faithfulness	4, 5	♩=86–98 (♩)	WOV 771, LMGM 242, NCH 423, PH 276, NNBH 153, VU 288, AME 84, UMH 140
Forest Green	O little town of Bethlehem	4	♩=50–58	LW 59, WOV 725, H82 78, H82 398, H82 705, W3 6, NCH 110, PH 43, PH 292, PH 412, PH 414, VU 518, VU 530, UMH 152, UMH 539, UMH 709
Foundation	How firm a foundation	4, 5	♩=68–82	LBW 507, LW 411, H82 636, W3 585, LMGM 102, NCH 407, PH 361, NNBH 21, AME 433, UMH 529
Freu dich sehr	Comfort, comfort now my people	4	♩=54–72	LBW 29, LBW 470, LW 28, LW 387, LW 390, PH 3
Galilee	Jesus calls us; o'er the tumult	5	♩=66–80	LBW 494, NCH 172, NNBH 167, VU 562, AME 238, UMH 398
Gather Us In	Here in this place	4, 7	♩=48–62	WOV 718, W3 665
Gaudeamus pariter	Come, you faithful, raise the strain	4	♩=69–84	LBW 132, LBW 193, LW 141, H82 200, H82 237, W3 355, W3 456, PH 114
Gayom ni hi-gami	Lord, your hands have formed	10	♩=46–56	WOV 727

TUNE NAME	COMMON ENGLISH TITLE	CHAPTER	TEMPO	WORSHIP BOOK
Gift of Love	*see* O Waly Waly			
Gloria	Angels we have heard on high	4	♩=56–64	LBW 71, LW 55, H82 96, W3 376, LMGM 17, NCH 125, PH 23, NNBH 54, VU 38, AME 118, UMH 238
Go Tell It	Go tell it on the mountain	6	♩=52–62	LBW 70, LW 504, H82 99, W3 397, LMGM 22, PH 29, NNBH 66, VU 43, AME 122, UMH 251
God Be With You	God be with you	5	♩=40–48	LMGM 309, NCH 81, NNBH 361, VU 422, AME 45, UMH 672
Greensleeves	What child is this	4	♩=44–50	LBW 40, LW 61, WOV 701, H82 115, W3 411, LMGM 29, NCH 148, PH 53, VU 74, UMH 219
Haleluya! Pelo tso rona	Hallelujah! We sing your praises	9	♩=104–110	WOV 722
Hanover	Oh, worship the King You servants of God, your master proclaim	4	♩=102–112	LBW 548, LW 458, H82 388, NCH 305, PH 477, VU 235, UMH 181, UMH 708
Hanson Place	Shall we gather at the river	5	♩=69–80 (♩)	WOV 690, LMGM 103, NCH 597, VU 710, AME 486, UMH 723
He Leadeth Me	He leadeth me: oh, blessed thought!	5	♩=46–52	LBW 501, NNBH 209, VU 657, AME 395, UMH 128
Here I Am Lord	I, the Lord of sea and sky	4, 7	♩=52–62	WOV 752, LMGM 283, PH 525, VU 509, UMH 593
Herzlich tut mich verlangen	O sacred head, now wounded	4	♩=68–76 (metric) ♩=58–66 (rhythmic)	LBW 116, LBW 117, LW 113, LW 427, WOV 733, H82 168, H82 169, H82 669, LMGM 52, NCH 179, NCH 202, NCH 226, PH 98
Holy Manna	God, who stretched the spangled heavens	4, 5	♩=50–58	LBW 463, H82 238, H82 580, W3 648, NCH 376, NCH 556, PH 268, VU 460, UMH 150
How Can I Keep from Singing	My life flows on in endless song	5	♩=48–58	WOV 781, VU 716
Hyfrydol	Alleluia! Sing to Jesus Love divine, all loves excelling	4	♩=102–120 (♩)	LBW 158, LBW 288, LBW 315, LBW 424, LW 286, LW 402, H82 460, H82 657, W3 588, W3 737, LMGM 67, NCH 182, NCH 257, NCH 355, PH 2, PH 144, PH 376, NNBH 7, VU 333, VU 486, AME 103, UMH 196, UMH 648
Hymn to Joy	Joyful, joyful we adore thee	4	♩=56–64	LBW 551, H82 376, W3 467, W3 525, LMGM 197, NCH 4, PH 104, PH 464, NNBH 6, VU 232, AME 75, AME 163, UMH 89, UMH 702
I Want to Be a Christian	Lord, I want to be a Christian	6	♩=48–62	LMGM 119, NCH 454, PH 372, NNBH 490, AME 282, UMH 402
Id y enseñad	You are the seed (Sois la semilla)	8	♩=54–62	WOV 753, NCH 528, UMH 583
In dulci jubilo	Good Christian friends (men), rejoice	4	♩=60–70	LBW 55, LW 47, H82 107, W3 391, NCH 129, PH 28, VU 35, UMH 224
It Is Well	*see* Ville du Havre			
Italian Hymn	Come, thou almighty King	4	♩=40–46	LBW 400, LBW 522, LW 169, LW 317, LW 471, W3 486, W3 487, LMGM 76, NCH 275, PH 139, NNBH 4, AME 7, AME 565, UMH 61, UMH 568
Jesus Lifted Me	I'm so glad Jesus lifted me	6	♩=48–63	WOV 673, LMGM 171, NCH 474
Jesus Loves Me	Jesus loves me! This I know	5	♩=48–60	LMGM 106, NCH 327, PH 304, NNBH 465, VU 365, AME 549, UMH 191

TUNE NAME	COMMON ENGLISH TITLE	CHAPTER	TEMPO	WORSHIP BOOK
Kedron	Creating God, your fingers trace Lord save your world	4, 5	♩=58–63	LBW 420, H82 10, H82 163, NCH 568, PH 124, PH 283, UMH 109
King's Weston	At the name of Jesus	4	♩=60–70	LBW 179, LW 178, H82 435, W3 499, NCH 255, NCH 586, PH 148, VU 97, VU 335, UMH 168, UMH 592
Kings of Orient	We three kings of Orient are	4	♩=50–60	WOV 646, H82 128, W3 406, LMGM 27, PH 66, NNBH 64, UMH 254
Kingsfold	I heard the voice of Jesus say	4	♩=50–58	LBW 391, WOV 730, H82 292, H82 480, W3 490, W3 607, NCH 51, NCH 308, NCH 434, NCH 601, VU 625, VU 626, UMH 179, UMH 285, UMH 606
Lafferty	Seek ye first the kingdom of God	7	♩=48–60	WOV 783, PH 333, VU 356
Lasst uns erfreuen	All creatures of our God and King From all that dwell below the skies Ye watchers and ye holy ones	4	♩=66–76	LBW 143, LBW 157, LBW 175, LBW 527, LW 131, LW 149, LW 308, LW 436, LW 440, H82 400, H82 618, W3 469, W3 520, W3 707, LMGM 104, NCH 17, NCH 27, PH 229, PH 451, PH 455, NNBH 5, VU 217, AME 50, UMH 62, UMH 90, UMH 94
Lauda Anima	Praise, my soul, the King of heaven	4	♩=48–54	H82 410, W3 530, LMGM 198, NCH 273, NCH 567, PH 478, VU 240, VU 312, VU 399, UMH 66, UMH 100
Let Us Break Bread	Let us break bread together	6	♩=46–52	H82 325, W3 727, LMGM 135, NCH 330, PH 513, NNBH 488, VU 480, AME 530, UMH 618
Lift Ev'ry Voice and Sing	Lift every voice and sing	6	♩=44–52	LBW 562, H82 599, LMGM 291, NCH 593, PH 563, NNBH 477, AME 571, UMH 519
Linstead	Let us talents and tongues employ	8	♩=54–62	WOV 754, NCH 347, PH 514, VU 468, AME 536
Lobe den Herren	Praise to the Lord, the Almighty	4	♩=102–132 (♩)	LBW 543, LW 444, H82 390, W3 547, LMGM 196, NCH 22, PH 482, NNBH 8, VU 220, AME 3, UMH 139
Love Unknown	My song is love unknown	4	♩=54–62	LW 91, WOV 661, H82 458, W3 439, PH 76, PH 515, VU 143, VU 456
Marching to Zion	Come, we that love the Lord	5	♩=64–76	WOV 742, LMGM 316, NCH 382, NNBH 22, VU 714, AME 520, UMH 733
Marion	Rejoice, ye pure in heart	4	♩=54–66	LBW 553, LW 455, H82 556, LMGM 94, NCH 55, PH 145, NNBH 11, AME 8, UMH 160
Martyrdom	Alas! And did my Savior bleed	5	♩=108–126 (♩)	LBW 98, LBW 452, LW 97, H82 658, NCH 200, NCH 481, PH 78, PH 228, NNBH 367, AME 140, AME 151, AME 273, AME 324, AME 472, AME 539, UMH 294
McKee	In Christ there is no east or west	5, 6	♩=46–54	LBW 359, H82 529, W3 659, LMGM 301, NCH 394, PH 440, VU 606, AME 557
Mfurahini, haleluya	Christ has arisen, alleluia	9	♩=50–60	WOV 678, LMGM 61
Miles Lane	All hail the power of Jesus' name!	4, 5	♩=52–58	LBW 329, H82 451, VU 334, AME 6
Mit Freuden zart	Sing praise to God who reigns above With high delight let us unite Lord Christ, when first you came to earth	4	♩=66–84	LBW 140, LBW 421, LW 134, H82 408, H82 598, W3 438, W3 455, W3 528, NCH 6, PH 7, PH 483, VU 216, UMH 126
Near the Cross	Jesus, keep me near the cross	5, 6	♩=46–56	LMGM 45, NCH 197, NNBH 94, VU 142, AME 321, UMH 301

TUNE NAME	COMMON ENGLISH TITLE	CHAPTER	TEMPO	WORSHIP BOOK
Neno lake Mungu	Listen, God is calling	9	♩=88–96	WOV 712
Nettleton	Come, thou Fount of every blessing	5	♩=82–94	LBW 499, H82 686, W3 535, NCH 59, NCH 459, PH 355, PH 356, NNBH 14, VU 559, AME 77, UMH 400
New Britain	Amazing grace, how sweet the sound	5	♩=84–100 (♩)	LBW 448, LW 509, H82 671, W3 583, LMGM 173, NCH 547, NCH 548, NCH 617, PH 280, NNBH 132, AME 226, UMH 378
Nicaea	Holy, holy, holy	4	♩=48–56	LBW 165, LW 168, H82 362, W3 485, LMGM 78, NCH 277, PH 138, NNBH 1, VU 315, AME 25, UMH 64, UMH 65
Njoo kwetu, Roho Mwema	Gracious Spirit, hear our pleading	9	♩=46–54	WOV 687
Noël nouvelet	Now the green blade rises	4	♩=40–46	LBW 148, H82 204, W3 453, NCH 238, VU 117, VU 186
Now	Now the silence	4	♩=58–64	LBW 205, H82 333, W3 668, VU 475, UMH 619
Nueva creación	Walk on, O people of God (Camina, Pueblo)	8	♩=60–64	NCH 614, PH 296, UMH 305
O filii et filiae	O sons and daughters of the King	4	♩=46–54	LBW 139, LW 130, H82 203, H82 206, W3 447, LMGM 60, NCH 244, PH 500, PH 116, PH 117, VU 170, UMH 317
O Waly Waly	Though I may speak (The gift of love) When love is found	4, 5	♩=56–66	WOV 749, W3 710, W3 745, NCH 362, NCH 363, PH 94, PH 335, VU 372, VU 490, UMH 408, UMH 643
Olivet	My faith looks up to thee	4, 5	♩=50–56	LBW 479, LW 378, H82 691, LMGM 221, PH 383, NNBH 203, VU 663, AME 415, UMH 452
On Eagle's Wings	On Eagle's Wings (You who dwell)	4, 7	♩=44–52	WOV 779, VU 808, UMH 143
One Bread, One Body	One bread, one body	7	♩=52–58	WOV 710, LMGM 139, VU 467, UMH 620
Open My Eyes	Open my eyes that I may see	5	♩=50–56	PH 324, NNBH 129, VU 371, AME 285, UMH 454
Pescador de hombres	You have come to the lakeshore (Tú has venido)	8	♩=54–62	WOV 784, LMGM 116, NCH 173, PH 377, VU 563, UMH 344
Picardy	Let all mortal flesh keep silence	4	♩=52–60	LBW 198, LW 15, LW 241, H82 324, W3 437, W3 523, NCH 345, PH 5, VU 111, VU 473, VU 700, AME 598, UMH 296, UMH 626
Pilot	Jesus, Savior, pilot me	5	♩=56–69	LBW 334, LW 513, LMGM 251, NCH 441, NNBH 241, VU 637, AME 372, UMH 509
Precious Lord	Precious Lord, take my hand	6	♩=50–66 (♩)	WOV 731, LMGM 162, NCH 472, PH 404, NNBH 339, VU 670, AME 393, UMH 474
Rathbun	In the cross of Christ I glory	4, 5	♩=44–50	LBW 104, LW 101, H82 441, NCH 193, PH 84, NNBH 88, AME 153, UMH 295
Rockingham Old	When I survey the wondrous cross	4	♩=96–108 (♩)	LBW 482, LW 114, H82 321, H82 474, W3 433, PH 100, PH 189, NCH 208, NCH 414, NCH 465, AME 49, AME 340, UMH 299
Schmücke dich	Deck thyself with joy and gladness	4	♩=52–58	LBW 203, LBW 224, LW 239, LW 468, H82 339, NCH 334, PH 506, VU 463, UMH 612
Schönster Herr Jesu	Beautiful Savior	4	♩=44–54	LBW 518, LW 507, H82 384, NCH 44, PH 306, NNBH 110, VU 341

TUNE INDEX

TUNE NAME	COMMON ENGLISH TITLE	CHAPTER	TEMPO	WORSHIP BOOK
Señor, ten piedad	Lord, have mercy	8	♩=64–72	WOV 605
Shine, Jesus, Shine	Shine, Jesus, shine	7	♩=54–66	WOV 651
Showalter	What a fellowship, what a joy divine (Leaning on the everlasting)	5, 6	♩=50–60	WOV 780, LMGM 257, NNBH 211, AME 525, UMH 133
Sine Nomine	For all the saints	4	♩=54–60	LBW 174, LW 191, H82 287, W3 705, LMGM 105, NCH 299, PH 526, NNBH 424, VU 327, VU 420, VU 705, AME 476, UMH 166, UMH 711
Siyahamba	We are marching in the light of God	9	♩=48–56	WOV 650, NCH 526, VU 646
Slane	Be thou my vision	4	♩=80–88	LBW 469, LW 365, WOV 776, H82 482, H82 488, W3 568, NCH 451, PH 339, VU 642, AME 281, UMH 451
Soon and Very Soon	*see Very Soon*			
Splendor Paternae	O Splendor of the Father's light	3	♩=50–58	LBW 271, LW 481, H82 5, NCH 87
St. Anne	O (Our) God, our help in ages past	4	♩=40–44	LBW 320, LW 180, H82 680, W3 579, LMGM 230, NCH 25, NCH 278, NCH 359, PH 210, PH 255, NNBH 19, VU 806, AME 61, UMH 117
St. Catherine	Faith of our fathers	4	♩=40–44	LBW 500, H82 558, W3 571, W3 743, NCH 381, PH 366, NNBH 192, NNBH 193, VU 580, AME 429, AME 430, UMH 710
St. Denio	Immortal, invisible, God only wise	4	♩=102–120 (♩)	LBW 526, LW 451, H82 423, W3 512, NCH 1, NCH 427, PH 263, VU 223, VU 264, VU 660, AME 71, UMH 103
St. George's, Windsor	Come, you thankful people, come	4	♩=52–58	LBW 407, LW 88, LW 495, LW 499, H82 290, W3 759, LMGM 205, NCH 422, PH 551, NNBH 46, VU 516, AME 574, UMH 694
St. Theodulph	All glory, laud, and honor	4	♩=52–58	LBW 108, LW 79, LW 102, W3 428, W3 706, LMGM 30, NCH 102, NCH 216, PH 11, PH 88, NNBH 71, VU 31, VU 122, AME 129, UMH 280
Stille Nacht	Silent night, holy night!	4	♩=92–102 (♩)	LBW 65, LW 68, H82 111, W3 379, LMGM 26, NCH 134, PH 60, NNBH 56, VU 67, AME 116, UMH 239
Taulé	All earth is hopeful (Toda la tierra)	8	♩=54–64	WOV 629, NCH 121, VU 5, UMH 210
The King's Majesty	Ride on, ride on in majesty!	4	♩=48–54	LBW 121, LW 105, H82 156, PH 90, NNBH 69, VU 127
The Old Rugged Cross	On a hill far away	5	♪=74–86 (♩)	LMGM 37, NCH 195, NNBH 96, AME 143, UMH 504
Thuma mina	Send me, Jesus	9	♩=68–74	WOV 773, NCH 360, VU 572, UMH 497
To God Be the Glory	To God be the glory	5	♩=94–108	PH 485, NNBH 23, AME 21, UMH 98
Tokyo	Here, O Lord, your servants gather	10	♩=44–50	NCH 72, PH 465, VU 362, UMH 552
Toplady	Rock of Ages, cleft for me	5	♩=62–70	LBW 327, LW 361, H82 685, LMGM 51, NCH 596, NNBH 101, AME 328, UMH 361
Truro	Christ is alive! Let Christians sing Lift up your heads, ye mighty gates	4	♩=80–92	LBW 363, H82 182, H82 436, W3 363, W3 466, NCH 117, PH 8, PH 108, PH 332, VU 158, VU 207, VU 699, AME 94, UMH 213, UMH 318

TUNE NAME	COMMON ENGLISH TITLE	CHAPTER	TEMPO	WORSHIP BOOK
Tryggare kan ingen vara	Children of the heavenly Father	4	♩=64–76	LBW 474, NCH 487, UMH 141
Ubi caritas	Where true charity and love dwell	3	♩=58–72	H82 606, W3 598
Valet will ich dir geben	see St. Theodulph			
Veni, Creator Spiritus	Come, Holy Ghost, our souls inspire	3	♩=40–44 (♩.)	LBW 472, LW 158, H82 502, H82 504, W3 475, W3 479, LMGM 70, PH 125, VU 200, VU 201, UMH 651
Veni, Emmanuel	Oh, come, oh, come, Emmanuel	3	♩=48–60	LBW 34, LW 31, H82 56, W3 357, LMGM 3, NCH 116, PH 9, NNBH 53, VU 1, AME 102, UMH 211
Very Soon	Soon and very soon	6	♩=52–58	WOV 744, LMGM 4, UMH 706, LMGM 4
Vexilla regis	The royal banners forward go	3	♪=120–144	LBW 125, LW 104, H82 161, H82 162, W3 435
Victory	The strife is o'er, the battle done	4	♩=112–132 (♩)	LBW 135, LW 143, H82 208, W3 451, LMGM 64, NCH 242, PH 119, VU 159, AME 162, UMH 306
Victory Hymn	Jaya ho! Jaya ho!	10	♩=96–104	VU 252, UMH 478
Ville du Havre (It Is Well)	When peace, like a river	5	♩=52–60	LBW 346, LMGM 256, NCH 438, NNBH 189, AME 448, UMH 377
Vineyard Haven	Rejoice, ye pure in heart / Lift up your heads, O gates	4	♩=48–54	WOV 631, H82 392, H82 557, W3 481, W3 552, NCH 71, PH 146, PH 206, UMH 161
Wachet auf	Wake, awake, for night is flying	4	♩=66–76 (rhythmic) / ♩=63–72 (metric)	LBW 31, LBW 247, LW 177, LW 303, H82 61, H82 62, H82 484, H82 485, W3 371, NCH 112, PH 17, VU 111, UMH 720
Wait For The Lord	Wait for the Lord	3	♩=80	VU 22
Waterlife	I was there to hear your borning cry	4, 5, 7	♩=46–54	WOV 770, NCH 351, VU 644
Webb	Stand up, stand up for Jesus	5	♩=54–60	LBW 389, LW 305, NCH 609, NNBH 394, AME 412, UMH 514
Wen-ti	May the Lord, mighty God	10	♩=60–72	PH 596
Were You There	Were you there	6	♩=76–88 (♩)	LBW 92, LW 505, H82 172, W3 436, LMGM 43, NCH 229, PH 102, NNBH 485, VU 144, AME 136, UMH 288
Westminster Abbey	Christ is made the sure foundation	4	♩=40–44	LW 186, WOV 747, H82 518, W3 617, W3 643, NCH 47, NCH 308, NCH 576, PH 416, VU 325, VU 678, UMH 559
Wie schön leuchtet	O Morning Star, how fair and bright!	4	♩=64–74 (rhythmic) / ♩=76–86 (metric)	LBW 43, LBW 73, LBW 76, LBW 138, LBW 459, LW 73, LW 160, LW 325, LW 437, LW 520, H82 496, H82 497, W3 389, W3 390, NCH 158, PH 69, VU 98, UMH 247
Wondrous Love	What wondrous love	4, 5	♩=50–60	LBW 385, H82 439, W3 600, NCH 223, PH 85, VU 147, UMH 292

INDEX

a cappella, 15, 53, 59
accent, 18, 46, 75
accompanying, 21–23
  African, 117, 118
  African American, 79
  Asian, 134–37
  chant, 33–34
  early American, 68
  folk hymns, 53–60
  revival, 70–71
  shape note, 68–69
acoustics, 17, 41
African, characteristics of, 116–17, 120
Afro-Cuban, 98
agocic, 46, 138
alternation practice, 51–52
alternative music, 85
Amen, 41
amplification, 23–24
Andean, characteristics of, 100
Anglican chant, 28
anxiety, 18
Argentinean, characteristics of, 100
arsis, 29
articulation, 18, 19, 43, 45–50, 77
Asian, characteristics of, 138–39
ballad, 60
ballade, 38
bamboo flute, 135
bass guitar, in contemporary, 91–92
beat (*see* tactus)
Billings, William, 67
Bliss, Philip, 65
blue notes, 78
bolero ranchero, 103
Bonhoeffer, Dietrich, 22
Brazilian, characteristics of, 100
breathing, 11, 94
Byzantine chant, 28
call and response, 70, 74–75, 99, 117–18
calypso, 98
camp meeting songs, 64, 65
cantor, 14
Caribbean, characteristics of, 100
changgo, 134
ching, 135
choir, 20, 52–53
chorale preludes, 16

chorales, German, 37, 39, 42
chorus, 65, 66
conducting chant, 32
copyright, 8, 87
country music, 86
Crosby, Fanny, 65
cross-cultural dynamics, 113–15
dance forms, 100
dance hymns, 55–56
duet songs, 70
duets, organ and piano, 69
ecclesia, 15
ehr-hu, 135
electronics, 23–24
environment, 7
episema, 29
equalism, 30
erh-hu, 135
estribillo, 99–100, 104
fauxbourdon, 34
Feliciano, Francisco, 129, 136, 138–39, 140
finding musicians, 95
Fiori musicali, 29
flamenco, 99
flexibility, 17
flute, 135
folk hymnody, 37–39
folk music, 5
fuging tunes, 63, 67
Gajard, Dom Joseph, 31
gamelan orchestra, 135
Generation X, 85
Genevan Psalter tunes, 37, 39, 42
global music, 9
gospel songs, 65, 74
Gregory I, 27
guaracha simplificada, 104
guitar
  in Asian, 136
  in contemporary, 90–91
  in Latino, 106
guitarra, 101
Hammond organ, 77, 79
handbells, 54, 69
harmonizations, 58
harmony, 22–23, 78, 129
harmony, functional, 34
Haya, 120

hazzan, 14
Hillert, Richard, 31
hocket, 119–20
Hurd, David, 33
hymn helps, 19
Hymn Society, The, 19, 68
ictus, 29, 30, 31, 32
idiophones, 122
improvisation, 79, 122
instrumental leadership, 19–21
instruments, in African, 122–24
interpolations, 76
introductions, 6, 13, 16, 57
jazz and blues, 86
keyboard
  in Asian, 136–37
  in contemporary, 89–90
  in Latino, 104–06
lament, hymns of, 56–59
language, non-English, 108
leadership, 18–19, 124
legato hymn playing, 43
Liber Usualis, 32
lied, 14
Loh, I-to, 128–29, 139, 140
lullabies, 59
Luther, Martin, 129
mainstream hymnody, 39
mariachi, 98, 100
Mason, Lowell, 64–65
mazurka (*mazurca*), 100
melody, 67–68, 131–33
membranophones, 123
mensuralism, 30
merengue, 98
meter, 78
metrical hymn, 37, 39
Medicean Gradual, 29
Mexican, characteristics of, 100
MIDI, 24
movement, 80
neume, 29
notation, chant, 28
obbligato, 21
Orff instruments, 69
Olson, Howard, 114, 125
organ and piano duets, 69
Orgelbüchlein, 16

158

1 Divinum mysterium

LBW 42
Tune: plainsong, mode V, 13th cent.

2 Veni, Creator Spiritus

LBW 472
Text: attr. Rhabanus Maurus, 776–856; tr. John Cosin, 1594–1672
Music: Sarum plainsong, mode VIII

3 Veni, Creator Spiritus

LBW 472
Text: attr. Rhabanus Maurus, 776–856
Music: Sarum plainsong, mode VIII

4 Glory to God in the highest

LBW Setting I © 1978, admin. Augsburg Fortress

5 Ubi Caritas

W3 598
Text and music: © 1986 GIA Publications, Inc.

6 Kingsfold

WOV 730
Music: English melody, arr. Ralph Vaughan Williams, 1872–1958

7 The Ash Grove

LBW 557
Music: Welsh folk tune

8 Easter Hymn

LBW 151
Music: *Lyra Davidica*, London, 1708

9 Es ist das Heil

TLH 377
Music: *Etlich christlich Lieder*, Wittenberg, 1524

10 Es ist das Heil

TLH 377
Music: *Etlich christlich Lieder*, Wittenberg, 1524

11 Es ist das Heil

TLH 377
Music: *Etlich christlich Lieder*, Wittenberg, 1524

12 Noël nouvelet

LBW 148
Text: John M. Crum © Oxford University Press, New York
Music: French carol; arr. Marie Rubis Bauer © 1998 Augsburg Fortress

13 Freu dich sehr

LBW 29
Music: *Trente quatre pseaumes de David*, Geneva, 1551

14 Ein feste Burg

LBW 229
Text: © 1978 Augsburg Fortress
Music: J. Klug, *Geistliche Lieder*, 1543

15 Ein feste Burg

LBW 229
Text: © 1978 Augsburg Fortress
Music: J. Klug, *Geistliche Lieder*, 1543

16 Hanover

H82 388
Text: Robert Grant, 1779–1838
Music: *Hanover*, att. William Croft, 1678–1727

17 Hanover

LBW 548
Text: Robert Grant, 1779–1838, alt.
Music: William Croft, 1678–1727

18 Hanover

LBW 548
Text: Robert Grant, 1779–1838, alt.
Music: William Croft, 1678–1727

19 Hanover

LBW 548
Text: Robert Grant, 1779–1838, alt.
Music: William Croft, 1678–1727

20 Hanover

LBW 548
Text: Robert Grant, 1779–1838, alt.
Music: William Croft, 1678–1727

21 Hanover

LBW 548
Text: Robert Grant, 1779–1838, alt.
Music: William Croft, 1678–1727

22 Hanover

LBW 548
Text: Robert Grant, 1779–1838, alt.
Music: William Croft, 1678–1727

23 Bunessan

H82 8
Text: Eleanor Farjeon
Music: Gaelic tune; arr. Mark Sedio © 1998 Augsburg Fortress

24 Bunessan

H82 8
Text: Eleanor Farjeon
Music: Gaelic tune; arr. Mark Sedio © 1998 Augsburg Fortress

25 Assurance

WOV 699
Music: Phoebe P. Knapp, 1830–1908

26 Assurance

WOV 699
Music: Phoebe P. Knapp, 1830–1908

27 Coronation

UMH 154
Text: Edward Perronet, 1726–1792
Music: Oliver Holden, 1765–1844

28 Pilot

LBW 334
Text: Edward Hopper, 1818–1888
Music: John E. Gould, 1822–1875

29 Jesus Lifted Me

WOV 673
Music: African American spiritual; arr. *With One Voice* © 1995
Augsburg Fortress

30 Jesus Lifted Me

WOV 673
Text: African American spiritual
Music: African American spiritual; arr. *With One Voice* © 1995
Augsburg Fortress

31 Very Soon

UMH 706
© 1976 Bud John Songs/Crouch Music

32 Showalter

WOV 780
Text: Elisha Hoffman, 1839–1929
Music: Anthony J. Showalter, 1858–1924

33 Showalter

WOV 780
Text: Elisha Hoffman, 1839–1929
Music: Anthony J. Showalter, 1858–1924

34 Jesus Lifted Me

WOV 673
Music: arr. © 1995 Augsburg Fortress

35 Lord, I lift your name on high

Text and music: Rick Founds; arr. © 1997 Marantha! Music,
admin. The Copyright Company

36 Lord, I lift your name on high

Text and music: Rick Founds; arr. © 1997 Marantha! Music,
admin. The Copyright Company

37 Lord, I lift your name on high

Text and music: Rick Founds; arr. © 1997 Marantha! Music,
admin. The Copyright Company

38 Lord, I lift your name on high

Text and music: Rick Founds; arr. © 1997 Marantha! Music,
admin. The Copyright Company

39 Lord, I lift your name on high

Text and music: Rick Founds; arr. © 1997 Marantha! Music,
admin. The Copyright Company

40 Lord, I lift your name on high

Text and music: Rick Founds; arr. © 1997 Marantha! Music,
admin. The Copyright Company

41 Id y enseñad

WOV 753
Text and music: © 1979 Cesareo Gabarain, published by OCP; tr.
© The United Methodist Publishing House, admin. The Copyright
Company

42 Id y enseñad

WOV 753
Text and music: © 1979 Cesareo Gabarain, published by OCP; tr.
© The United Methodist Publishing House, admin. The Copyright
Company

43 Cantad al Señor

WOV 795
Text: Brazilian folk song; tr. Gerhard Cartford, b. 1923
Music: Brazilian folk song; arr. Mark Sedio © 1998 Augsburg
Fortress

44 Cantad al Señor

WOV 795
Text: Brazilian folk song; tr. Gerhard Cartford, b. 1923
Music: Brazilian folk song; arr. Mark Sedio © 1998 Augsburg
Fortress

45 Cantad al Señor

WOV 795
Text: Brazilian folk song; tr. Gerhard Cartford, b. 1923
Music: Brazilian folk song; arr. Mark Sedio © 1998 Augsburg
Fortress

46 Cantad al Señor

WOV 795
Text: Brazilian folk song; tr. Gerhard Cartford, b. 1923
Music: Brazilian folk song; arr. Mark Sedio © 1998 Augsburg
Fortress

47 Guitar strumming technique

48 Señor, ten piedad

WOV 605
Music: Jose Ruíz, © 1995 Augsburg Fortress

49 Neno lake Mungu

WOV 712
Text: Tanzanian traditional, tr. © Lutheran Theological College
Music: Tanzanian tune, arr. © 1986 Austin C. Lovelace

50 Mfurahini, haleluya

WOV 678
Text: Bernard Kyamanywa, b. 1938, tr. © 1977 Howard S. Olson
Music: Traditional Tanzanian

51 Mfurahini, haleluya

WOV 678
Text: Bernard Kyamanywa, b. 1938, tr. © 1977 Howard S. Olson
Music: Traditional Tanzanian

52 Mfurahini, haleluya

WOV 678
Text: Bernard Kyamanywa, b. 1938, tr. © 1977 Howard S. Olson
Music: Traditional Tanzanian

53 Khudaya

SB 120
Text: Traditional; Pakistan
Music: © 1990 Asian Institute for Liturgy and Music

54 Jaya ho

UMH 478
Text: Anon. Hindi; trans. by Katherine R. Rohrbough, 1958; pho-
netic transcription from the Hindi by I-to Loh, 1988 © 1989 The
United Methodist Publishing House
Music: Trad. Hindi melody; arr. by Victor Sherring, 1955

55 Dapit hapon

WOV 663
Text: Moises Andrade, tr. © James Minchin, admin. Asian Institute
for Liturgy and Music
Music: © Francisco Feliciano

56 Dapit hapon

WOV 663
Text: Moises Andrade, tr. © James Minchin, admin. Asian Institute
for Liturgy and Music
Music: © Francisco Feliciano

Recording singers: Norma Aamodt-Nelson, Lorraine Brugh, Robin Cain, Carol Carver, Marta Edman, Ryan French, Kathy Fristad, Dave Goulette, Laura Hannah, Lynette Johnson, Wendy Kuharik, Dean Niquette, Charlie Payne, Sue Peterson, Martin Seltz, Maggie Speich, Tim Swanson, Eric Vollen, Scott Weidler, Lani Willis

Percussion: Dave Henzel, Dean Niquette, José Antonio Machado
Guitar: Dean Niquette, William Dexheimer Pharris
Bass: Bill Chouinard
Organ/Piano: Phil Kadidlo, Mark Sedio, Frank Stoldt, Scott Weidler

Music Directors: Lorraine Brugh, Mark Sedio, Scott Weidler
Producer and Digital Editing: Kathrine Handford
Engineer and Digital Mastering: William Lund
Executive Producers: Norma Aamodt-Nelson, Scott Weidler
Narrator: D. Foy Christopherson

Recorded May/June 1998, Trinity Lutheran Church, Stillwater, Minnesota